Praise for *Self-Worth to Net Worth*:

This warm, wonderful book shows you how to **build your self-esteem, self-image and self-confidence** to the point where you can **accomplish any goal you set** for yourself.

– BRIAN TRACY
Author, Earn What You're Worth

This **wise and comprehensive book begs to be read**—and digested—very slowly. In it, Cia Ricco and Belinda Rosenblum have managed to make **important and highly sophisticated psychological concepts very, very accessible**. From the get-go, they emphasize the importance of personal responsibility, going so far as to ask the reader to sign an agreement to further his or her commitment to a life that works.

Ideas like the cost of comfort and the cost of inaction **help the reader learn to analyze the cost/benefit ratio of any decision**. The authors offer an **abundance of user-friendly and effective tools** for restructuring non-supportive beliefs into supportive ones, for recognizing and moving beyond non-self-responsible communication, and for expanding the tolerance of joy. **Rich discussions and colorful examples** illustrate the key concepts; the authors' stance toward the reader is **unwaveringly empathic and compassionate**.

While psychological and financial skills and strategies are an integral part of this book—while it is, as its title suggests, about the movement to net worth through self-worth—its most powerful contribution lies in **its dogged focus on the cultivation of true wealth**, those non-financial assets that invigorate and vitalize.

– DR. APRIL LANE BENSON
Author, To Buy or Not to Buy: Why We Overshop and How to Stop

Achieving real wealth is an inside job first. This must-read book is the **step-by-step plan** to show you **how to embrace your own worthiness and get on the fast-track** to realizing your financial goals.

– **DR. JOE VITALE**
Author, *Attract Money Now*

If you're ready to take a deep dive into your financial reality, this book is for you! The authors **hand hold you through your process to permanent financial success.**

– **JULIE MURPHY CASSERLY**
Author, *The Emotion Behind Money: Building Wealth from the Inside Out*

Cia and Belinda have melded their talents and invested their energy wisely and well, returning to us this **savvy program** that will **help not only to heal yourself but to finance your new wishes.** Read it and get **energized and educated**, and you're on your way!

– **DR. SAMUEL SHEM**
Author, *The House of God, The Spirit of the Place,* and *Bill W. and Dr. Bob*

Read the news! Even great nations are struggling with financial literacy. This book is a **must-read for us all**, and Belinda is THE go-to expert on How to Own Your Money.

– **ORVEL RAY WILSON**, CSP
co-author of the Guerrilla Marketing series

OWNING YOUR LIFE

No book, therapist, financial plan, doctor, guru, pill, or program will change your life or your financial situation without your participation. Your involvement in and responsibility for your money and your life are what makes the difference. No one and no thing is responsible for your well-being except for you. To further your commitment to this process, we ask that you make the following agreements with yourself:

I am 100% responsible for my well-being.

I absolve others, living or dead, present or absent, from any responsibility for my well-being—financial or otherwise.

I am in charge of my financial destiny.

I agree to be 100% responsible for my participation in and creation of my experience of this book, as I choose to be with my life. If there is something about the book which is disturbing to me or does not meet my needs, I have the option of contacting the authors to discuss it.

I am willing to experience learning and transformation in ways that are loving and kind to me and everyone else.

I understand that the content contained in this book is intended for general informational purposes. I will verify pertinent information with my broker, dealer, agent, bank, financial institution, lawyer, doctor, or other service or information provider.

I am open to owning my money and owning my life.

Signed:_____

Date:_____

Your signature above is a declaration to yourself that you are claiming ownership of this book—and of your own life.

Cia Ricco
www.Live-Life.com
www.RanchoRicco.net

Belinda Rosenblum
www.OwnYourMoney.com
www.SelfWorthBook.com

TABLE OF CONTENTS

Introduction. ix

The 12 Keys

1. Be Willing to Change 1
2. Claim Responsibility 35
3. Feel Your Feelings 57
4. Accept WHAT IS 91
5. Set Your Boundaries 115
6. Transform Your Self-Talk .143
7. Learn to Love Yourself .167
8. Harness the Power of Choice 191
9. Commit and Follow Through 213
10. LET GO. 237
11. Stand in Your Truth 257
12. Develop a Tolerance for Joy 279

Conclusion. 303

Appendix I – Getting The Most Out
Of The Exercises In Each Key 305

Appendix II – Your Net Worth Belief
Assessment – At The Beginning. 317

Appendix III – Your Net Worth Belief
Assessment – At Completion 323

About the Authors 329

INTRODUCTION

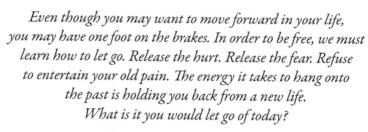

*Even though you may want to move forward in your life,
you may have one foot on the brakes. In order to be free, we must
learn how to let go. Release the hurt. Release the fear. Refuse
to entertain your old pain. The energy it takes to hang onto
the past is holding you back from a new life.
What is it you would let go of today?*

—MARY MANIN MORRISSEY

Imagine this: You are running as fast as you can, only to reach the edge
of a cliff. You can run no more, turning back is not an option, and you
must decide whether to leap or languish. Do you jump? Or do you dig in
your heels, conflicted and helpless, permanently hovering near the edge of
new possibilities? This book begs you, implores you, and encourages you to
jump—and to take flight. Your life and financial well-being depend on it.

We live in an abundant universe, rich and giving to those who live in that
recognition, and a mystery, or often seemingly an enemy, to those who exist
in conflict with this basic fact. Why can some tap into abundance while
others live in constant struggle and lack? This book will help you to examine
your self-imposed barriers to abundance. You will explore the true nature

and origin of your personal sense of lack and how to heal it. You will begin to change your limiting beliefs about money and about your self-worth into a courageous, unrestricted vision.

As you believe in and appreciate your own worthiness (your self-worth), you will ignite your motivation to move powerfully on your journey towards greater abundance in your financial situation (your net worth) as well. Feeling empowered and in a fully realized state of self-worth will support you to manifest and sustain the attitudes, behaviors, and activities that will allow you to grow your net worth. Self-worth and net worth are actually quite linked as both are natural parts of who you are and what is possible for you. Each of the 12 Keys to Creating Wealth Inside and Out outlined in this book (the "Keys") will provide you strategies, exercises, and techniques to advance you towards embracing your natural self-worth and growing your net worth and abundance. We will be on this bold new path with you as you read and implement each Key within this book.

What is money?

Knowing what money is, what it isn't, and what it means to you will transform your entire relationship with prosperity in your life. Belinda often asks audiences at her speaking engagements, "What does money mean to you?" She puts an image on the projection screen saying "Money = " and then she waits for the responses. The audience often calls out responses including freedom, security, power, control, love, happiness, fighting, and vacations. Rarely does Belinda hear that money is a means of exchange or a form of currency. Seeing only the emotional side of money blocks your ability to be objective about your attitudes, habits, and actions. Mistaking money itself for your emotional well-being, thus trusting your security and happiness to this inanimate object or concept, puts the power outside of yourself. Instead, this book is your opportunity to empower yourself to first own your relationship with yourself and, in the process, own your money and grow your net worth. This book weaves the lessons of each together to enable you to process through two previously challenging areas in your life.

What is wealth?

True wealth is clearly not just about money or possessions. In most cases within this book, whether we refer to personal well-being, financial well being, joy, self-worth, or in general to the quality of your life, we are using these terms somewhat interchangeably. We do not buy into the assumption that financial wealth creates happiness. However, we have noticed that the Keys revealed in this book can create great joy in many aspects of your life. When followed with regard to fiscal health, as well as other forms of self-care, these Keys contribute to a life that works.

Each person reading this book will have his or her own values, dreams, desires, and vision of what constitutes a "life that works." Please feel free to substitute your own priorities whenever we use wording that is not precisely applicable to your personal vision. What we are looking for is your happiness and an authentic acceptance of the life you have as well as the life you are creating.

The Keys

We noticed that the Keys, drawn from Cia's book *Living As If Your Life Depended On It: Twelve Gateways to a Life that Works*, were important steps to enable Cia's life, and the lives of her clients, to find joy and to manifest the life of their dreams. In Belinda's year of discovery and reflection, she met Cia and also used the Gateways to create a deeper sense of self-esteem and fulfillment. Once Belinda launched Own Your Money LLC, there was a natural fit in their work. The original Gateways from Cia's book have been expanded to support your new and profoundly powerful relationship to money, true wealth, and true worth.

As the saying goes, "You can't take it with you." This book is not about how much you can accumulate in your lifetime. For what? Do you truly know? What makes you happy? What brings you joy? Is it peace of mind you are after? What is the *feeling* you want? Once you can truly answer these questions, your wealth can become a tool for supporting you in achieving the feelings and mind states you want in your life, not simply as an end in itself.

Consider this: Would you rather use your financial situation as a tool for living fully or as an excuse not to? Be careful not to answer too quickly. It is all too easy to say, "Well, of course I would rather use it as a tool for living fully, but . . ." We are here to help you drop the *buts*. They are only limiting what is possible in your life. In the following pages, we'll take a deeper, judgment-free look at where you are and where you want to be—no excuses. You may allow your financial situation, and your "B.S." (which stands for Belief Systems, by the way) about it, to hold you back. Finances often become an excuse for not living fully or getting what you want in your life, rather than allowing your wealth to support and facilitate you *creating* the life you want. For instance, I can't do X because I don't have enough money; when in reality, you may have the money but be afraid to take the risk, step outside your comfort zone, or fear your success in realizing completion. Thus, it is not actually about you having money at all.

The message you will find in this book is about living fully—about living every day and every moment as if your life depended on it. The 12 Keys will *reveal* and *transform* the mechanisms which keep you from financial and psychological freedom. Releasing these blocks frees you to stand up and be counted—to be truly present for your life.

How are you living your life on a daily basis? You may find yourself waiting around thinking, "if only" something would happen or "When I have _____, then I will be able to change my life." Is there some small step you can take today in the direction of how you want your life to be? Perhaps reading this book is your next step.

In these pages, you will discover what your barriers are to a deeper sense of self-worth and relationships with money, prosperity, and true abundance where *you* have choice over your life. What stands in your way? The 12 Keys will become your step-by-step toolkit for creating breakthrough. There is no situation or challenge that will arise in your life that cannot be addressed with one or more of these tools.

If you regard a certain net worth as a destination or end goal, this book will help you broaden your view. You will begin to shift your focus to living the life you have today in the moment, as you start thinking about what feelings and qualities you want. What actual thoughts, things, or activities help you to get those feelings and qualities? Once you've identified these, *you can powerfully set your financial intentions and take the actions which will help you get there.* This book provides the opportunity to truly come to terms with what you think you want money *for*, as well as what your true and authentic vision is about your life and your life's purpose—and then how money fits into that vision.

You will notice that we don't suggest you set "goals" to realize the worth you are seeking, as we prefer the word *intention* to *goal*. There is a great deal written and discussed in self-help circles about goal setting. We have observed, over a long period of working on ourselves and helping others, that the concept of a goal tends to create an unconscious *should*. With every "I should" we inflict a sense of pressure and thus resistance. "Intention" is far more gentle and supportive. It comes from what *you* truly want, i.e., what you feel, rather than what you think you "should" do or achieve, or what you believe someone else thinks you "should" be, do, or achieve. Human nature is designed for forward movement and the excitement is in the momentum, the process, the journey, and the anticipation. "Goal" usually implies something static and "intention" is something which is ongoing.

The more you move through the 12 Keys in this book and put them into practice, the more joy you will feel in your life. The cliff of possibilities will not be frightening any more. It becomes the cliff of opportunity and transformation. The value of your life is not about the destination or how much you have in the bank. It is about you being present, alive, wealthy (in the fullest sense of the word), and abundant—and feeling that way in this moment. There will be plenty of cliffs, but you will jump gladly, and as you do, you will learn to spread your wings.

This book will put you on the pathway to a more affluent life. How opportune that even the word "affluent" comes from the root word for "flow." Our hope is that, through your progression in experiencing this book, you will open yourself to the flow of life, prosperity, and abundance that you so rightly deserve.

As you open the doorway to the life you want, don't ever forget that life itself is the journey. The essence of life is in the living. It is how you live—not where you get to or how much you accomplish. A focus on money alone can take you out of the moment and into the past or the future in ways which can affect how you show up for your life in the present. Consider the present literally as a *present*—a gift you can give yourself each moment. Celebrate the *process* as you explore the pages of this book and the tools offered herein, and make them your own. Your journey through these pages will be unique, as unique as you are. One of the things you will do as you read and process these teachings is come to a more complete recognition of that uniqueness.

Getting Started

Each person has one or more Keys she or he is most in need of at any given time, and this may change as you progress through the book and through your life. You may wish to read the book once through without doing the exercises, and then go back and focus on the Key or Keys you are most in need of at the time. Or you may choose to take one Key per week and thoroughly integrate it into your life, doing the exercises completely and contemplating the impact of the applicable Key on your life each day that week. Using the latter approach, you will be able to complete this entire program in 90 days.

Remember to come back to this book at challenging times in your life and review the Key that is most applicable for that situation.

Getting Support

Your life will begin to change (for the better) as you travel this path. Of course, that process may be a bit scary at times. Know that you are not alone. Support on your journey is available. Many people have found it helpful to form a mastermind or support group with weekly or monthly meetings and go through the book together one Key at a time, discussing its impact on their lives, where they are with it, and perhaps doing the exercises together. Please feel free to contact one or both of the authors for additional support.

Reach out. Ask for help. Asking is not disempowering; it is empowering. Asking for what you want is one of the principles we will explore as a means for significantly increasing your odds of having what you want, because if you don't ask, then the answer is always "no."

On this journey, you may find and attract others like you who are committed to living fully and creating wealth inside and out. Even if not in a formal group, you may be amazed at the different people and conversations you now begin to have.

The term *financial independence* can be misleading. You may have been conditioned to believe that what you want is independence when, more and more, the challenges in your world and in your life, point toward the fact that what you are truly seeking is connectedness or interdependence (i.e., true community). In our final Key, "Develop a Tolerance for Joy," we will talk about the importance of giving back, which is so integral to an acknowledgement and celebration of our interdependence. In order to achieve true connectedness with yourself, with others, with your life's purpose, and perhaps with some universal force greater than any individual or group of individuals, what is required is that you truly show up for your life and live each moment fully valuing your own worth.

The Exercises

The exercises and related tools, such as visualizations, conscious breathing, body centered statements, and journal joggers, in this book are an extremely valuable adjunct to the work. You will experience deeper transformation if you complete the exercises and journal after each Key. Do not short-change yourself by reading without taking the time to reflect and do the exercises, even if you do a full read-through first and then come back to them. Also, if you are having additional insights not specifically mentioned in a journal jogger question, please don't feel limited by the questions. Make them your own. Write about your discoveries and changes, possibly even each day, as you move forward with your life and this journey.

In general, there are two types of exercises: those that will require material (usually just pen and paper) and those that will require visualization practice.

We suggest that you write directly in this book or use a journal or workbook for the exercises you do along with this book. Allow yourself more time and space to consider and explore the insights. Please read Appendix I at the back of this book before you begin your exercises. In particular, notice the section on Body Centered Statements, as it provides helpful information in better understanding the connection between your beliefs, your feelings, and life affirming statements. We've got some great tips for you—especially if you haven't done this level of transformational work before.

What to Expect

In preparing to read this book and to move through the powerful changes you are invited to create for yourself, you may have some uneasy feelings regarding your relationship with your self-worth, your net worth, and even the discussion of your money in such a candid and honest way. This is normal! It's great, actually, as it means that you are opening to the process and willing to move forward. Something in you knows that exciting change is on the way. It means that you are ready to dig deep and perhaps to pull some skeletons out of the closet—again, without judgment. Embrace the feelings and know you are in exactly the right place and time to be going through this. On the other side of these potentially uncomfortable feelings are peace of mind, relaxation, and joy.

With your full participation and involvement in this book and process, you will be able to:

- choose the way you want to live your life,
- choose the relationship you want to have with money and your own worth,

- recognize all that is within your power and what is not,
- choose to do something different from this moment on, and
- create a new level of wealth and abundance in your life starting right now.

This is your wake up call for your life.

Good luck. See you in the realm of abundance.

Wishing you much joy and succe$$!

—Cia and Belinda

Arrange whatever pieces come your way.
—Virginia Woolf

KEY ONE

BE WILLING TO CHANGE

I will go anywhere as long as it is forward.
—DAVID LIVINGSTON

You may believe that once you have more money in your life, then you will be happy or happier. Yes, money can help urgent needs or problems. Yet in the medium-term and long-term, you have likely just treated the symptoms and added more zeroes to the same underlying issues or dis-ease. Essentially, you are counting on your net worth to create your self-worth.

In fact, it is the other way around! Say it out loud: My self-worth leads to my net worth. What would it take for you to be joyful now—right in this moment? If you have trouble speaking this statement with a bodily-felt sense of belief and empowerment, perhaps you are not yet fully willing to change. This is not a criticism or judgment. We are only willing when we are willing. Resistance has many causes and many purposes. Our intent is to support you to acknowledge any resistance you may have—not to judge it.

Willingness is the doorway to change; the only way in is through. If you really want to change, if you want a life filled with joy, pleasure, aliveness, affluence, riches, and abundance, you must be willing to open the door and go through. Go for it! This is the key to being able to do anything in your life. When you are willing to change, you create a new context for your life—especially and including your life with money—and launch yourself upon the path to true worth.

On what do you base your self-worth? Is it related to what you do, what you buy, or how much stuff you have? If so, is that appropriate? Is that real self-worth? As a start, take a moment to appreciate who you are, what you have accomplished, and who you have become in your life. Practice living in the present moment and enjoying the experience of gratitude. It is the moment by moment, day by day choice to be fully who you are that will create your sense of self-worth for you, not what you have (or don't have) in the bank, or what you do for a living.

In this Key, the kind of change we're talking about is not that sort of little by little "I'm doing things differently now" change. We're talking about the radical change which comes from making a clear decision and sticking with it. You know the kind we mean: You wake up one morning and you're a different person! We are talking about a change that comes from the inside out—not waiting on external factors to change you—what Gottfried Benn called "primal perception."

Such a change often comes in the form of an epiphany, an insight, an inspiration, or a flash. Gottfried Benn said that such a perception gives the world a sense of "matchless clarity"—a "fresh minted" look. The "flash" sends out a signal which is carried by your delightfully complex system of neurotransmitters to every cell in your body. Each cell gets the message— Eureka! You are different. You are new. The change may be subtle, but it is real. It has occurred in physical reality.

Cia tells the story of how she had been an incredibly shy person with no sense of self-worth during her childhood and young adulthood, and of having just such an epiphany. Her breakthrough came when she suddenly realized that it was up to her to change the lack of belief in herself which was causing her misery. In a moment, she chose to own her full sense of self-worth. She went, virtually overnight, from being unpopular to being popular without a single external change—only a very powerful internal one. People couldn't explain what suddenly seemed so different about her. Many who had known her for a long time came up and asked her if she had changed her hair or done something differently. She simply smiled and said, "No," yet nothing was ever the same for her after a fundamental internal change that took a split second to make. Healing can happen for you in an instant as well.

Naturally, you have resistance to change. Your comfort zone consists of what is familiar, even if what is familiar isn't pleasant and isn't working. Isn't there a saying that, "The devil you know is better than the devil you don't?" You, like all of us, suffer from a deep-seated fear of the unknown, and all change essentially involves the unknown.

Your Reptilian Brain

The brain contains a deeply primal segment, often called the Reptilian Complex because it is the most ancient part of the conscious brain, thought to have evolved from human's reptilian ancestors. It is the part of the brain which higher mammals (such as humans) share with reptiles, the functions of which are based solely on survival instinct. Scientists from Paul D. McLean to Carl Sagan have written about the role of the Reptilian Complex, often abbreviated as the R-complex. It is sometimes also referred to as the Reptilian Brain and resides at the top of the brainstem—the very base of the brain which supports the pure autonomic functioning.

The theory is that millions of years ago, the brain began to gradually evolve around the stem, thus adding layers. The most recent layer is the one used for making conscious choices and is known as the neo-cortex. However, unconscious, instinctive, and automatic behaviors come largely from the Reptilian Complex, where the survival instinct is paramount. The most base of human emotions are attributed to this part of the brain—hatred and fear of that which is different from us (i.e., prejudice) and unfettered rage—because these are no more than the extension of the primitive survival instinct. This is often collectively referred to as the "fight or flight response."

Often, the R-Complex can override the more rational function of the brain and result in unpredictable and even primitive behavior in otherwise evolved humans. A well-developed and healthy neo-cortex, and specifically the orbitofrontal cortex which is responsible for social and emotional processing, can monitor R-Complex activity in conscious beings. Are you willing to exercise and strengthen this conscious control by making healthy decisions not based on survival alone?

The reptilian brain has only one goal and that is to keep you physically alive. Quality of life doesn't enter into its instinctive nature. So this part of the brain says, "If you are alive, it means it is working. Therefore don't change a thing because, if you do, I can't guarantee your survival." As in the saying, "If it ain't broke don't fix it," the reptilian brain believes that "it ain't broke" because you are still alive. Yet do you really want to let that part of your brain run your life and make your decisions for you? Or do you choose to get more out of life than simple survival? Notice when you are being *reactive* rather than *proactive* and ask yourself if that is your pure survival instinct kicking in. Notice when you are reacting from fear, which can then lead to anger. Can you evoke a more conscious response? Would you rather leap off that cliff into the unknown and take your chances, knowing you have weighed the pros and cons and you have decided that the potential reward is worth the risk?

"Death" of Your Identity

So, why *don't* you change or give up undesired habits and behaviors around wealth and worthiness? The answer we hear most often is that people lack discipline. This is not the reason. In fact, the rigidity of discipline opposes true transformation. The reason lies not in what you lack, but in what you fear with the support of your reptilian brain. You, or at least that part of your brain, are afraid of death. You fear letting go of the known—the familiar—because it would represent death to a part of yourself that you have come to identify with.

Most people would rather cling to their thoughts, patterns, and habits, no matter how uncomfortable, because they believe that in them their identity, and therefore their safety and security, lies. To relinquish that identity is to step into the unknown, and risk that you die to a part of yourself. To become fully alive, you must risk this "death" and take this leap of faith. If you can allow your old habits, personae, and belief systems to die, you will be making room for new ones. Only then can your essence, your true self-worth (the person you are deep down at your core), begin to shine.

While this is ultimately simple, we realize that it can be anything but easy. Not only do you (all of us, actually) have an instinctive fear of change—of stepping out of our old familiar comfort zone—but in addition, you may feel that doing so is not worth the effort. This is just one more belief system! It most likely comes from what you have invested in your old beliefs, and not having tasted the possibility of another reality. It may stem from experiences of having tried and failed, so that something in you, somewhere along the way, made a decision to stop trying. The sacred journey revealed in this book will, among many other benefits, support your exploration of your belief systems (Key One), your self-talk and your money personae (Key Six), and then support you in discovering the process of letting go to create a clearing for the new (Key Ten).

Moving Toward Pleasure or Away From Pain

All beings either move toward pleasure (a more conscious choice) or away from pain (the more instinctive one). If you have never tasted the possibility of pleasure that comes from the success of choosing what you want to believe, you are likely to move away from the projected pain associated with the unknown. You do this simply because it *is* the unknown and therefore out of your accustomed comfort zone. Are you willing to become conscious of your choices? As you do, you may find yourself willing and able to step out of your comfort zone even if it means that there may be some pain along the way. Can you experiment with what is likely to bring you pleasure instead of letting your "automatic pilot" steer you away from anything which may bring discomfort? There is a wonderful world awaiting you outside of your comfort zone, yet first you need to overcome your instinctive habit of avoiding the pain associated with change.

Try this 5-step exercise now:

1. Take a blank piece of paper or use your journal/workbook. Across the top briefly describe a situation you want to change (or a specific part of it that you want to change).

2. Below this create two columns. Column one is "Pleasure," defined as the gains or benefits you will achieve by changing the situation. Column two is "Pain," defined as any discomfort or costs (physical, financial, mental, or spiritual) that you are currently experiencing about the situation and which may increase if no action is taken.

3. List in detail everything you can think of in each category relating to the situation you want to change.

4. Contemplate what you notice, then put the paper away. Do not use the exercise as an excuse to "should" on yourself, i.e., feel guilty or ashamed for not taking action. Simply "be with" your noticing. Give this some time and see if any new insights begin to appear.

5. When you are ready, go back to your paper and see it with fresh eyes. Ask yourself if you are truly ready and willing to take the leap and make the change. If the answer is "no," are you willing to avoid judging yourself for that and simply notice? As you accept what is real for you in this situation, you will then move closer to being able to change the situation.

You will be able to take this exercise to a deeper level as you begin to quantify the resulting impact.

Cost of Inaction

What is your inaction and unwillingness to change costing you? What is your resistance to being committed to yourself and your self-worth costing you? When it comes to your net worth, your problem may be in not believing in something enough to save for it. Or it may be the opposite. You may hoard what you have out of fear of "not having" rather than risking for your passion—your inspiration. The link between self-worth and net worth is already becoming clear. As you solidify your own worthiness, appreciate your true aspirations, and release your fears, your path to a greater net worth will become more apparent and actually easier.

Thus, the most important part of inspiring yourself comes from visualizing and getting a very clear sense of what it is you want in your life, what that would look like, and how that would feel. How does what you want from life further who you truly are and who you are evolving into? What is your true and great purpose in life? Are you willing to "live into that" without using your net worth, or the lack thereof, as an excuse not to? Money often becomes more of a block than a tool for fulfilling your dreams. Turn that around by focusing on what you want, who you are, your true purpose, and your mission in life first. Inspiration comes when you are in alignment with your true calling. Never let money stand in the way of that. Instead, allow money to support that flow.

See Exercise A at the end of this Key to explore your "Cost of Comfortable" and better understand what the impact of your inaction truly is.

Growth and the Search for Meaning

Growing pains are called that for a reason. Growth means change and change usually comes with some discomfort. Think about when a baby gets a new tooth. It grows under the gums and then one day breaks through. While the tooth is breaking down the tissue under the gum, it is also preparing for a break through. The same goes for you. To overcome your discomfort related to issues around money and life choices, you will need to grow past your comfort zone. This may feel painful or scary at times. Staying comfortable often feels easier than change, even if *comfortable* isn't a happy place. Many of us would rather stay comfortably unhappy in a familiar malaise than take steps toward happiness and prosperity if that involves risk (feeling discomfort, for example). In short, Belinda says, "People often unconsciously choose to be comfortable and unhappy rather than a little uncomfortable and truly happy." The more you get the positive rewards of experiencing the difference in your life, the easier it becomes to step out of your comfort zone. Then notice how your comfort zone expands.

Most people claim to be searching for the "meaning of life." Here's our radical answer to the eternal search. Life *has* no meaning in and of itself. The meaning of life is what you bring to it. Knowing this, you can decide— what is the meaning of *your* life? What is your worth? What is your value? What are your values? If you haven't found out these things, create them. Discover them! Most people are not truly happy unless they are fulfilling their purpose in life. What if you were, in fact, born with that purpose but lost sight of it? What if it has always been there? Then your job is like that of Michelangelo who said that all he was really doing was chipping away the stone to find the sculpture which already existed within. As you move through this book, you will begin to clear the way for discovering your life's purpose. In Key Eight, you can specifically clarify your own life purpose through one of the exercises provided.

Willingness = Alignment

If the doors of perception were cleansed,
everything would appear to man as it is, infinite.

—WILLIAM BLAKE

True willingness happens only when your body, mind, and spirit are in total alignment. To be in true alignment is to be free from cognitive dissonance (the feeling that two or more parts of yourself are in disagreement). It is a balanced, clear feeling, where you are open to the unlimited possibilities and the abundance that life has to offer. It is to have thought, speech, and action in body, mind, and spirit, all united for a common purpose—YOUR PURPOSE, i.e., YOUR TRUE SELF-WORTH. Imagine the feeling of being at the beginning of an exciting journey into that abundance. If you have trouble getting this sense inside yourself, ask yourself, "What's in the way between me and having what I want?" Are you willing to release and move past what is in your way?

These Keys will support you in eliminating those obstacles, and encourage you to take the leap into the life you have always wanted. Willingness is not conditional. To be effective, it must be a total commitment. Willingness to change is a sudden core internal shift that takes place in your body, mind, and spirit; you feel comfortable standing up tall and presenting who you are to the world; you feel ready to embrace joy and abundance, and to change any belief systems which stand in your way. The world looks different. The physical, mental, emotional, and spiritual aspects of your being come into focus. That focus combines with energy, motivation, enthusiasm, and creativity to form INSPIRATION, as the Inspiration Formula diagram below illustrates:

FOCUS
+
ENERGY
+
MOTIVATION $=$ INSPIRATION
+
ENTHUSIASM
+
CREATIVITY

What moves you into alignment? What truly inspires you? We regularly see people who say they want to be doing something different, but aren't. Often that is because they don't have a clear vision of why they want it to be different, or what they want at all. The desire for things to be different alone is not enough. Having a clear vision of how you want your life to look, in financial and other aspects, will be instrumental to your true willingness and inspired action. As your vision grows, so will your confidence, belief in the possibilities, and positive expectations/thoughts/intentions.

We will support you with your visioning as we take you through the visualization exercises presented throughout the book. An excellent way to get started is to create a Vision Book or Board, like a scrapbook or collage of images. You collect images, words, or other clippings from magazines and other sources which emotionally touch you, as you wish to manifest what the image represents in your life. Note, we say "touch" you. It is important that this be connected with your heart and spirit and not just some cultural idea of what "success" looks like.

It is ok if you don't have a crystal clear vision before you begin a vision board or book. Often this process helps you to gain the clarity you seek. Belinda has found this to be true many times over. She used a vision board when she was clarifying who she wanted to be in a relationship with, how she wanted to feel in this relationship, and the images that demonstrated her desires. Then, when in transition out of her 15-year corporate accounting roles to a new venture, she initially felt "out of control" and "all over the place." She first chose to use separate scrapbooks to help organize her life and new goals emerging from this interim period. As she would find images from magazines, newspapers, or even mailings or cards received, she would put them into one of these vision books. She created different books for the romantic relationship she desired, one for her new career, and the third for her home, health, and self-worth. Belinda would look at these each morning and each night, reminding herself where she was headed and what touched her. When images were no longer meaningful, they would come out and would be replaced by new, more relevant ones. Her energy was aligning with her vision each day. As she got clearer on her career vision, and her book started to overflow, Belinda took her favorite images and glued them onto a vision board to appreciate the depth and clarity that was emerging. Shortly thereafter, her new company of Own Your Money LLC was born, as was a meaningful relationship resulting in marriage, a new home, and an ever increasing sense of self-worth.

Inspiration and Motivation

Inspiration generates further motivation in a positive spiral. Motivation is what moves you—what gives you the impetus and the courage to dare—to act. So if you find yourself wondering why you are not moving in the direction you say you want your life to go in, take notice of where you may lack motivation and, ultimately, inspiration. Belinda was speaking with Gail, who was outwardly unhappy with her financial situation and called Belinda for help. Gail was particularly frustrated with earning less than she was capable, and barely making ends meet each month. Her hours as a massage therapist had been cut from 35 to 20 so things financially were about to get much worse. She said that she wanted to make things better, but she had gotten stuck in blaming her employer (for the shorter hours and inconsistent work) and judging her husband (for not making a decision about a potential move).

Belinda helped Gail realize that this blaming and judging was giving her more of what she didn't want and not moving her closer to what she did want. Once she realized that, Belinda encouraged her to look at why she wasn't motivated to take more productive action, and how she could get in touch with her inspiration to add action to her words, followed by a "kick in the pants" to get moving. Gail's response: "It was really great speaking with you and your partner. It was like a kick in the pants and a breath of fresh air. It's unfortunate that my hours have been cut and I'm in this situation, especially when I left a previous job for it, but I do believe this implies even more so how I need to find something more—and now I'm inspired to do it!"

The more grounded you are in a solid purposeful inspiration, the more intentional you will be about moving forward through this book and taking the risks and actions necessary to move forward in both the self-worth and net worth aspects of your life. It is then that you allow your whole being to come into alignment.

Inspiration comes from the Latin word, "inspirare," to draw in breath or spirit (in Latin "spiritus" also means breath). When you are inspired, you have drawn in spirit, energy, and motivation. All of your forthcoming actions take on a new level of grace and ease. Allow yourself to be inspired and find your "great purpose" as Patanjali suggests in the quote below. (Patanjali is the best known of the ancient Hindu authors of Yoga Sutras.) You may amaze yourself once you see your true capabilities.

"When you are inspired by some great purpose, some extraordinary project, all your thoughts break their bonds: Your mind transcends limitations, your consciousness expands in every direction, and you find yourself in a new, great, and wonderful world. Dormant forces, faculties and talents

BE WILLING TO CHANGE

1

become alive, and you discover yourself to be a greater person by far than you ever dreamed yourself to be."

Since "inspirare" means to draw in breath, use this as an opportunity to take in deep breaths as you recite this quote aloud. Allow your body to feel the impact of being inspired by a purpose greater than your likely previously limited vision of yourself. As you breathe deeply, you'll be generating more energy which will enhance your inspiration in the largest sense of the word.

Refer to Exercise C – Part I at the end of this Key to personally identify where you want to be in your life, allow yourself to embrace those areas, and then begin to move into alignment and abundance in each of those areas.

Three Levels of Inspiration

Considering the importance of connection, take a look at the possibility of your inspiration on three levels:

1. YOU—Yourself, which expands on your sense of self and who you are.
2. YOUR RELATIONSHIPS—How you demonstrate who you are by showing up in your relationships.
3. YOUR COMMUNITY—How you connect with your larger community, which may start as small as your own family and/or grow as big as the global community itself. How do you want to give back in a way that is in alignment with who you are and what you are passionate about?

As you expand your inspiration beyond Level One, you will also increase your commitment to change and to realizing your intention(s). Exercise C – Part II will provide you the framework to connect with your own inspiration on all three levels.

Connect with your inspirations and intentions early and often. That is where you will require the commitment and follow-through that you will read about in detail in Key Nine. Write them down and read them out loud to yourself every day. Do this in front of a mirror whenever you can. Observe your body language. Feel your feelings. Notice how you grow into the process day-by-day until the statements become an extension of who you are. (See Appendix I on Body-Centered Statements for more support in understanding how your statements can be felt and demonstrated in your body.)

Resisting Change

Why do you stay in prison when the door is so wide open?

—RUMI

Having something you *want* to change in your life, even if you feel inspired to do it, is not the same thing as *willingness*—a radical whole-self commitment. Saying to yourself, "I can't stand where I'm at, therefore, if A, B, and C would change I would be willing to change," is not true willingness to change. Nor is saying, "I can't stand where I'm at, so, therefore, I must be willing."

What is not working in your life? What is it you want to change? When it comes to your financial situation, maybe you can't pay your bills but are addicted to spending on things which aren't really serving you. Maybe you are not keeping your agreements with yourself or others. Whatever it is, if something is out of alignment in your life, you are probably experiencing resistance to change. Real change takes stepping outside your comfort zone. If you want to have a continuously positive relationship with money, it requires consistently stepping out of your comfort zone as well.

Notice if you tend to find every excuse to avoid changing something in your non-supportive money behaviors. These behaviors may include not opening your credit card statements, not managing your bank account to avoid fees, or using your credit card even when you don't have the money to pay it. By avoiding changing these activities, you are ignoring the long term consequences these will have on your life. Further, there are feelings associated with those behaviors to consider. What feelings are behind your actions or your inactions when it comes to your money? Very often, people just like you experience guilt, self-judgment, and shame, which lower self-worth and lead to more procrastination.

As you notice your feelings, don't despair or give yourself a hard time about them. That won't help. Instead, have some compassion for yourself and especially for your feelings. Your feelings are there for a reason and those reasons may be quite ingrained. See if you can understand what they are and where they came from. Understanding happens through compassion, not through criticism. The carrot works better than the stick.

For example, you may realize that opening your credit card statement will help you to pay it on time and not suffer late fees, but the pain and shame associated with opening it may feel like too much for you in the moment. Or you may realize that if you were to open up your bank statement, you'd again realize that you have too much sitting in cash and yet you haven't made the call to find a financial advisor or consult your current advisor. Or perhaps, if you opened your bank statement, you would have to face that you, once again, are bringing in a good amount of money, but seem to be scraping by each month.

Examples of self-defeating behaviors which may stem from such feelings are:

- Not opening the mail
- Avoiding bill collectors
- Using your credit card when you know it will anger your partner
- Not making calls to get changes on credit lines, levels of service, or decreases in fees or coverage
- Ignoring or resisting talking about money with your partner
- Living in denial of your financial situation

Do any of these apply to you? Can you think of others that might?

Why do you continue non-supportive behaviors, even once you recognize them as not serving you? Often, the dysfunctional behavior comes from fear, shame, guilt, anger, and rebellion, even if you are unaware of it. You may fear being judged by the person who would advise you, for example. You may use your credit card and ignore the fact that you don't have the money, because you have shame around facing your lack of money. You may be unconsciously rebelling against a spouse or a parent who was or is tight-fisted with money. Explore this concept through the questions within the Journal Joggers section at the end of the Key.

What's Your "B.S." (Belief System)?

Man is what he believes.

—ANTON CHEKHOV

The source of your non-supportive *behaviors* is likely in your non-supportive *beliefs*. You may even feel imprisoned by your own beliefs, consciously or unconsciously, as many of your beliefs, especially when it comes to money and wealth, are probably quite non-supportive. Your beliefs generally stem from messages you got from your parents as you were growing up, from your culture and society as a whole, and from what you have taught yourself or learned from peers. As this book focuses on your worth and your wealth, examples of such beliefs relating to money are:

- I'm not good at money or math.
- In order to have wealth of any kind, I have to work hard (effort, struggle, try, "it doesn't grow on trees," etc.).
- I won't be able to make money doing what I love.
- If I try and I don't succeed (at making money), I'll be a failure.
- If I do succeed at making money, I'll lose my friends and I won't be able to handle the responsibility.

Developing a deeper understanding of your own "B.S." is essential to the development of your perspective and your willingness to change.

Perception Is Reality

When you change the way you look at things, the things you look at change.

—WAYNE DYER

A belief forms a *reality filter*. It causes us to see the world through a narrow lens or filter. That lens is actually only capable of seeing what we believe. It filters out that which does not match our pre-existing belief. Therefore, the saying "You have to see it to believe it," is actually backwards. You have to believe it to see it!

The remarkable film, *"What the Bleep Do We Know,"* directed by William Arntz, offers a vivid portrayal of how this works. This documentary, based on quantum physics and the potential of the mind, tells a story, believed by some to be true, about the approach of Columbus' clipper ships to the Caribbean Islands. The fascinating part of the story is that the Native Americans were unable to see the ships on the horizon, because they had no model or experience (i.e., belief system) to match the existence of such things. In other words, they didn't see it because they didn't believe it. The shaman of the tribe, it is told, saw the ripples on the water. He went each day to watch these ripples and attempt to imagine what was causing them. Finally he was able to see. Once he saw the ships, because the other members of the tribe believed in him, they were then able to see them as well.

> *For those who believe, no proof is necessary.*
> *For those who don't believe, no proof is possible.*
>
> —STUART CHASE

We also attract what we believe. Sound like magical thinking to you? Actually it is really quite simple when you think in terms of that reality filter. Imagine that the universe around you is full of abundance and awash with anything you could ever dream of or desire. Like those Native Americans who couldn't see the ships, you can only dream of or desire that which you believe in—that which your reality filter allows you to focus on. Then what you see is what shows up! For example, have you ever purchased a new car and suddenly you see the same make and model everywhere? Where were they before? Apparently they weren't there and yet we realize, of course, "I just didn't notice them because that wasn't what I was focusing on." So, if you don't like what is showing up in your life, would you be willing to try a new reality filter—a new focus? Would you be willing to choose a new belief—one more likely to serve you?

What is the reality filter through which you view the world? If you were to consider your beliefs or reality filter like a pair of glasses that you've put on, what color are *your* glasses? In other words, what story keeps you stuck in an old belief system which may no longer be serving you? Many just like you spend their entire life gathering evidence and building a case to prove what you already believe, yet they are essentially limiting their own potential. Can you see how you may be doing this too?

With the help of your reality filters, you find evidence for what you believe to be true, so that you can build a case against change. Therefore your very case, your body of evidence, is nothing more than an example of your own reality filter at work again. As you explore your own individual belief systems, consider how they fit within the framework of following the four core belief systems.

Four Core Beliefs

If you look closely enough, you may see that most of your beliefs stem from one or more primary over-arching beliefs. We call these your *core beliefs*. The seeds of these beliefs were planted early in life, generally by one traumatic event, or a repeating series of small traumas, which locked a certain conviction into our consciousness. In keeping the principle of *you get what you are expecting*, or *you see what you believe*, your unconscious mind tends to put you into situations which reinforce your conviction in that belief.

Don't be too hard on your unconscious. It means well. It thinks that if you keep repeating the experience, you will eventually get it right. It is like waking from a bad dream and wanting to go back to it so that you can work your way out of it. Unfortunately, all this is getting you is more pain and a further conviction that your beliefs are right and valid.

The four primary core beliefs, under which all others tend to fall, are:

1. Not good enough
2. Deprived
3. Abandoned
4. Betrayed

Most people incorporate a mixture of more than one of these beliefs. For example, you may have been emotionally and/or physically abandoned by a parent who felt ashamed that he or she could not support you properly. Instead of speaking that truth, he/she may have given you a direct or indirect message that you did not deserve more. If that was your experience, you would likely have core beliefs about not being good enough, being deprived, and being abandoned. Or you may have told a secret to a sibling who then ridiculed you publicly for it, which would likely give you core beliefs about being betrayed and not being good enough.

Again, if you look carefully, you may find that one of these is the primary underlying belief beneath all your subsequent beliefs. Given that you are reading a book about improving your sense of worth, you have probably been challenged by at least one of the first two beliefs:

- not good enough = issues of self-worth
- deprived = issues of net worth

Let's look at how each of the four core beliefs functions and how each may play itself out with regard to you and your finances.

1. *Not good enough*

Somehow, most likely early in life, you got the idea that you had to live up to someone else's standards, be equal to someone else's gifts, or do something to earn love and appreciation. No matter how hard you tried, you never quite made it. Whatever you tried, it (or you) just wasn't quite good enough. As you embodied that belief, it was as if you went through life with a sign (invisible to you and in bright neon lights to everyone else) on your forehead saying "I'm not good enough." Other people's unconscious can read that sign and will expect you to play that part.

You may be likely to attract other people who want to feel good about themselves by putting you down in some way. Not that you need someone else to do that for you—you do a pretty good job of putting yourself down. You don't believe you have worth. In the realm of finance, that translates to not believing you deserve to have all the good things in life you would like to have. Devaluing yourself leads to an unconscious blocking of your flow of abundance and greater net worth, and often includes a physical manifestation through underearning or undercharging.

2. Deprived

If, early in life, you didn't have enough, or were unable to get what you wanted, you may have internalized a sense of deprivation. No matter how much you have in your life now—no matter how much wealth and goodness—it may be extremely difficult for you to take it in and fully enjoy it. A parallel would be a child who grows up overweight and is taunted or feels uncomfortable about it. As an adult, that same person may be thin by other's standards, but, when she looks in the mirror, she still carries the old image of herself and sees the ghost of that image.

If you believe you are deprived, no amount of wealth will change that belief inside you. We have known multi-millionaires who were convinced that the "poorhouse" was only one step behind them if they weren't hyper-vigilant. Only you can change your belief. Just like the deep-seated fear of being overweight can lead to anorexia, so, too, can the deep seated belief in deprivation lead to financial anorexia. (See Key Seven for a further explanation and understanding of the impact of financial anorexia.) You don't let yourself enjoy what you have. The place to start is with the small things—practice allowing yourself to really appreciate and take in something special that you have in your life, and let it grow from there until you grow an internal sense of your own true wealth.

3. Abandoned

Many people have experienced some degree of abandonment in life. It can happen in subtle and almost unnoticeable ways, such as in emotional abandonment, or in a more dramatic way, such as a parent disappearing abruptly from your life or your parents divorcing. Whatever the cause, if you have experienced abandonment in your life, you are likely to have an exaggerated fear of loss. Ironically, your fear of loss may actually drive people away from you, thus reinforcing your belief system that you will lose what you love.

The fear of loss may extend to more than just human beings. You may fear the loss of your net worth as well. This may lead to a hyper-focus on holding on to what you have and possibly feeling comforted by holding onto or having material items. This may lead to stinginess, clutter, or even hoarding. Or it may have seemingly the opposite effect where you believe, unconsciously, that you need to buy love and friendship, and you may overspend in your belief that you can hang on to others by gifting or caretaking them in some way.

4. Betrayed

If you have been betrayed in life by someone close to you (and, as we have described above, this pattern may have repeated itself), you are likely to harbor the belief that you will continue to be betrayed by others. Naturally this leads to a lack of trust. You may then make mistakes with your finances out of an unwillingness to trust the advice of others. You may become obsessed with amassing means of your own so that you will never be dependent on another. If you are successful at this, you may hoard your wealth so that no one can ever take it away from you. If you are unsuccessful at your strategy, you may place an inordinate amount of blame on someone else. You may even become reclusive so that you don't have to share or run the risk of being betrayed again, financially or otherwise.

These belief systems are not life sentences. Bringing them to your attention and into your awareness will help you to begin to change them. Celebrate the good news—you have choice over your thoughts. Your thoughts stem from your belief systems. Be mindful of your thoughts and trace them back to the underlying beliefs, note where those beliefs come from, and recognize that you can choose a different belief. You *can* start fresh. You actually *can* undo the past, since it exists only as neurochemical storage, or patterns planted in the brain. Plant a new "memory."

The Truth

The good news is that your belief systems are nothing more than made up stories that you have created—stories that you have full choice over. We know that may be difficult to comprehend. You have a lifetime invested in your beliefs. How wonderful it would be if you learned in second grade that you actually have choice over your attitudes and beliefs! Alas, those who taught you were probably too busy cramming down the acceptable or popular beliefs as truths themselves.

Ultimately, we can never know the absolute truth. Galileo was tried by the Inquisition for maintaining that the earth circled the sun. Columbus was turned down multiple times in his request for ships because of the absurdity of his belief that the world was round. What has recently been proven by quantum physics was thought for years to be hocus-pocus, except perhaps for some of the ancient Eastern philosophies which early on recognized similar principles, such as the malleability of truth and the nonexistence of matter.

People are so attached to their beliefs that they literally fight and die for them every day. If you will grant that you can't really know the ultimate Truth, would you be willing to choose a belief which is more likely to attract to you what it is that you truly want—a belief which truly serves you? Consider what it would be like to have a belief that serves both your self-worth and your net worth, such as "I am deserving of abundance." Try saying it to yourself with conviction and note what it feels like. Be aware of any part of yourself that resists or argues. That is where you have some work to do.

The Antidote

What can you do with your old belief system(s) and how do you choose a new one? Start by finding an antidote. Below are sample belief/antidote pairs relating to your beliefs around money to help you develop your own antidotes. (This is a good time to review Appendix I on Body-Centered Statements at the back of the book. Consider a Body-Centered Statement as one of your antidotes.)_____

BE WILLING TO CHANGE

Non-Supportive Beliefs: Bring disempowerment, helplessness, hopelessness, and panic	Supportive Beliefs: Provide encouragement, empowerment, and positive feelings
I'm not good at money or math.	I have access to the resources I need.
I have to work very hard for money.	Making money is easy, joyful and fun.
I won't be able to make money doing what I love.	I love what I do for money and I deserve to have it.
If I try and I don't succeed at making money, I'll be a failure. If I do succeed, I'll lose my friends and I won't be able to handle the responsibility.	People love me for who I am and encourage my success. I am capable and confident with my money, wealth, and well-being.

Here are some other sample non-supportive beliefs about money:

- I don't have enough money. I'll never have enough to feel secure or satisfied.
- I don't deserve it.
- There's not enough to go around.
- If I have something it will be taken away from me.
- It's too late for me to get better with my money.
- I'll be a bag lady.
- I'll never be able to retire.

See Exercise B at the end of the Key to complete your own list of beliefs and antidotes about money.

Beliefs Underlie Thoughts

If you are plagued by a troublesome thought pattern, explore the belief system associated with that particular thought pattern. Recurring thoughts stem from recurring beliefs. Core beliefs generally stem from early childhood messages and experiences. For example, your childhood experience may have created a belief that "The world is not a safe place." Without your conscious awareness of the connection, this belief may be resulting in some present thought such as, "This is a dangerous situation." The thought then results in a feeling—in this case *fear*.

Our overarching belief systems determine our thoughts. The power of our thoughts is tremendous. Our thoughts create our feelings. (More on understanding how to better feel your feelings in Key Three.) If you doubt this assertion, try this simple exercise. Close your eyes and imagine someone sitting in front of you sucking on a lemon. Did that create a feeling in your own body, such as salivation or puckering? Feelings consist of both sensations and emotions, as shown in the lemon example. It works the same way with emotions; the connection may, however, be less obvious to you at first.

If we do not become conscious of our feelings and able to sit with and observe them, they may result in actions and events counter to our aspirations. Next, complete the assessment of your current belief systems detailed in Appendix II to help you identify your beliefs, thoughts, and feelings about money in more detail.

There is nothing you need to *do* to deserve happiness and abundance in life. It is your natural birthright. Who you are, sitting here today, is amazing and wonderful and you deserve all the best. What would it take for you to believe that, and thus to begin to transform your belief system into something that serves you? Do you find yourself saying, "I wish I could stop overspending," or "If only I hadn't bought that," or "If only I had bought that?" These are very disempowering messages. The reality is that you don't stop because the part of you that wants to continue outweighs the part of you that wants to stop right now. That's okay—don't beat yourself up about it. You can, however, recognize that there is *choice* involved. That in itself is empowering. Messages like "I can't stop" take away your choice. Acknowledge that a part of you is choosing not to and you reclaim your power as you recognize you have the power to choose. This is all part of stepping into and embracing the willingness to change.

Of course, it's scary to change—to let old beliefs and habits die inside you. When the beliefs through which you have always viewed the world change, it may be a little frightening. That is understandable and appropriate. Change is a shock to your system, even if you desperately want things to be better.

Role of Focus and Gratitude

What can you do if you find yourself out of alignment, unmotivated, uninspired, or still stuck in old beliefs? Start by practicing gratitude as a way of strengthening the muscle of appreciation and building your focus on what you want, as opposed to what you don't want. Often you may spend more time on what you don't want, and then, not so surprisingly, that is all you create. In the process, you don't actually clarify what you want. Then you may find yourself again building more and more evidence that you are only worthy of what you don't want—as more and more of your evidence seems to indicate that is true.

You can stop this bitter cycle. Not only does your reality filter affect what you see of what is all around you, what you focus on actually expands. Your vision becomes more expansive, creating your reality. You actually attract and get more of what you focus on. This is not a new concept. Teachers, writers, and leaders such as Napoleon Hill, Wallace Wattles, John Assaraf, and Abraham-Hicks have spoken of it in many ways for decades. More recently, due to the media popularity of "The Secret," many refer to it as the Law of Attraction. As you expand your gratitude for what you do have in your life, you create an opening to receive in a flow of worthiness, both internally and externally.

Whatever the mind of man can conceive and believe it can achieve.

—NAPOLEON HILL

Further, the act of acknowledging what you have already manifested in your life (even if sometimes it was negative) can help you with the impetus and recognition of your power to create what you want. As you begin to observe this working in your life, your sense of inspiration, possibility, and potential will begin to grow. Use gratitude as a tool for noticing what it is you are attracted to, and deepen your clarity about what you want.

Taking the Leap

The greatest thing in this world is not such where we are, but in what direction we are moving.

—Oliver Wendell Holmes

Have you ever jumped off a diving board? A cliff? There are people who do it for a living—diving off cliff edges into the water below. You might think, "Wow, that person is fearless." This is almost certainly not true. Most human beings will feel fear before they are about to jump off a cliff's edge. But a high-jump diver has the courage to be afraid, feel the fear, and jump. Courage is not the absence of fear, because without fear there is no courage or sense of danger. It is the willingness to feel the fear and do it anyway—to recognize that something else has priority for you over staying in the fear. This is what willingness to change is all about: staying present with your feelings, welcoming them even if they feel scary, and then taking that leap of faith.

There Is No Try

It is not the strongest of the species that survives, nor the most intelligent, but the one most responsive to change.

—Charles Darwin

You don't change by *trying* to change. You change by changing. We get hung up on the trying or wanting to change. We join groups for people who are trying to change. We talk to our friends about how difficult it is and "if only" we could make things different. You can! The minute you are 100% willing to change, change has taken place. There is nothing in the way.

Discard the word *try* from your vocabulary. Do it or don't do it. The character of the wise one, Yoda, in the first *Stars Wars* episode said "Do or do not. There is no try." The word *try* gives you a back door—it lets you off the hook because there is no true commitment associated with it. "Try" to do something right now. "Try" to pick up an object off a surface near you, such as a cup off a coffee table. No, we didn't say "pick it up." We said "try." What does that look like? What does that feel like? Now imagine you are going through your life making that kind of an effort with no result. Your results (or lack of results) may become much less surprising.

Perhaps you are making things harder than they need to be. You have been programmed to think it must be hard in order to mean anything. A common belief system is that in order to earn money, you have to work hard—you have to struggle. Does that sound familiar to what you may have been taught or taught yourself? What is it you are struggling for right now? Probe your belief system. Especially when it comes to creating net worth, do you make it harder than it needs to be?

Jumping: A Life Without Regrets

As you move forward into your life, you will come upon a great chasm. Jump. It is not as wide as you think.

— ADVICE TO A YOUNG ZUNI
UPON INITIATION INTO ADULTHOOD

We have essentially asked you to leap off a cliff. What have you been waiting for? Why have you been standing on the edge, or the sidelines, of your life? The cliff may feel safe because it is old and familiar. But if what's familiar is not bringing you joy and abundance, is it worth it to keep standing there? Weigh the pros and cons of standing on that cliff—the risk/reward ratio. Is staying safe worth giving up the potential reward of living the abundant and affluent life?

Let yourself dive into your stuck places and allow yourself to be who you truly are. Take that leap of faith. It's a leap of faith because you are diving into the unknown. The new is always unknown. You may first need to let yourself believe that the cool water below is better than the rocky edges of the cliff. We are guessing that, by now, you are discovering that the payoffs of staying where you are aren't worth the costs, and that is a very good place to be. Keep reading and taking action!

It has been said that we don't regret things in life that we have tried and failed as much as things we have never tried. All of your life has brought you to this moment. It is yours and you can do with it what you will. Not one moment of your life has been wasted since it has all in some way been working toward this moment. We invite you to spread your wings and soar.

EXERCISES

Note: Before you begin work with the exercises in this book, please refer to Appendix I. We strongly encourage you to do that now so you maximize the impact of your time and energy. Next, complete Appendix II to document your current Belief Assessment at the beginning of this *Self-Worth to Net Worth* process.

Exercise A: The Cost of Comfortable

What is staying comfortable costing me?

Make a list of the benefits of staying where you are and not changing.

Make a list of what you are (consciously and previously unconsciously) giving up in order to stay comfortable.

In actual dollars, what are your current beliefs and behaviors costing you?

Full range: Minimum:_____ and Maximum:_____

Average per month:_____

Per year (multiply per month times 12):_____

Over the next 5 years (multiply per year times 5):_____

Make a long list of what else you could be doing with that money.

Exercise B: Shift to Supportive Beliefs

Make a list of some of the beliefs which are no longer serving you and replace them with ones that are. Here are some of the most frequently encountered beliefs to consider when you are discovering your own. (Some of the most crucial were already included within the Key.)

Non-Supportive Beliefs: Bring disempowerment, helplessness, hopelessness, and panic	Supportive Beliefs: Provide encouragement, empowerment, and positive feelings
EXAMPLES:	
I'm not good at money or math.	I have access to the resources I need.
I have to work very hard for money.	Making money is easy, joyful, and fun.
I won't be able to make money doing what I love.	I love what I do for money and I deserve it.
If I try and I don't succeed at making money, I'll be a failure. If I do succeed, I'll lose my friends and I won't be able to handle the responsibility.	People love me for who I am and encourage my success. I am capable and confident with money.
What happened to me has made me non-functional around money.	I choose what I believe.
There's no way out of this situation.	I seize opportunities with my eyes wide open.
It's too late for me to regularly save money and I am doomed to struggle for the rest of my life.	I create my own bright future starting today.
I can't let go of the fact that I lost so much money.	I live in gratitude and unlimited wealth possibilities.

I'm too confused about what I want and what I should be doing to think straight.	My daily choices align easily with my priorities and my purpose.
I'm too scared to change anything.	I strive to expand my comfort zone.
I'm paralyzed by the mistakes I have made.	I courageously face my fears.
I don't deserve to be wealthy.	My strong self-worth leads to my abundant net worth.
I have to do it all myself.	I am supported by a powerful team.
I am angry with myself and others for the situation I'm in.	I forgive past mistakes and celebrate all wins.
I'm not good with money or with decisions, so I prefer to let someone else handle all that for me.	I am the hero and the creator of my own life story.
I am powerless over my financial situation and my whole life is based on trying to keep up.	I own my money—my money doesn't own me.
FOR YOU:	
Non-Supportive Beliefs: Bring disempowerment, helplessness, hopelessness, and panic	*Supportive Beliefs: Provide encouragement, empowerment, and positive feelings*

Exercise C

Part I: Where do you want to be in your life?

This is a four-part written exercise to further understand where you are, where you want to be, appreciate the disparity, and explore what is in your way. Take the opportunity to contemplate and journal about the questions below.

1. Where you are: Describe your current situation in life. Then, specifically describe your current *financial* situation, including your emotional relationship to money as well as the actual financial circumstances you are in.
2. Where you want to be: Describe where you want to be in relation to both your life and your money (Self-worth and Net Worth). State your intention in the present tense positive, for example: "I have an income of _____, and am experiencing great gratitude and joy in all areas of my life."
3. For each item you have identified in Step Two, list what is in the way between where you are and where you want to be. Be as thorough as possible, taking into consideration both internal and external blocks.
4. What is one step you can take in the next 48-hours to eliminate each item from Step Three to move closer to where you want to be?

Exercise C

Part II: Inspiration: What would you do with more abundance and money in your life?

Write down 5–10 specific things you want to do with more abundance in your life for each of the three identified areas of inspiration:

1 = You

BE WILLING TO CHANGE

1

2 = Your Relationships

3 = Your Community

Identify the number one priority for yourself in each category.

Then, with your top three inspirations identified, choose one that truly touches your soul. Write it below in large lettering and refer to it often to help you maintain your motivation. Use this as a starting point—the start of a new level of deeper inspiration to both move forward through this book and through your life.

Visualization

From the exercises above, having picked the number one thing you want to do with more abundance in your life, visualize actually having that abundance and doing what it is you want to do. Bask in being the person this abundance has helped you to become.

Conscious Breathing

In this Key, we have invited you to understand the link between breath and inspiration. We have encouraged you to read Appendix I which talks more about breath. Clearly, breathing is important to your process of transformation. Yet so few people are aware of their breathing. It is a very special bodily function as it is conscious if you make it, and autonomic when you don't. This meditation practice can provide one way for you to honor the breath of life that is your great gift.

An ancient and very simple form of meditation and creating mindfulness is simply watching the breath. That is the place for you to start. If you develop a sitting meditation practice even for five minutes a day of following your breath with your awareness, it can change your life. You may focus on your nostrils as the air moves in and out, or focus on your belly, rib cage and chest, as they expand and contract. As thoughts arise, your breathing pattern changes. Note that every single thought has an effect on your breath. When you think negative or fear-based thoughts, your breath tends to become shallow, which in turn creates a greater sensation of fear and "smallness" in your body. The practice of conscious awareness and focus on the breath, even for five minutes a day, can carry into your daily life. You begin to develop the habit of breathing into your feelings and thus avoiding allowing your thoughts to take away your power, cause you to feel smaller, and minimize your worth.

Body-Centered Statements

1. I am willing to change. I am changing. It is safe.
2. I deserve abundance in my life.
3. I love my work and money flows easily to me.
4. I am worthy of abundance and affluence.
5. People love me for who I am and encourage my success. I am capable and confident with money.
6. When my body, mind, and spirit are in alignment, I feel calm and all possibilities for change become possible.
7. I give myself permission to wonder.

Journal Joggers

Use the following questions to lead you into your journal entries for this Key, or choose your own.

- What would you most like to change regarding your relationship with your own worthiness (your self-worth)?
- Why haven't you changed it? What's in the way?
- Would it be worth it to you to eliminate that obstacle?
- What are some steps you would be willing to take to do so?

- What would you most like to change regarding your relationship and situation with your money (your net worth)?
- Why haven't you changed it? What's in the way?
- Would it be worth it to you to eliminate that obstacle?
- What are some steps you would be willing to take to do so?
- What are your dysfunctional patterns around your Self-Worth and Net Worth?
- What are the underlying beliefs that accompany each of those dysfunctional patterns/behaviors?
- Then, for each one, what is one small step you are willing to take in order to remedy your pattern?

For the items identified in Exercise C above, what feelings arise when you experience the hope and possibility of these new beliefs becoming your reality? Imagine and describe in vivid detail what this will look, taste, smell, sound, and kinesthetically feel like. See if you can breathe in a sense of excitement and possibility.

You must be the change you wish to see in the world.

—MOHANDAS GANDHI

KEY TWO
CLAIM RESPONSIBILITY

The moment you are old enough to take the wheel,
responsibility lies with you.

—J. K. ROWLING

The cause of most dissatisfaction with your self-worth and net worth stems from a failure to take full responsibility for them. The reverse is also true: Feelings of satisfaction with *your* self-worth and net worth occur when you take responsibility for *your* actions and decisions in *your* life, especially with *your* money. So, you can create your own satisfaction. How?

Planting the Seeds of Worth

Think of the *act* of claiming personal and financial responsibility as planting *seeds of worth* in your garden of life. François-Marie Arouet, the French Enlightenment writer, historian, and philosopher better known by his pen name of Voltaire, said, "We must cultivate our own garden." How true this is for every one of us. When we take care of ourselves, we can grow. And what

CLAIM RESPONSIBILITY

2

happens when seeds are lovingly cared for? They grow strong, healthy, and vibrant. Nurturing your *claiming responsibility seed* helps you grow an increased sense of wholeness, creativity, and aliveness in your body, mind, and spirit. Your entire being becomes empowered. On the other hand, blaming and complaining almost instantly eliminates your power.

Do you claim responsibility for your sense of self-worth? For your net worth? Ask yourself this question: on a moment-to-moment basis, do I take responsibility for my choices, my actions, and their consequences? If you can't clearly declare "Yes!" then claiming responsibility is an area you are going to want to nurture.

Playing the Victim

When you plant lettuce, if it does not grow well,
you don't blame the lettuce.

—THICH NHAT HANH

You assign yourself the role of victim when you choose to focus on complaining, and blame external forces, circumstances, or people for your situation. In essence, you relinquish your power over your own life, especially your worthiness.

There is but one (wonderful) way out of the victim role: the act of claiming responsibility! Claiming responsibility for yourself—your choices, your actions, your self-worth, and your net worth—is a deeply freeing experience.

Have you ever played the victim? Have you ever made a decision and found yourself complaining "poor me" to everyone, as well as to yourself? Did being the martyr, or the victim, feel good in your body? Did your body feel alive when it was complaining? Staying stuck in the victim mode will not bring you happiness or financial gain. You will go through life looking over your shoulder and carrying around a bag of toxic resentment and regrets that you don't know what to do with.

This doesn't mean that you haven't suffered losses. It doesn't mean that life is fair. It doesn't mean that you haven't been taken advantage of.

It doesn't mean that you haven't been deprived or betrayed. But if you're putting energy into holding on to those stories, you're claiming the victim role. And then, you fail to become unstuck. You don't change, because you think if you do change then you would be letting "so-and-so" off the hook, i.e., "so-and-so" being the one who wronged you. Even if "so-and-so" is the stock market, God, or life itself, it's easy to stand in victimhood. But you can end this disempowerment, scarcity mentality, and resulting unhappiness. You can liberate yourself by claiming responsibility in and for your life. Trust in your power to take ownership of your sense of self-worth as well as your net worth.

Identifying with Blame

Blame of self and/or another is an easy way to avoid claiming responsibility for the way you are spending your time, your life, *and* your money.

If you can't blame someone for what has gone wrong financially, for example, and you don't want to blame yourself, you may find yourself without a clear sense of identity—of who you are and where you stand. Blame, shame, judgment, guilt, and complaining often become building blocks for your financial identity, as well as your sense of self-worth or lack thereof. Though they are negative hooks, they still tie you into your perceived and unconsciously chosen role.

Just as letting go of your identity may have been blocking your willingness to change, the concept of letting go of those blaming feelings, and the accompanying stories, can be scary too. The unconscious fear that doing so will leave you without an identity can be paralyzing. You realize, at least unconsciously, that you will be forced to claim responsibility for yourself and your part in having created your present circumstances, as well as your ability to create your future. The positive side is that the more willing you are to claim responsibility for both the positive and the negative you have created in your life, the more you empower yourself to claim responsibility for creating your future. Often, people will cling to their current sense of identity, even when it clearly doesn't serve them, rather than take the risk of stepping into the unknown and unfamiliar.

2

The Blame Game

How can you halt the vicious cycles of bitterness, resentment, and regrets over your losses, lack, and backstory that seem to never want to go away? Stop blaming. Many people confuse taking responsibility with blaming oneself. "I take responsibility. I know I'm to blame," is a typical response. If you do not accept responsibility through blame, how then do you claim it? What is the difference? Remember, we said that taking responsibility causes satisfaction. This is a key to ending blame. Blame cannot cause satisfaction because blame is a form of negativity. Negativism cannot create something positive any more than darkness can create light. Blame and responsibility are, in fact, opposites. Responsibility means claiming ownership, and blame is pushing off ownership as beyond you. In fact, we call claiming responsibility the no-blame stance.

Take this example: You've been consistently saving money, you've done your research, and you've invested it in the stock market based on historically consistent returns. In a 12-month period, your diversified portfolio has gone down by 40%. Outside blame: "The politicians and bankers have mismanaged the economy." "We are paying for the botched jobs of top CEOs." "People who were trying to keep up with the Joneses spent more on homes, cars, and toys than they could afford." Self-blame: "I should have seen the market decline coming. I should have pulled my money out sooner." "I'm just not good at money management." "I can't do anything right." Taking responsibility: "I did the best I could with what I knew at the time." "When I invested, I knew that there were risks and I looked at a long-term average return."

Blame will turn every situation sour. Blame is like a dance with a "hot potato." First, you blame yourself, but then the hot potato of blame that you are holding gets too hot, so you throw it to someone else and blame them. Soon you feel guilty because you see their hands burning, so you grab the hot potato back and blame yourself again. But then that potato gets hot again in your hands, so you throw the blame to someone else. Sound familiar?

The Language of Blame

Don't find fault, find a remedy.

— HENRY FORD

A self-blamer's life and language is full of *shoulds* and *shouldn'ts*. An outside-blamer's life and language is full of *can't* and *have to*. Both of these approaches alienate people and are barriers to communication as well as to experience. This tends to lead to a lack of abundance and a decreased sense of self-worth. While a self-blamer confuses responsibility with blaming herself, an outside-blamer confuses responsibility with duty, which is part of her *have-to*. She can then blame the duty itself for her lack of time, freedom, or money, heaping layers upon layers of blame and guilt in an endless cycle of defeatism. "I take responsibility. I pay my bills on time," she may say from between clenched teeth. What happened to choice, freedom, and the natural flow of affluence? The outside-blamer denies that any of these are possible due to external circumstances. The self-blamer feels that these are beyond her ability and control.

Children are taught to blame in every situation and this pattern continues into adulthood. You were likely asked, and now you ask yourself, "Whose fault was it?" You may go on stubbornly itemizing each incidence of dissatisfaction that touches your consciousness and look for a cause to blame your dissatisfaction on. This perennial hunt for objects of blame narrows your window of perception on the world when applied to money, events, and people around you. When this hunt for objects of blame is applied to your own dissatisfaction, the consequences are even more serious. It breeds bitterness, hatred, and resentment of self, others, and even money (or the lack thereof). This reaction, in turn, causes further alienation, more bitterness, and more dissatisfaction.

Imagine a life where the concept of "fault" doesn't exist—where everyone is simply doing what they believe will bring them the most happiness and satisfaction, even if the path they choose has led them astray. The Buddhists say that all creatures have one thing in common—they seek pleasure and happiness. Some know the trick of how to find it. Other's actions bring the opposite result. Yet fundamentally, everyone is striving for the same thing. If you have, or someone else has, chosen a path that has not resulted in what you want, can you forgive yourself? Can you forgive the other? Holding onto the blame doesn't hurt anyone else but you.

Punishing Through Blame

One reason you may be placing blame on someone is to punish them or prove a point. Your thinking may be something like this: "If I allow myself to let go of this and make a lot of money, or if I allow myself to be happy, 'they' will have won because I have failed to prove that 'they' ruined my life." Can you see the irony of this statement? By not letting go of the situation, you are not allowing yourself to have the life of financial or emotional freedom you deserve! You have not won anything: In fact, your body will feel defeated and your sense of aliveness will slowly disintegrate. What is the cost to you, to your financial future, and your sense of aliveness when you place blame on someone, something, or on yourself?

Many people spend years trying to change a spouse or other loved one. Consider these examples: You can see so clearly all the things he or she does wrong with money. "If only" she would be willing to make minor changes, our family finances could work. "If only" he wouldn't be so defensive and we could talk about it. "If only" she would listen. "If only" he would keep his agreements. And what do you get for your efforts? You get more of the same. The harder you push, the harder your partner pushes back, and the more the dysfunctional behavior becomes entrenched. Change only comes when you claim 100% responsibility for changing yourself and drop any agenda to change the other. You then create the space for them to also claim 100% responsibility for themselves.

It may have seemed easier to give up freedom through a process of withdrawal and not claiming responsibility than to risk a sense of shame, regret, or failure. You begin to turn this situation around by taking matters into your own hands. Does the relationship with your partner over money get better right away? No. In fact, at first it may get worse. From Cia's work in counseling couples, she has come to call this the *rocking the boat* phase.

When *you* change, it creates ripples that affect everyone near you due to the effect that it has on *their* status quo.

For example, if you decide that you no longer want to be the only person managing your family finances, that will certainly have an effect on your spouse and you are likely to notice some resistance. Since they are not the initiators of this change, they are likely to resist it. This may cause a period of stress and friction in the relationship. But focusing on *you* begins to help *you*. Then learning to communicate what you need in a self-responsible way will enable your partner and those around you to better understand the nature of your shift.

Self-Responsible Communication

Self-responsible communication is communication which uses "I" language and is not attacking, belittling, or blaming. This extends to body language and tone of voice as well. It is possible to use perfectly self-responsible words while the tone and body language express sarcasm, hostility, and so on. The basic format of self-responsible communication is: "When you said or did _____, I felt _____." Gay and Kathlyn Hendricks refer to speaking the truth of what we feel as the "microscopic" or "unarguable" truth, because it boils everything down to the one truth that no one can seriously argue with—what you feel. Everything else is arguable. Marshall Rosenburg, best-selling author of *Non-Violent Communication* and *Speak Peace in a World of Conflict*, expands upon this technique and skillfully turns it into an art form.

When a couple comes to see Cia as clients, they are required to make an agreement to speak self-responsibly during the sessions. Cia explains in brief that this means no name calling, no raising of voices, no aggressive body language, and no blame or verbal attacks. It is interesting to watch the number of couples who are stuck for something to say, as it has been so long since they consciously engaged in fully self-responsible communication.

When Kara and Cole first met with Cia, money was tight and Kara had just received a small inheritance of $30,000 from her grandmother.

Kara, who married young and became pregnant soon after, had never had money of her own. Kara felt beholden to Cole for the money he earned to support the family. Although Cole did nothing overt that would make her feel that way, Kara based these feelings on stories she carried with her from her past. She begrudged herself the right to ask for spending money for little treats or indulgences. When she did ask, she imagined a scowl on Cole's face as he wrote out the check. Though he rarely mentioned that it was a squeeze getting the monthly bills paid, she imagined that he would resent the check he wrote her at the end of the month when he wrote out the other checks. So Kara very much wanted to put her inheritance away into her own account, so that she could then use the monies for personal items which felt important to her, but might not feel important to him.

Cole was incensed. He wanted to put that money into the family "pot" to help defray the expenses they were struggling to meet. It was beyond him to understand how "after all these years of selflessly supporting the family," "hardly ever taking a day off," and "hardly ever buying a single thing for himself," that Kara would want to keep that money to herself. His mind took off on him. Before long, he had an internal dialogue going about Kara hoarding money for herself, so that she could eventually leave him. He became suspicious and tightened the reins even more, which, of course, only made Kara surer that it was vital for her to have her own account.

Like so many clients, each one was convinced that Cia would tell them they were "right" and would "explain" to their partner the error of his or her ways. Since Cia doesn't coach for "right" and "wrong", the good news is that after the first session, the couple often walks away both angry at Cia! Why is this good news? They suddenly have something in common. They start talking again. That leads to their coming back for their next appointment with a glimmer of willingness and hope.

Here are some examples of non self-responsible communication which came out of the session, with a proposed more self-responsible alternative.

Non Self-Responsible	Self-Responsible Communication
You are wrong.	In my way of looking at it, that way of thinking has some flaws in it which are not serving us. For example, . . .
You are selfish.	I understand that you are feeling afraid and therefore trying to protect yourself. So am I.
You OWE this to me.	What I want for us is . .
You always (or you never) . . .	I am concerned about what seems to be a certain pattern in our relationship. From where I stand it looks like . . .
You don't care about me.	I notice that right now I am projecting that my feelings are not important to you. I feel . . .
It's my right, and not fair.	I notice that my way of looking at it is different than yours. I imagine that . . .

CLAIM RESPONSIBILITY

2

Notice that the non self-responsible communication usually involves the word "you", whereas the self-responsible communication always uses "I" statements. The non self-responsible speaker focuses all of his or her energy on what their partner is doing wrong, rather than trying to see clearly the two points of view, which might bring them closer to reconciliation. When the sentence starts with "You", or is an ultimatum, demand, or states a supposed "fact" as if it is irrefutable, the partner has no opening for a dialogue and will only respond with his or her most familiar coping strategy (fight, flight, freeze, or faint). (These coping strategies will be discussed in more detail in Key Seven.)

In the end, Kara and Cole wound up dividing the money. Half of it went to pay down mutual debts, thus lowering their monthly payments, and the other half went into an account for Kara. Both were very happy with the final arrangement.

The Impact of Blame on Your Partner

To engage in true self-responsible communication, you will need to clear your blame for your partner. Susan Jeffers, author of the internationally acclaimed best-selling classic book, *Feel the Fear and Do It Anyway,* poses a very helpful question: "What am I not doing in my life that I could be doing that I am blaming him for not doing for me?" She attributes much of the success of her marriage to her application of this question. This technique can work for anyone you are blaming—not only a spouse.

As you think and act smarter with money (starting to "own your money"™), you will begin to feel more confident, make more powerful choices (leading to a sense of self-worth), and learn to create more net worth and abundance in your life. Over time, your partner may see the benefit of this change. He/she may even stop resisting it and follow the momentum of the change. Day by day, he/she may start taking his/her lunch to work, helping write out checks to pay the bills, and even initiate conversations about your financial future. We can't promise that will happen in every relationship, but if the relationship is worth sticking around for, it will. Either way, claiming responsibility for your own life and financial transformation is the only way to go, no matter what. You are worth it.

Believing that someone or something else, whether it is a spouse, the stock market, the universe, or even God, is responsible for what you are feeling or for your current emotional and financial situation is disempowering. It is also addicting. It is much easier to have something outside of yourself to blame for your own lack of satisfaction, self-esteem, or financial success. You may find it hard to even imagine what it would be like to embrace an alternate view. What would this mean about you?

Wouldn't you feel like a failure if you didn't have something to blame your situation on? Yet deep down inside you feel like a failure for harboring blame. Letting go of blame is empowering.

Autobiography in Five Short Chapters
Poem by Portia Nelson

CHAPTER 1

I walk down the street.
There is a deep hole in the sidewalk.
I fall in.
I am lost . . . I am helpless.
It isn't my fault.
It takes forever to find a way out.

CHAPTER 2

I walk down the same street.
There is a deep hole in the sidewalk.
I pretend I don't see it.
I fall in again.
I can't believe I am in the same place.
But, it isn't my fault.
It still takes a long time to get out.

CHAPTER 3

I walk down the same street.
There is a deep hole in the sidewalk.
I see it is there.
I still fall in . . . it's a habit.
My eyes are open.
I know where I am.

It is my fault.
I get out immediately.

CHAPTER 4

I walk down the same street
There is a deep hole in the sidewalk.
I walk around it.

CHAPTER 5

I walk down another street.

Reprinted with the permission of Atria Books, a division of Simon & Schuster, Inc., from THERE'S A HOLE IN MY SIDEWALK: THE ROMANCE OF SELF-DISCOVERY by Portia Nelson. Copyright © 1993 by Portia Nelson. All rights reserved.

The Waiting Game

One way of avoiding responsibility is the strategy of waiting for something to be different. The person or thing we are waiting on to change becomes our scapegoat—our excuse for staying stuck. For example, one of Belinda's clients, Margaret, approached Belinda with some dissatisfaction about her current financial approach. Belinda helped her realize that she had created the stock market as her scapegoat. Instead of taking any responsibility for her life or her own portfolio, she sat around and waited for the Dow to top 12,000 again before she would act. She delegated her power of choice and action to a factor completely beyond her control. Who (or what) is your scapegoat and what are you waiting for?

Often you may put on a good show, and believe it yourself, of trying to change that person or situation that you are blaming. Deep down, however, if you are willing to look carefully, you may see that there is a part of yourself invested in *not* having that person or situation change. If they, or it, changed, you would lose your scapegoat! You might even have to change yourself! Even if you succeeded in changing that outside entity, it would not really serve you in the way you think it would. For change to be meaningful in your life, it needs to come from within yourself. Only then can change be fully integrated in your life and allow you to grow. External change can trigger an internal response. As you claim responsibility for your response, you grow.

Where to Start (Hint: Claim Responsibility)

How can you begin to take greater responsibility for your wealth, your worth, and your life? Begin by observing how you speak and think, including *have to* and *can't*. With practice, you will see subtle thought patterns and faulty thinking such as: "all or nothing," exaggeration, guilt, shame, over-generalization, should, predicting the future, focusing on the past, judging, and especially, blame. Also, noticing your body language helps you tune in to your mind-state. Watch for patterns in your life, especially connections between events such as getting sick every time you have to pay your bills or go on a job interview. Once you gain more awareness of your words, body language, and past patterns, you have become an observer of your present actions. We referred to mindfulness in Key One as a tool for becoming aware of your thought patterns. Thought, speech, and action are a connected trinity. Becoming aware of any one of them—thinking before your speak or act, for example—can help you claim responsibility for all of them.

Always aim at complete harmony of thoughts and word and deed.
Always aim at purifying your thoughts and everything will be well.

— MOHANDAS GANDHI

By becoming more aware of thought, word, and deed, you will become empowered to make conscious choices about how you will carry your sense of healthy responsibility into action. One by one, change your actions to align with your newfound ability to claim responsibility for your self-worth and your net worth—essentially for your life and your money!

CLAIM RESPONSIBILITY

2

Claiming Responsibility For Your Feelings

How can you claim responsibility for your feelings? By acknowledging that it is not the person or event that is *causing* our feelings, but it is your response to that person or event. The person or event is the trigger. We call it the domino effect. Think of a long row of dominoes set on end. The *trigger* is just barely touching the domino closest to you. Once you trigger this first domino, the whole row, no matter how long, topples. Each domino represents a time in your life that you have felt the same feeling. The very last domino represents the first time you ever felt that particular feeling. Often that is the most impactful. If you can follow the row all the way back to its beginning, you can start to own that what seems like it is all about the current event, is actually also about something much deeper; therefore, your reaction may be way out of proportion to the circumstance.

Here's an example: Cathy noticed she was losing her temper with her contractor and building subcontractors because they weren't doing what she told them to do. Cia coached her by asking: "How is this familiar? What does this remind you of?" What Cathy got is that she didn't feel heard. She was then flooded with childhood memories of how much it hurt that her voice wasn't heard and she didn't feel understood. Once she grasped this, she was able to claim responsibility that this was her issue stemming from her belief, based on childhood experiences, that she wouldn't be heard. Cathy was thus manifesting that over and over again in her life, and getting angrier and angrier each time it happened. Now when/if Cathy loses her temper, she pauses to ask herself, "Am I not feeling heard?" She now knows something very important about herself by understanding this trigger. It doesn't mean that she doesn't lose her temper, but she now realizes that this is her trigger. Then she can catch herself faster and change the pattern. Cathy can say "I'm not feeling heard right now. How can I be more clear so I am better heard?" Cathy has experienced amazing compassion for herself and others through this realization, as well as increased power in being able to more appropriately respond in these trigger situations. The net result is that she, in fact, is more likely to be heard.

Are You the Owner or the Renter in Your Own Life?

In your life, you are either choosing to play the part of the owner or the renter. Being the renter in your own life means that you are treating your life as if you weren't going to be there very long. You complain about the circumstances but fail to claim ownership of them. (In Key Four, we will further explore the impact of complaining and how it serves to bring you more reasons to complain.) As an owner, on the other hand, you claim full responsibility for and authority over the circumstances of your life and your reactions to those circumstances.

Once you own your life, then you can utilize the power of that ownership to claim ownership of your money and your entire net worth. When you step up as the owner, you leave your blame, shame, judgment, complaining, and guilt at the door. You don't get to hide behind them any longer.

Become the CEO of Your Life

No one can make you feel inferior without your consent.

— Eleanor Roosevelt

As a true owner, you are the Chief Executive Officer ("CEO") of your life. Accepting this opens up a whole new world of possibility. You get to create your life the way you want it to be. Think of your life as an organization and you as the CEO. Claim ownership! Who's the boss here, anyway? Are the mission and vision statements of your life/organization clear and in order? Are your goals and priorities clear and in order? Of course there are obstacles. Noticing how you can begin to take responsibility for handling those obstacles in a way that works for you is empowering. No one has power over you unless you give it to them. You have a *right* to be responsible for your life.

As you step into your rightful role as the CEO of your life, you will discover that a primary stepping stone to realizing your worth and its related power is in owning your money. Ask yourself, "Do I own my money, or does it own me?"™ If you've never asked yourself that question, you are not as wealthy, in all aspects of your life, as you can be. Owning your money and owning your life are closely intertwined. As you own your money, you own your life. As you own your life, you own your money.

Here are five keys to Own Your Money™:

1. Taking responsibility for your financial situation without judgment, blame, or shame.
2. Creating a positive relationship *to* money and abundance.
3. Discovering how to easily and effectively use money to create the life you desire and deserve.
4. Becoming smart with money.
5. Clarifying what you truly value so that you stress less and spend better.

What impact would it have on your life if you started implementing these keys to owning your money into your life starting today? Choose one small step that you can do to start incorporating this new empowered ownership into your life.

100% Responsibility

"They cannot take away our self-respect if we do not give it to them."

—MOHANDAS GANDHI

Self-responsibility is a balance. It's not about taking more than your share, and it's not about taking less than your share. It's about finding what 100% responsibility is for you. Not 200%. It's just as much of a problem if you start taking responsibility for more than your share, than it is if you take responsibility for less. If your partner isn't paying the bills on time and you take over the job, even though you hate it and it gives you anxiety attacks to do it, you are claiming more than 100% responsibility.

Drs. Gay and Kathlyn Hendricks, psychologists and the authors of *Conscious Loving* and numerous other books, with whom Cia studied and who strongly influenced her Keys, talk about the 100% model of responsibility. In their relationship trainings, they discourage the tendency of people to look at shared responsibility as "I have 50%, so you should carry 50%." Their powerful model calls upon each one of us to carry 100% responsibility for ourselves. When we are ready to own that full 100% responsibility, we are ready to show up in life and in relationship in a powerful way. The Hendrickses also point out that carrying more than 100%, such as taking responsibility for someone else, can be just as detrimental as claiming less than 100%.

There is a saying: *If you don't watch out, you will wind up where you are headed.* It pays to be careful of what you focus on because you are likely to get it. If you are focusing on the negative, then that is what you will tend to manifest.

There is another saying: *If someone calls you an ass, ignore it. If two people call you an ass, consider it. If three people call you an ass, get a saddle.* If something keeps showing up in your life in various forms, claim responsibility for it!

There is a final saying: *You are the common denominator in all of your relationships.* If there is something or someone that is not working, look in the mirror and then do something about it.

Paralyzing Fear

Often you may be so paralyzed by your fear of making a mistake, that you are afraid to claim responsibility. So you turn to someone or something else for the answers, for direction, or to tell you what to do. Some people won't make a move without consulting their financial advisor, for example. We are not opposed to financial advisors. The problem is not with the advice; it is with the frequent dependency and consequential credit or blame to the advisor instead of owning your decision to act on the information provided. This becomes an avoidance of responsibility. You insulate yourself from the outside world. You create a false sense of security because you have no vested risk.

When you act on the guidance of others, without owning the decision yourself, then you falsely believe you cannot be blamed or held accountable

2

CLAIM RESPONSIBILITY

for the consequences of those actions. You gradually lose your capacity for decision-making and then you forget how. Once this happens, you become paralyzed when faced with important decisions. You lose touch with what it is you really want. What results is a loss of connectedness with yourself and even your money, as well as with others. This loss of connectedness in turn results in a loss of meaning.

You are haunted by the agonizing feeling that your life lacks meaning. Yet since you do not recognize this as the by-product of your unwillingness to claim responsibility, you fail to take the first step to reverse the process. Lack of connectedness with money is rampant in the current age of credit card spending. Once upon a time, when people were only paid with real cash or trade and then paid for things in the same real cash or trade, individuals were more connected and in touch with their money.

Liberate Yourself

Success and failure. We think of them as opposites, but they're really not. They're companions —the hero and the sidekick.

—Laurence Shames

Claiming responsibility for your worth (both internally and externally) is quite a liberating experience. Without it, in a mistaken quest to rid yourself of regrets, pent-up blame looking for an object is always just beneath the surface ready to explode. You may find yourself living in fear of that explosion; in fear of finding an object and in fear of *not* finding one. What a relief it is to lay that burden down by accepting responsibility. You have the *right* to blame no one—to be blame-free.

Taking responsibility may be initially challenging, but it is well worth it. We're talking about taking back your life, regaining your innate sense of self-worth, and standing for who you are.

If you have trouble taking responsibility for your actions, start with just the smallest steps and watch how quickly you start to gain a sense of mastery and self-confidence with your life and your money. This is a key step to empowering your sense of self-worth and growing your net worth.

It is like building a muscle which has been long unused. Your right and ability to act is one of the most precious of human capacities—to act fully and of your own accord, and to claim responsibility for that action. The benefits of claiming this right include heightened aliveness, creativity, self-esteem, and an increased openness to the flow of abundance in your life. Claim responsibility now.

CLAIM RESPONSIBILITY

2

EXERCISES

Exercise A: What does this have to do with me?

This written exercise helps you explore how you can claim responsibility for a particular situation in your life.

Pick a situation in your life that you are having trouble with, especially in the area of wealth and worthiness, and explore these questions:

1. How is this familiar?
2. What does it remind me of?
3. What is it about me and my thinking (or beliefs) that tends to create or re-create this kind of circumstance?

As you answer the questions above, allow yourself to see the connections and patterns that may exist between you and the circumstances of your life.

Exercise B

Part I: Payoffs for Not Claiming Responsibility (What you gain by staying stuck in the Blame Game)

Pick a situation in your life (the same as in the previous exercise or a different one), particularly in the area of wealth and worthiness, in which you are claiming less than 100% responsibility.

Make a written list of your *payoffs* for not claiming responsibility.

Examples:

When/if things go wrong, I don't blame myself as much.
I get to look like the good guy for going along with what others want.
I don't have to deal with as much conflict or resistance.
It's safe. I know what to expect.
Things seem manageable.

For you:

Part II: Costs for Not Claiming Responsibility (What you lose by staying stuck in the Blame Game)

Take the same situation from Part I and make a written list of the *costs* for not claiming responsibility.

Examples:

I rarely get what I want.

I don't even remember anymore what I really want.

I experience a sense of internal conflict and of life being out of my control.

I still blame myself but at a deeper level.

I blame others and that tends to keep me feeling distant from them.

For you:

Part III: Choose to Claim Responsibility

For the situation or situations identified in Parts I and II, reflect and journal on whether the payoffs are actually worth the costs. Having reflected, are you willing to claim responsibility for your part in the situation (and the related costs) in your life and make appropriate changes? Do the costs outweigh the payoff? Have you fully acknowledged that something about you has created this to show up over and over? Once you can answer affirmatively to these questions: congratulations—you have claimed responsibility.

Visualization

Get a visual image and bodily felt sense of what your life would look and feel like if you were claiming responsibility for what showed up. Journal about what you notice and take a *sense memory photograph* of the feeling you get. Can you get a sense of being more fully empowered?

Conscious Breathing

Pick something for which you have not been claiming responsibility (an area where you feel angry and are blaming someone, for example). As you think about your hurt, anger, and blame, notice what happens with your breath. Now step into responsibility by letting go of any blame and expanding into a sense of ownership and responsibility. Are you able to fill yourself with more oxygen as you claim this more empowered stance? Practice breathing in this more powerful owner role now.

Body-Centered Statements

1. I have a right to _____.
2. Claiming responsibility, not blaming _____ or myself, is creating more aliveness and joy in my life.
3. I am supported and celebrated for claiming responsibility in all situations.

Journal Joggers

Use the following questions to lead you into your journal entries for this Key.
- What am I telling myself that keeps me upset? Why do I think I need to tell myself these things?
- What would I have to give up or change in order to be self-responsible in this situation?
- What are some other, more direct ways I can get or replace what I would give up?
- What small steps can I take to incorporate these changes into my life?

I've lived through many difficult times in my life,
and some of them actually happened.

— MARK TWAIN

3

FEEL YOUR FEELINGS

KEY THREE

FEEL YOUR FEELINGS

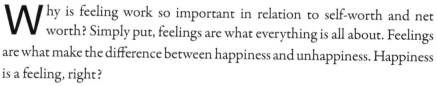

Our feelings are our most genuine paths to knowledge.

— AUDRE LORDE

W hy is feeling work so important in relation to self-worth and net worth? Simply put, feelings are what everything is all about. Feelings are what make the difference between happiness and unhappiness. Happiness is a feeling, right?

Do you control your feelings or do they control you? Actually, it is our *thoughts* that determine our feelings. Test this out. Think of something very pleasant right now. How do you feel? Now think of something unpleasant. It's a different sensation, isn't it? Remember the lemon exercise in Key One? Nothing changed around you in the minute it took to do the experiment. The only thing that changed was what you were thinking. This may sound like an oversimplification, but it is really a big deal—an important life lesson! If you truly grasp the implication of this exercise, you can change your life. You never need to dwell in unhappiness again. You have the magic key. Nikos

Kazantzakis, the Greek writer and philosopher, declared, "We have our brush and colors—paint Paradise, and in we go."

Please notice that we said, you "never need to *dwell* in unhappiness," not "never need to feel unhappy." Thoughts arise spontaneously, and therefore, so do feelings. The problem is not caused by the thought or even the feeling. Thoughts cause problems when we follow them in self-defeating directions. They tend to take off like a runaway train, and we fail to apply the brakes or switch the track. There is choice involved. You can pursue thoughts that don't serve you in that they trigger negative feelings, or you can switch the track.

See Exercise A at the end of this Key for additional examples and to consider this belief/thought/feeling relationship in your life.

You, the Architect, and You, the Blueprint

Mr. Duffy lived a few feet from his body.

—JAMES JOYCE

Feelings live in our body. Feelings consist of both sensations and emotions, and often they overlap. An earache is a feeling, while anger is also a feeling. The word "feeling" can relate to your sensations and emotions. They do, indeed, live in the body and can cause all manner of trouble there. Anything from a stiff neck, to a backache, to a real medical problem may be the result of repressed or unfelt feelings, as well as more psychological symptoms such as anxiety, depression, and addictive behavior. Your body is the gateway to your feelings and your feelings are the gateway to your spirit or your higher purpose. The body has an inner knowing which will guide you in the direction of what you truly love.

You are a blueprint that you are creating yourself, with your own thoughts, feelings, words, and actions. With each thought, feeling, word, and deed you are creating an imprint and, most often, underscoring one that already exists. Your body is a manifestation of that blueprint. Louise Hay illustrated this principle of the mind-body connection in her ground-breaking book, *Heal Your Body: The Mental Causes For Physical Illness and the Metaphysical Way to Overcome Them.*

In the same way, your life is also a manifestation of the blueprint you have been creating, including your financial well-being or lack thereof. You are the one creating your life. Just as you came to understand in Key One that "you have to believe it to see it," so are your thoughts and beliefs imprinting and thus creating your life all the time. Your thoughts and beliefs are placing all your experiences within your unique frame of reference, like putting an order in to the universe. What you think, feel, say, and do combine to create what you are going to get in return from your life. You are the one making that input—creating that blueprint and placing that order—nobody else!

In an intriguing Wall Street Journal article, *Expectations May Alter Outcomes Far More Than We Realize* (November 7, 2003 by Sharon Begley), 479 studies are cited which have found that teachers' expectations of students actually affect how they perform. In one typical experiment noted, teachers were told which school children were expected to make remarkable academic gains based on a test predicting their capacity to learn. After a few months, the group of children that were predicted to do well had in fact exceeded other students in the class academically. In reality, the test was of the teachers and the effect of their expectations. The group of "successful" children had been randomly chosen across a broad spectrum demographic. It was something in the teachers' expectations which created the results.

> *The minute you settle for less than you deserve,*
> *you get even less than you settled for.*
>
> —MAUREEN DOWD

We see examples all the time of people manifesting what they expect for better or for worse. You are constantly setting expectations and finding evidence so that you can validate your expectations, whether your expectations are, in fact, positive or negative. Here is how Belinda summarizes this phenomenon: "It's not likely that you are aiming too high. You likely are

FEEL YOUR FEELINGS

3

aiming too low, getting only that, and then reinforcing the belief that is all you deserve and will ever receive in life. When in reality, if you aimed and thought on a bigger level, then much more could become available." Consider how this feeds your unwillingness to change and what the resulting impact may be having on your life.

Projection: Ignoring Your Feelings

Ignored feelings are often also a cause of projection. They color your view of the world, as the reality filter of your belief systems causes you to build evidence for what you already believe. If you are angry, the world looks like an angry place. When you are sad, the world seems full of suffering. When you are afraid, the world feels scary. When you are without money (or even simply *afraid of being* without money), you may see scarcity everywhere and everything seems expensive. If you are feeling the effects of a down economy, all you see are more effects of a down economy. When you are afraid to risk, the world feels dangerous and risky. You become attuned to the things that you already believe and often don't want to admit. How do you view the world? Can you deduce from that what your feelings and the belief systems behind them may be?

Holding On

There is a Buddhist story that we love. Two monks, an old one and a young one, were walking together down a muddy road. A heavy rain was falling and they came to a place where the road was severely flooded. On the far side of the road stood a lovely woman in a silk kimono and sash, who was unable to cross the intersection. The older monk waded through the water, picked the woman up, carried her across the flooded road, put her down, and then continued on his way. The younger monk, who had not moved during all of this, rejoined him but appeared sullen, distressed, and wouldn't speak. His mind was running away as he obsessed over what just happened. Finally, as they neared their destination, the younger monk could contain himself no longer and blurted out, "Oh brother, we monks are not supposed to have anything to do with women, especially not young and lovely ones. It is dangerous. Why did you do that?" The older monk looked surprised and replied without hesitation, "I left the woman behind two hours ago. Are you still carrying her?"

If you are holding on to past decisions you have made which have affected your worth (internal or external), maybe you are still carrying them across the metaphorical river! Another way to put it is that your mind might be like a dog chasing its own tail. Are you going around and around in circles and not getting anywhere except to stress yourself out? Do you feel like a record or a CD player stuck on repeat and thus playing the same song (or scripts) over and over?

Obsessing

Instead of staying on this runaway train, why *don't* you switch tracks? In addition to the fact that you may not even realize this was a possibility, you may tend to stay with that out-of-control train because it is stimulating, or is allowing you to avoid something that feels scarier or harder. Think about a time you felt really angry, jealous, scared, ashamed, or obsessed—very stimulating feelings, right?

For example, Belinda's client, Jessica, holds a portfolio that includes mostly individual stocks. She is not planning on withdrawing these monies for twenty or thirty years. Yet, she is completely obsessed with the daily prices of these stocks and can barely take herself away from her computer when any of the stocks are having a volatile day. It is similar to people who obsess about their weight and so they get on the scale twice a day. In the same way that the daily fluctuations on the scale are irrelevant, so are the day-to-day up and down swings in the market for most investors. This is especially true for Jessica as she is a long-term investor. Yet investors can become obsessive about individual stock prices and the overall indexes, such as the Dow Jones Industrial Average or the S&P 500 Stock Index. Yes, there is a healthy time or way to monitor the stock market. The important point is to notice the tipping point—the point at which you cross over into unhealthy obsessing about it.

Think back. Did you ever find yourself obsessing? Did you keep thinking thoughts which, in turn, kept stimulating and building upon uncomfortable feelings? Did you even reach a state of panic? Most likely, you were experiencing an actual addiction to those feelings. Strong feelings release brain chemicals called neurotransmitters, neuropeptides, and hormones, such as adrenaline. We get an actual physical reaction. The primary principle of Cia's specialty of body-centered therapy is that feelings live in the body. This is where it begins.

Humans are wired for stimulation. You have more receptor sites in the brain for highly stimulating emotions (usually the more unpleasant feelings) than you do for happiness and joy. You can turn this around. You can actually begin to change the way your nervous systems are set up. You can develop more receptor sites for joy and high self-esteem. You can decrease your dependency on the stimulation of unpleasant feelings. You can do this by mastering your own thought processes. It is simply a matter of willingness and practice. Just as Cathy, in Key Two, claimed responsibility for her trigger of not being heard by her contractor, so can you catch yourself and create much more positive outcomes.

Switch Tracks

Practice switching tracks. At first the train may be a long way down the track before you remember to switch. You may even experience an internal battle over whether you really want to or not. As you gradually realize the benefits of the exercise of *choice*, you will start to catch that train earlier and earlier on the journey, until it becomes almost automatic. Eventually you'll check the tracks before the train of thought even leaves the station.

For instance, Marie recognizes that when she has a slow commission month, she triggers feelings of fear, shame, and scarcity. After working with Belinda, she now catches herself as she begins to experience those feelings, and reminds herself not to dwell on them as that will only yield more of the same. Instead, Marie gets into action to increase her commissions and has started to build other sources of income.

No Negative Emotions

There actually are no negative emotions! Isn't that refreshing? There are unpleasant feelings and pleasant feelings. There are feelings that are so powerful they can compel behavior that does not serve you or another. Yet no feeling is, in and of itself, bad. Our resistance to feelings causes more problems than the feeling itself. Every emotion you feel is sending you a message.

A feeling may be pleasant or unpleasant, mild or intense, but the nature of feelings is that they pass quickly; that is, of course, *unless* we resist them. That is when the trouble can start for you. The saying goes, "What you resist, persists." That is very true when it comes to feelings. When you resist them, you make them wrong. What feelings about your relationship with your worthiness, your money, or your success are you resisting? Once you see what feelings you are resisting, you may be able to see the connection between those repressed feelings and the results you are getting, or failing to get. Your true self-worth and net worth depend on it.

Pain as a Path to Growth

You suffer because you try to reject the pain in your search for the joy.
Pain is a partner to joy and enhances its beauty, like the night enhances
the beauty of the day. As you embrace the darkness of life,
so much greater will be your joy.

— Barry and Joyce Vissell

Emotional pain is a reality of life. When not resisted, that pain can be used as a positive force for growth and change. A friend of ours says, "Everything in life is either a lesson or a gift." Pain is life's lesson. Just like physical pain exists so that you will know when you are in jeopardy and do something about it, so too, emotional pain indicates where something is wrong in your life—a place where you are living out of integrity perhaps. Instead of fighting it, begin by going right to the heart of the pain and ask it, "What is this sadness, fear, anger, or combination thereof really about? What can I learn from it? What needs change or attention in my life?"

It's not an accident that you're having a repeated undesirable outcome, if you are continuing to stuff down and ignore a feeling which, in fact, has an important message for you. When you accidentally place your hand on a hot stove, that painful sensation is there for a reason—to get you to remove your hand. Emotion is the same way. If you are unhappy and suffering a feeling of low self-worth, it is telling you something. You can resist it and ignore it, but in the end, that is like grimacing and leaving your hand on the stove until you become scarred.

Resisting Feeling Your Feelings

We should take care not to make the intellect our God; it has of course, powerful muscles, but no personality.

— ALBERT EINSTEIN

You may experience resistance to the very idea of feeling your feelings at first, yet your feelings are the gateway to who you are. They provide an uncontrived glimpse of your real self. You may be unprepared to see yourself as you really are. Herman Hesse said, "Nothing in the world is more distasteful to a man than to take the path that leads to himself." The good news is that this is only true in the beginning—in the anticipation stage. It is exhilarating and totally freeing to get a taste of your own true nature. You will not want to revert back for anything. That, in fact, is the essence of true self-worth.

Resistance feeds the thing you are resisting. In the case of unpleasant feelings, you may tend to push them away, thus creating resistance and then actually increasing your hook into the feeling. The more you resist the feeling, the more powerful it becomes. The message you give yourself is, "I *have* to feel good," or whatever pleasant feeling you think is the opposite of the one you are resisting. As soon as you tell yourself that, it makes the unpleasant feeling worse because you are labeling it as wrong. The antidote is to feel the feeling. Give yourself permission to have it. When you allow yourself to do this authentically, the feeling passes.

Feelings as a Signal

Feelings are a *signal* and as such are important to listen to. They may be a message that your rights and your boundaries are being violated, that your wants or needs are not being adequately met, that you are not addressing an important emotional issue in your life, or that you are somehow compromising too much of yourself. Just as, in the previous example, physical pain prompts you to take your hand off a hot stove, emotional pain alerts you to threats to the very integrity of your being.

For example, Belinda had a client, Pam, who was proceeding through her career, replaying an agonizing and almost identical dynamic each time. Pam was chronically underearning and thus having a hard time paying her bills. To avoid confronting the pain and sense of unworthiness directly, she either jumped into another low-paying job immediately, or stayed stuck in the same one too long. Once Pam got in touch with her feelings and interpreted the signals they were sending her, she could act as an observer and recognize the pattern that she was creating. Belinda sourced Pam's patterns to one original incident when she felt overlooked and less than a peer while in school. Once she could heal and forgive both herself and the teacher from this situation, Pam took a huge step forward in claiming her inner worthiness and soon charged her true worth in the marketplace.

The Flow of Feelings (And How They Get Stuck)

The natural flow of feelings are like waves. They are always in motion. Emotion (or E-motion) equals Energy in Motion. Feelings have a beginning, middle, and an end. When we allow them expression, they have their own crescendo and denouement. Our internal critic, learned early in life, tells us that certain feelings are unacceptable. Then the feelings do not move through us. They get stuck. A lump in the throat, the heaviness in the chest, the tightening in the stomach, are all examples of what happens to a stuck feeling.

Another analogy that might help is the weather. Where we both grew up in New England, there is a saying about the weather (which also holds true for feelings), "If you don't like it right now, wait five minutes and it will change." Feelings are like clouds in the sky as well. It is their nature to move on. But most of us learned to repress our feelings, keeping them hidden away and stifled. This clogs up our internal weather so it no longer moves freely through us.

The Pressure Builds

Imagine yourself as a pressure cooker. If you don't allow the release of some steam in an appropriate manner, you will eventually explode. Notice we say *an appropriate manner*. We are not talking about dumping. There is a way to speak the truth of your feelings self-responsibly and without blame (as discussed in Key Two). Sometimes the most self-responsible way to release steam is to let it out on your own—not in the presence of the person who triggered your reaction.

Remember there is a difference between a trigger and a cause. That person didn't cause you to feel your feelings. The immediate cause was your *thoughts*—your reaction to the situation. The long-term cause goes way back to the very first time you ever felt that feeling and all the times between then and now.

The Ticking Time Bomb

Unaddressed feelings are psychological (and financial) time bombs that can have devastating effects. At best, they cause you to go through life with only part of your aliveness and awareness intact. What remains of your energy is being wasted keeping your feelings at bay, like having guards at the gate or standing on top of a pressure valve on the street. You lose a sense of creativity, freedom, joy, expansiveness, and abundance. You also lose your ability to make wise decisions with money, in particular, and your worthiness, in general.

You may be carrying around a lot of unnecessary baggage. This baggage can get very heavy and costly as it keeps you in inaction. What you are doing is bringing the old baggage into your current behaviors and decisions. It is with you all the time through everything that you do. Heavy gobs of old stuck energy live in your body. You acquired them in the form of past traumas and have been lugging them ever since at great cost to your energy, joy, and aliveness. You must get this material to the surface in order to heal it and let it go. Like teething, the body has to get used to the new tooth, but in the process may be uncomfortable and feel pain. You have to allow it to come up and break the surface.

What is the baggage that you personally are carrying around? How does it weigh you down, hold you back, or get in your way? Specifically around money, what feelings have you stuffed down so deep that no one (not even you or your partner) would have to face them again? Many clients first come to Belinda feeling scared, embarrassed, or ashamed, and yearning for a safe space to express their feelings. Their baggage has turned into a dangerous ticking time bomb, causing them unnecessary stress and anxiety.

Financial Stress Causing Depression or Anxiety

It may be helpful to know that the majority of people, when stressed about money experience either depression or anxiety, depending on their predisposition. Depression and anxiety, for example, are really unaddressed and unfelt feelings—a deadening and dullness which come from keeping the lid on. Generally depression is repressed grief and/or anger, and anxiety is repressed fear. In a worst case scenario, unaddressed feelings may even be life-threatening. As mind-body medicine is rapidly gaining credibility, doctors are beginning to recognize the statistical correlation between people who have very little outlet or support for their feelings and a high incidence of life-threatening illness. If it is not physical illness that manifests, the result may be mental illness.

Dr. Alice D. Domar, Executive Director of the *Domar Center for Mind/Body Health* and co-author of *Live a Little*, is recognized as an international leader in the field of mind/body medicine and women's health. The Domar Center for Mind/Body Health helps people create measurable, positive changes in their health, and their lives, by enhancing the mind-body connection. They understand that emotional well-being has a powerful effect on physical health.

Dr. Domar explains, "In a recent study in Asia, it was determined that when the stock market went up or down more than 100 points in one day, deaths that day from cardiovascular events went up more than 5%. This study illustrates that worrying about finances can in fact kill you, but note that it happened when the stock market went up as well as when it went down, suggesting that we get highly stressed from either extreme. This means that you need to assess your emotional reaction to your financial situation no matter how well, or badly, you are doing. Check in with yourself, both physically and psychologically, on a regular basis. Notice what your stress warning signs are, and when they appear, do whatever you need to do to counteract the level of stress you are feeling."

Specifically, according to a 2011 survey by Financial Finesse, a leading provider of workplace financial wellness programs, based upon questioning more than 1000 people, 86% of all respondents reported experiencing financial stress. Interestingly, 90% of women reported feeling "some," "high," or "overwhelming" financial stress, with 28% of women and only 17% of men reporting "high or overwhelming levels of stress." At the "overwhelming" financial stress level (the highest level listed), women were found to be three times as likely to experience "overwhelming" financial stress.

Further, an estimated 60% of illnesses, directly or indirectly, are caused by financial stress and the American Psychological Association has identified it as the leading cause of unhealthy behaviors such as overeating, smoking, and alcohol and drug addiction. As an aside to be considered, this financial stress is costing you, your business, or your employer millions of dollars per year in (avoidable) health care expenses. The clear message: Don't let your feelings fester. Fortunately, there is an alternative to this financial repression. By all means, please find healthy ways to address your financial stress, including acknowledging and releasing any related pent-up feelings you may have not fully dealt with in your life as well as educating yourself financially.

Shake Up and Scare Up

So, how do you avoid having your feelings get stuck and causing you trouble? Simple. Feel them! "We are healed of the suffering only by experiencing it to the full," said Marcel Proust, a French novelist, critic, and essayist. While *simple*, this may not be *easy* at first. There is a difference between simple and easy. If you are totally unfamiliar with what it means to really feel your feelings, then this is new territory for you. Chances are the message that you have received from society, or wherever, is that feelings are bad and should be avoided. Didn't your parents tell you with all good intentions, "Don't be scared. Don't be angry. Don't be sad." And how about, "Big girls (or big boys) don't cry?"

While you are stirring things up, you may find yourself scared or not feeling good. Think about having a glass of carbonated water, and what you really want is still water. You are very thirsty. How do you get the bubbles out of the carbonated water? You stir it! The more vigorously you stir or shake, the more bubbles come to the surface. At first it looks like you're making your water even more bubbly, but what you're actually doing is releasing the bubbles. The faster you allow them to come to the surface and disappear into the air, the sooner you will have the glass of still water you are longing for.

The good news is that feelings move through your system surprisingly quickly once you are willing to acknowledge and feel them, and the release feels great. For the price of a brief but intense confrontation with your own deep feelings, the reward is a lifetime of increased aliveness and awareness. This awareness creates a powerful new perspective and sense of self-worth.

Men, Women, and Feelings

Men in our culture are typically discouraged from expressing sadness or fear, and therefore believe that there is something wrong with having those feelings. Women are typically discouraged from the expression of anger with the same results. Our cultural heroes have been the James Bond or John Wayne types. Society emphasizes doing and achieving rather than feeling, and admires people who seem to ride through life's challenges as if they were unaffected. Turning away from your own feelings, however, leads to a decline in your self-worth, while accepting your feelings and working through them leads to increased self-worth along with a better relationship to your own issues and to your true self.

Your Cellular Memory

Your body remembers the intensity of past feelings. This is called *cellular memory*. The memory is encoded in the very cells of your body and is often unconscious. Thus, it is scary to begin with the process of really feeling your feelings. When you try, at first, you may go into shutdown or resistance. It may take the form of numbing out, denial, getting sleepy, finding yourself very distracted, saying, "this is stupid," or addictive behavior, such as shopping or eating, as a way to avoid experiencing the feelings. For example, you may feel empty and your unconscious believes that shopping or eating will cause you to feel satisfied. You may naturally take the easy way out and attempt to fill the void without truly dealing with the issue.

When those things happen, view them as a sign that you are probably close to a breakthrough and seek some support for pushing through the resistance. Resistance is not a bad thing in itself. It has been there for a reason and has probably served you in some way. However, you may not need it anymore in the way you did. If it flares up, it may be a sign that your unconscious mind knows you are on to something important! Try moving in the direction of whatever you find yourself resisting, instead of away.

Attaching Your Identity to Your Pain

An opposite but equally insidious response to emotional pain that we see often is an *attachment* to it—clinging to pain. The pain itself becomes an addiction, as we described earlier. When this occurs, it becomes part of your identity and you are afraid that if you let go of it, you will no longer be yourself. When it comes to self-worth and net worth, you may often define yourself and your value by what you do (as an occupation and/or for accomplishments), how much money you have, and/or how much money you earn. Changing your (painful) story alters your definition of your self and your worth, thereby confronting you with losing your familiar identity. Thus, you may fear losing the pain because the loss of the pain to you represents a kind of death to the known. Your identity has many layers. Think of it like an onion and each Key along this journey is helping to peel away each layer to reveal the authentic you.

If you have experienced impoverishment for a long enough period, or during a formative period of your life, you may have grown used to the idea of it and hold onto that identity. Similarly, someone who grew up fat may never feel slim or see herself as slim no matter how much evidence there is to the contrary. There is a certain victimhood to not having sufficient worth, either the inner worthiness or actual money, to which you may become attached.

For instance, you may come into money, perhaps through inheritance or a significant pay increase, and not be able to hold onto it because it doesn't match who you believe yourself to be. If you have not established your sense of self-worth first, you will not believe fully in your own entitlement to that sufficiency. As well, your friends may be people who don't have money. You want to be accepted by them and being different would put that at risk. The result is that you may do whatever you can, primarily unconsciously, to rid yourself of your money. You may get into bad investments, give your money away, or frivolously spend. That is why, statistically, most people who win the lottery lose all or most of their money within a remarkably short period of time.

Perhaps you hold onto pain as a negative way of staying attached to (and perhaps blaming) other people in your lives, whether they are living or not. So you get to play the victim and collect evidence that you have been victimized. The focus of your blame could be on your spouse or partner, an ex, your parents, or someone else you feel has betrayed you. For example, some people put their attention on what their parents *didn't* teach them about fiscal responsibility, or how their spouse or partner is *not spending* responsibly. This kind of outward blaming continues to reinforce your pain, repeatedly proving you right. You may, in fact, be victimizing yourself. So, would you rather be right or happy?

Pain Is Inevitable; Suffering Is Optional

There is no time like the present to allow ourselves to feel the grief of missed opportunities. Our grief and pain are ours. We have earned them. They are part of us. Only when we let ourselves feel them is it possible to open ourselves to the lessons they teach.

—ANNE WILSON SCHAEF

Pain is a part of life—an important part. Like any other feeling it comes and goes if we allow it. Suffering is what we create when we play a broken record over and over in our mind, clinging to that pain as our story—as part of our identity.

Clinging to pain is not what we mean by feeling your feelings. We are talking about allowing the waves of emotion to move through and then releasing them. Feelings in their natural state come and go. Let them. It is the clinging to them or identifying with them (versus feeling and releasing them) that creates the problem.

Joy and Pain

Emotional pain is the flip side of joy. We can't have one without the other. Time and time again, we find that people who have the greatest capacity to feel any emotion, including the so-called negative ones, are the people who have the greatest potential capacity to experience joy and abundance—a true sense of self-worth. The deeper you can feel pain and other less comfortable emotions, the more you have access to, and capacity, for joy. So allow yourself to be a person who feels deeply and fully about life and all it has to offer. Start today.

Belinda personally found that it was only after she was able to release her negative feelings about her father that she was able to experience deeper positive feelings. She had been harboring significant sadness and anger about her father having a stroke when he was 59 and then passing when he was 68. (She was only 21 and 30 years old, respectively.) Once she allowed herself to feel her own feelings, and she found a safe way to release her own pressure cooker of emotions, she was pleasantly surprised how her feelings of joy and abundance (relating both to her father and to life) were deeper and more meaningful. The protection had been lifted and all her feelings deepened. Where are you protecting yourself? What don't you want people to know about you? What feelings have you been suppressing for fear that they would be too painful to release, yet are actually limiting the joy and abundance available to you?

Four Categories of Emotions

It is helpful to know that all our human emotions can be roughly divided into four basic categories: anger, sadness, fear, and joy. Each of the four categories of feelings contains a myriad of subtle shades, ranging from barely perceptible to intense. For example, the category of anger contains feelings ranging from irritation to rage, sadness ranges from a flat and dull feeling to profound grief, fear ranges from mild timidity to terror, and joy from a mildly pleasant sensation to ecstasy.

There are certain feelings which are actually a combination of two feelings, or a combination of a feeling plus a thought. If you notice that a particular feeling is a combination of a feeling and a thought, that is good news. As you have choice over your thoughts, you can therefore choose to think differently and therefore to feel differently. For example, the feeling of hurt is a combination of two feelings—generally sad and angry.

Combinations that are particularly harmful and demonstrate the pairing of a feeling with a thought result in guilt and shame. So stop telling yourself the story (thought) that is perpetrating those feelings. (We often use the word *story* to describe a cluster of thoughts woven together.)

Be Curious and Present

In body-centered work, what you do with feelings is to approach them in a friendly, curious way and simply be with them. This is a practice known as *presencing*. Try it now. Again, take a moment and get a handle on what you are feeling right now. Let your attention rest on that sensation without doing anything else. Don't do anything except allow yourself to take an attitude of curiosity toward your own feeling. Breathe deeply to help you stay present and explore your feeling. Where do you experience it in your body? Does the feeling itself have a sensation associated with it: an image, a memory, a word or phrase, a gesture, sound, shape, size, color, or texture? Notice everything there is to notice about this feeling, and anything that might be associated with it.

Take the questioning process begun in Key Two to a whole new level. Ask yourself, "How is this familiar? What does this remind me of? When was the first time I ever felt this feeling?" Or, perhaps, "What was the original memory or event that is being triggered?" Sometimes these questions will propel us back in time to a core memory. By going back and healing that original wound, often all the layers of feeling stuck to it snowball-style will fall away, including whatever feeling we are experiencing at this moment. This questioning process can shed tremendous light on behavior patterns and associated emotions.

As you allow yourself to truly experience the feeling, follow it into the very heart of its being—listen to it, ask it deeper questions such as: What originally happened that created you? What is it that you need right now? How old are you? Where are you in my body? How are you familiar to me? What do you remind me of? What triggers you? Is there a way that I can see you as a little child and send some love to you? As you ask each question, just wait.

Don't accept an answer from your mind, which is really just a rationalization or story. Wait until your *body* answers. If there is no answer, be patient as you would with a small child, and gradually go even deeper. Do not judge the feeling. As odd as this approach may sound, give it a try the next time you are feeling an intense feeling. You may discover some remarkable results. See Exercise C for a full list of questions and space to follow this process for one of your own particular feelings.

Breathing Into Your Feelings

One of the very best ways to be with or presence feelings is through the breath. When seized by a strong feeling, such as fear or shame when you are confronted with any irresponsibility with money, you may tend to hold your breath. That keeps the feeling stuck and keeps you from moving forward. We have seen that with deep, intentional breathing, our clients are often able to interrupt their patterns. This creates an opportunity to insert a new perspective—a perspective that allows them to be in control, rather than lost in the whirlwind of emotions.

As an example, whenever Cia's client, Jan, would think about her current work environment, she became stressed, her speech pattern became faster and louder, and she appeared overcome by an intense emotional wave of anger and frustration. By taking that extra moment to breathe deeply and feel her way into the feeling, she recognized a way to become bigger than the emotion rather than overcome by it. As soon as she did that, Jan caught a glimpse of the way her belief system about being mistreated and undervalued at work caused a sense of rage. This in turn had made her less effective at her work and clouded the faculties she might have used for making other choices. Eventually Jan discovered that her belief system about being undervalued at work was a projection stemming from her own internal lack of self-worth.

For those of you who suffer from panic/anxiety disorder, deep breathing is especially helpful. If you can catch yourself at the beginning of an attack, or even better, right before it begins, you can often short-circuit the automatic mind/body response that leads to full-blown anxiety.

Safe Support To Feel

If feeling your feelings is unfamiliar to you, we urge you to create some support for yourself first. Excellent sources of support for this process are individual or group therapy, support groups, and 12-Step programs, such as Debtors Anonymous, etc. Any of these places will help by providing validation for your feelings, which will support you to push through to completion. You will recognize that you are not alone and that you have what it takes to feel your feelings, work through them, and thrive in an environment that feels safe. If your feelings are related to your overall self-esteem or well-being, contact Cia for personal attention or resources. If your feelings are related to money or your relationship with it, then contact Belinda and join the Own Your Money community. We are here with suggestions to support your success.

How do you create a safe environment for your feelings? Your conscious mind may tell you that a feeling in itself is not dangerous. Your body doesn't know this. Did you ever have a feeling so intense that it felt like you could die from it? Perhaps you felt that way back in childhood. Maybe even the memory is blocked. Did you ever do something you deeply regretted later while in the midst of some intense feeling? So, allow your consciousness to speak to the scared part of you, often the child within, and to let her know that she is safe now. Let her know that you are with her and that she can get through this feeling without dying from it or doing something catastrophic. Create a safe and secure environment for you to do this work.

Love—Don't Judge—Yourself

The advanced version of presencing your feelings is to love yourself for feeling them. This suggestion generally elicits a strong negative reaction in most people. How can I love myself for feeling angry, or scared, etc. about my money and my worthiness? Won't that be condoning the very situation I am trying to change? We'll talk more about this in the next Key on "Accept What Is" and Key Seven on "Learning to Love Yourself," where we point out that loving and accepting yourself is the way through. It is actually a prerequisite to permanent change. It creates the platform that makes change possible. That same principle applies here.

Binge Spending

If you can set aside resisting the concept of loving yourself for feeling your feelings just long enough to try it, you will find this to be true. For example, do you have a problem with binge shopping? If so, have you ever noticed that after you have gone out on a spree you tend to come home and beat up on yourself? Notice, as well, that this judgmental behavior doesn't serve to prevent you from going out and doing it again. If anything it makes the behavior worse. Here are two reasons why that is:

1. You get what you focus on. When you beat up on yourself, you are focusing on, and therefore reinforcing, the belief that there is something wrong with you—not exactly a self-worth-enhancing activity. The more you reinforce that belief, the more you will act from that place. Repeating this pattern feeds a sense of hopelessness regarding any possible change.

2. Binge spending (or eating) comes from an inner (and usually unexpressed and unsatisfied) feeling of lack, deprivation or love, probably one acquired early in life. When you give yourself a hard time for it, you are actually increasing your own sense of deprivation and other unpleasant feelings and beliefs. What is it you really longed for back then when you were a child? Might it be that you are still longing for the same thing? Often that thing is love. No outside love is capable of filling that void as effectively as your own capacity to love yourself, just as you would give love to a small child who is feeling deprived and in need of being loved. (Key Seven will further explore this concept as well.) This example will apply to other behaviors for which you tend to chastise yourself. Here is an exercise to support you in this process.

Begin by repeating the phrase to yourself, "I feel sad about _____," and fill in the blank with as many things as come to mind. Don't just do this from your mind, but really try to feel the feelings in your body as you do it. Once you run out of things to fill in the blank with, stop and take a minute to love yourself for feeling sad about all those things. Follow the same process using "I feel angry about" and "I feel scared about." (See Exercise B at the end of this Key.) You are allowing yourself to feel the feelings that have been holding you back from realizing your worthiness.

Let Them Out

How about *expressing* feelings? It is always important to speak the truth about feelings. There is a big difference, however, between speaking the truth about your feelings and simply reacting. If you are simply reacting, you are likely taking a defensive and non-self responsible stance. The alternative and more powerful approach is to speak the truth of your feelings once you have allowed yourself to feel them and clearly identify what they are and where they are coming from.

For example, your reaction may be coming from a belief system or wounding formed early in childhood which is causing you to speak from projection rather than from the unarguable truth. Speaking the truth about your feelings implies that you've taken the time needed to own your feelings. Owning your feelings usually slows you down enough to prevent a reaction that you might regret later—one that could be harmful to yourself or others.

Your Emotional Triggers

Let's say that someone says something that "makes" you really angry. Actually, what they said *triggered* your anger, which is different than "making" you angry, yet in the moment may feel similar. Can you claim responsibility for that? The domino effect articulated in Key Two can blow up one minor and apparently insignificant event or action into a much larger surge of feelings. The person who triggered you may be thinking, "Wow, what the hell did I do? That is certainly an overreaction." You may find it very difficult in that moment to understand that it is an overreaction because you are convinced that all the anger comes from what your companion just said.

Through working on this book, Belinda realized an ongoing impactful trigger for her personally. Whenever she thought about getting hungry (in terms of the physical wanting of food), she would have a visceral and painful reaction. She would do whatever she could to avoid being hungry, even if this caused her to be late (so she could prepare food), overpay for food, eat more than was necessary at a sitting, or always carry multiple snacks with her wherever she went. Through employing the techniques in this book to her avoidance of hunger, Belinda recognized that she avoided feeling hungry because she was creating a negative meaning for the hunger, specifically that she was poor and couldn't afford food. This would then trigger a sense of scarcity and lack.

This belief stemmed back from a childhood memory of living with her mother post-divorce when they had trouble affording fresh food, and recalls her mother saying they had to buy "day old turkey" as that is all they could pay for. At the time, Belinda's mother had little money left after the costs of the divorce and her struggling entrepreneurial venture. In attempting to resist falling into a poverty feeling, Belinda would be sure she always stayed physically satiated or "full." After this realization, Belinda can now address the trigger, become aware when it occurs, and create a new meaning for being hungry.

If you take the time to pause before reacting strongly, you can say, "I notice I am feeling really angry right now and I want to go take some time to process it." Then you can remove yourself from the situation and go ask yourself (or journal), "What was the first time I ever felt this feeling? What does it remind me of? What is the little child in me really feeling now?" Do this until you get some insight into your reaction. Then it is time to go to your companion and ask if you can talk. (Calmly please.) Share what you noticed. Make requests, if appropriate, regarding future communications and be real about the current and the past feelings arising for you. (We will further explore effective communication techniques with your partner in Key Eleven.)

"I Feel" and Creating Safe Space

When you speak your feelings, use *I* messages. If you start your sentence, "I feel," and then state your feeling, you are using the basics of self-responsible communication. You are stepping into ownership. Watch that you don't follow the "I feel" with the word *that*, however. This is a basic test to tell the difference between a feeling and the thought. If the word "that" creeps in, you are no longer talking about a feeling, which means you are no longer telling the unarguable truth. For example: "I feel sad when you buy something that's not an urgent need even though we have agreed to prioritize paying down the credit cards" is self-responsible. "I feel that you have a complete disregard for our future," is not. You are describing an idea or projection, and a subjective or arguable one at that—not a feeling.

Is there ever a time for a more vehement expression of feeling—such as in a more extreme example of the above where your partner has just maxed the credit cards and you are enraged? Yes. The prerequisite is creating a safe space for yourself (and for your partner) where you can do this work. Then, by all means, let off some steam first so you can begin to get in touch with the real issues at hand—enough to communicate self-responsibly. If you do not have a therapist or a financial coach you can do this with, you can ask a friend to help you by being a stand-in for the person you want to communicate with or use the Gestalt technique, surprisingly effective, of talking to an empty chair.

Expressing Your Feelings Physically

The physical expression of a strong feeling, including a strong feeling about your financial matters, is often the most effective way to vent and allow it to move. As another example, if you have just lost your job and are experiencing deep sadness, do whatever you can to give yourself a chance to stop and let the tears come, even if it takes watching a sad movie to get them rolling. Anger may, sometimes surprisingly, arise for you regarding your finances. Perhaps you are angry about something you or your partner said, did, or even didn't do with money.

With anger, there are many options for physical expression. Tune into your bodily impulses to discover what form of safe physical expression feels right for you. Is it a hitting, striking, or punching movement? Try pounding pillows with your fist, a tennis racket, or a wiffle bat. Some people like to go out in nature and strike trees or chop wood. If the throwing motion is more satisfying, is there a place you could go safely to throw rocks or rubble? Perhaps a ripping motion feels right to you. Old phone books are wonderful for this purpose. Or, a wringing motion. Try wringing a sheet or a towel. Or whipping—use that sheet or towel as a whip. It may be that your legs want to be engaged. Stomping or kicking can be very effective. A safe way to kick is to do it lying down against a wall where you have leaned a mattress or lots of pillows. You will find what works best for you. Avoid reacting strongly in front of your partner until you have let off that initial steam.

Add Sound

Don't neglect the effectiveness of audible sounds with all these techniques. Let out as much of a groan, growl, or roar as you can manage. Or, try getting verbal and telling "so-and-so" just how you feel as you are pounding their effigy to a pulp. Use profanity if it helps you release. You are not hurting anyone by this. You are helping them because you won't be tempted to do it in front of them. If it is hard for you to let loose with any volume, you can yell into a pillow, or roll up the windows of the car and really holler or scream.

Once you really let it all out physically, you may feel a great sense of relief or peace with an open sense of increased aliveness and space inside your body. If you are ready to do any forgiveness work or to invite the flow of compassion, or gratitude, this is an excellent time to do so. Don't push it until you are ready.

Facing Fear

Fear is a very difficult emotion to work with and also often responds well to allowing yourself to get physical. Let's say you just got a bad performance review at work and your company is forecasting layoffs. Many of your friends are out of work. You are wondering how you will pay your mortgage and start seeing a vision of either being homeless or having no food on the table. You start telling yourself you are unsuccessful as a parent or a spouse. You have reached a state of profound fear.

When you are in the midst of the feeling and in a safe place, go with it. Actually begin by trying to exaggerate and outwardly express the fear. Let your body begin to tremble, vibrate, shiver, or shake. Let your teeth chatter. Let your body take the position it craves—very often with fear it is a fetal position. Again, be sure to use sound, even whining, and go with it until you push through to release.

If you catch a fear or anxiety attack early, often you can stave it off by remembering to breathe and thinking of it not as fear or anxiety, but simply as energy. Fritz Pearls, one of the first great body-centered therapists, said, "Fear is excitement without the breath." End your fear work with some form of self-soothing, such as an affirmation about the universe as a safe and supportive place, or spending a moment with the child within you—holding, soothing, and comforting that child.

Write It Down

If, after all of these techniques, you still don't trust yourself to speak the truth of your feelings self-responsibly to the person you need to clear something with, then write a letter. Writing a letter serves to help you get your thoughts in order and have them at arm's length—out of your system, so to speak. Whether or not you ever send or give someone that letter is secondary. You can decide that later. You may decide to rewrite it and then send it.

Both—We Can Be Happy *and* Unhappy

Another strategy that may help is the concept that you are big enough to contain both pleasant and unpleasant feelings. When you are happy, you tend to forget that you ever feel unhappy. Unfortunately, when you're unhappy, you may also tend to forget that you ever feel happy! It is human nature. So whenever you notice yourself feeling very happy, you might say to yourself, "I feel wonderful, *and* sometimes I don't." Whenever you notice yourself feeling down, you might say to yourself, "I feel terrible, *and* sometimes I don't."

Hold your two hands out in front of you, now, palms up as if you were holding two separate objects and comparing their weight. Hold them wide apart and imagine that one hand holds happiness and the other whatever unpleasant feeling you are most likely to experience. Feel yourself as big enough to contain both of these feelings. Realize that they are both within you and the potential to experience them is always there. The very fact that you can contain them both helps you grasp that you are more powerful than your passing feelings. Seemingly opposing feelings do *not* invalidate each other, nor need they overpower you.

Open The Door

These strategies are not solely for your feelings toward others. Oftentimes, when it comes to financial matters, you are your harshest critic. If it is yourself that you are angry with, for example, the previous exercises may also apply. Employing them may allow you to release the self-judgment and clarify what the real issues are that have been holding you back.

Your problem is seldom with the feelings themselves; it is how you feel *about* your feelings. By denying and ignoring your feelings, you lose the vital messages they are trying to bring you. On the other hand, by feeling, experiencing, and often expressing your feelings, you open the door to true awareness and enhanced perspective about who you are and how worthy you are as well.

EXERCISES

Exercise A: Belief, Thought, Feeling

Your beliefs create your thoughts, your thoughts create your feelings, and your feelings fall into one of the four categories of emotions (anger, sadness, fear, and joy). Here are some examples:

Beliefs	Thoughts	Feelings
I am unlovable.	You don't love me.	Sadness
I always get the short end of the stick with raises or promotions.	That wasn't fair.	Anger
I'll be abandoned.	You're not going to stay with me.	Fear
I am not good at math or money.	I'm doomed to my current situation.	Sadness
I don't deserve to have a lot of money in the bank.	Having money is for other people.	Fear or Anger

Now, consider this relationship in your own life. For each of your beliefs (as previously identified in Key One), complete the table below with the related thought and feeling connected to it. Use this format again and again as you start to become aware on a daily basis of how this process works in your life.

Beliefs	Thoughts	Feelings

Exercise B:
Understanding and Communicating Your Feelings

Think of some examples of something someone did or said (especially related to money, wealth, or your worth) that triggered primary feelings in you, and fill in the appropriate blanks for each primary feeling. You may want to share what you come up with by speaking with the appropriate party. This is excellent practice for getting in the habit of identifying and expressing feelings. The more you do it, the more quickly you will be able to identify what you feel and the more honestly you will be able to share without attacking or blaming.

Fear

When you say or do _____,
I feel _____
(for example, scared, terrified, shaky, afraid, withdrawn, etc.)

I feel anxious when _____

I feel afraid when _____

I feel tense when _____

I want _____

Sadness

When you say or do _____,

I feel _____

(for example, sad, alone, dejected, rejected, disappointed, crushed, lonely, empty, hollow, grief, etc.)

I feel apathetic when _____

I feel disappointed when _____

I feel sad when _____

I feel disappointed because _____

I want _____

Anger

When you say or do _____,

I feel _____

(for example, anger, resentment, rage, frustration, fury, irritation, etc.)

I feel frustrated when _____

I feel resentful when _____

I feel angry when _____

I want _____

Joy

When you say or do _____,

I feel _____

(for example, appreciation, happiness, gratitude, joy, warmth, affection, understanding, forgiving, loving, etc.)

I feel friendly when _____

Thank you for _____

I feel joy when _____

I want _____

Exercise C: Presencing Feelings

As discussed in this Key, the best thing to do with a feeling is to simply be with it. You might consider having a compassionate conversation with the feeling as if you were sitting and talking with a small child. Ask it some questions. Surely it has a message for you.

Here are some questions you might ask yourself about a given feeling when you are having it, that will help you to be with it and to get to the root of that feeling. You may not get answers to all of the questions, but be sure to allow the answers that come to arise from the feeling itself, rather than from a story that your mind makes up about the feeling.

1. How is this familiar?
2. Where and how do I feel this feeling in my body?
3. Does it have a size, shape, color, texture, or weight? (Be specific. For example, if you feel pressure, is it a downward, or inward pressure, or a sense of a vice grip? Exactly how much pressure is there? Is there an image associated with it?)
4. When was the first time I remember having had this feeling and what was going on?
5. How old is this feeling?
6. What did the child in me need the first time she/he had this feeling, and what can I say to her/him right now?
7. What does this feeling really want?
8. If I gave this feeling a voice, what would it say?
9. Is there something that I can do or say self-responsibly, that will help this feeling to release?

FEEL YOUR FEELINGS

3

Visualization – Your Thoughts Create Your Feelings

Close your eyes and find a comfortable position. Take a few deep breaths and sit with the feelings in your body. Do a simple body scan, starting with your toes and working your way up to the top of your head. Notice how you are feeling. We call this *getting a baseline* or doing a *body check-in*.

Now, while still in a relaxed position, imagine something unpleasant or upsetting. Do your body scan again and notice how you are feeling. Did it change?

Let that unpleasant thought dissolve and come back to a neutral relaxed position. Now imagine something pleasant, calm, uplifting—a feel-good visualization. Check in once again with your feelings. Did they change again?

Look around you. Notice that nothing much has changed in your external environment. Yet your feeling state may have shifted noticeably. What caused the change in how you were feeling? Your thoughts. That's right. Can you take responsibility for that?

Conscious Breathing

- Think of something that creates a feeling of *anger*. Notice what happens with your breath, your posture, and your muscles while you are immersed in that feeling.
- Think of something that creates a feeling of *fear*. Notice what happens with your breath, your posture, and your muscles when you are immersed in that feeling.
- Think of something that creates a feeling of *sadness*. Notice what happens with your breath, your posture and your muscles while you are immersed in that feeling.
- Think of something that creates a feeling of *joy*. Notice what happens with your breath, your posture, and your muscles while you are immersed in that feeling.
- The practice of noticing how your breath changes with each feeling, and how you are in your body, will help you identify when you are having a certain feeling, even before you are consciously aware of it.

Body-Centered Statements

1. It is okay to feel _____.
2. (Say the feeling.)
3. I know I am on a path towards happiness and wealth when I allow myself to feel _____ fully.
4. I feel _____
    (say the feeling) and sometimes I don't.

Journal Joggers

Use the following questions to lead you into your journal entries for this Key.

*   What am I feeling now? Can I experience the feeling and let it go? If I can't let go, why do I think I am holding on to the feeling? Will holding on be a positive thing for me?
*   What is the purpose of this feeling? What does this feeling want? What is underneath it? Where do I choose to go from here?
*   What feelings am I resisting? What would happen if I embraced and expressed these feelings?

When we were children we used to think that when we grew up we would no longer be vulnerable. But to grow up is to accept vulnerability. To be alive is to be vulnerable.

— Madeline L'Engle

KEY FOUR

ACCEPT WHAT IS

God grant me the serenity to accept the things
I cannot change, the courage to change the things I can,
and the wisdom to know the difference.

—SERENITY PRAYER

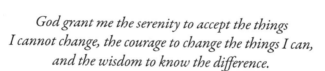

Before you can change your life, you have to get real about WHAT IS. We use the words WHAT IS in capital letters, because we mean them to encompass everything, including the full nature of existence, life, death, and your negative cash flow. They are not separate.

If you are in denial regarding your present reality, there is no way that you will have the clarity of focus to determine how you would like it to be. We get more pushback from clients on this Key than any other! Yet you can create massive change in your life through the one small act of accepting. The opposite of acceptance is resistance. You battle and struggle. You suffer and you are attached to that suffering. It may have become your raison d'être and your identity. Your mind often imagines that in accepting WHAT IS, you will lose who you are. So you hold on to the struggle and resist WHAT IS because you may feel gripped with the fear of no longer recognizing your life and yourself.

A couple came to Cia with something that would seem impossible for anyone to accept—the death of their seven-year-old only child, Ian, who had been hit by a car on his bike in front of their own eyes. Cia knew that statistically the odds of a couple staying together after the loss of a child were slim. The reason for this is that each person grieves in his or her own way. Already having been asked to accept the unacceptable (the death of their child), each member of a grieving couple feels like "hell be damned" if he or she has to accept the "non-supportive" and "unhealthy" way his or her partner is grieving (or not grieving as it sometimes appears).

This couples' case was no different. Marilyn wanted support. Her way of coping was to talk about Ian every chance she got—telling stories about things he did or said and the way he smiled. She had his photos enlarged and filled the house with them. She cried herself to sleep at night watching family videos. Her husband, Todd, had a private kind of grief. He did not want reminders. His own mind was full of them constantly and he wished they would go away. He was embarrassed about how Marilyn talked to other people about Ian and showed photographs, as he imagined the expressions on the faces of friends and acquaintances were strained and that they didn't know what to say. Todd resented Marilyn for keeping the loss so present, and she resented Todd for what she perceived as him not caring. Not only had they lost Ian, they had lost the sense of identity and self-worth they had as parents and as a couple and family. At the first birthday after Ian's death, the situation came to a head, as Marilyn wanted to go through all the motions of a celebration. Todd saw that as insane and torturous, and she saw him as callous and unreachable. Then they came to Cia for therapy.

What might seem from the outside like a given, that they each had their own grieving style, was a revelation to Marilyn and Todd. Ever so gently, Cia helped each of them to let down the defenses they had built up around their own pain just enough to catch a glimpse of the pain their partner was in, and how their partner coped with that pain. Over a series of several sessions, the miracle of compassion began to flicker with the first sign of light in their eyes since their son's death. It didn't mean that either of them had to change their own grieving style. It meant that the first step was to ACCEPT that their partner might have a different yet still valid one.

Acceptance opens the door to more acceptance. Over time, Marilyn and Todd were able to face that they had been through one of the worst tragedies anyone ever could. It happened. They were still alive. They had each other. Slowly, they were able to move on with their lives, growing a new sense of identity and self-worth both as individuals and, albeit forever changed, as a couple. The last Cia heard from them, Marilyn and Todd were expecting another child. We are happy for that child as his or her parents found enough acceptance in their lives that the new he or she would not have to come into the world to fill a void.

Resisting WHAT IS

And acceptance is the answer to all my problems today.
When I am disturbed, it is because I find some person, place, thing,
or situation—some fact of my life—unacceptable to me, and I can find no
serenity until I accept that person, place, thing, or situation as being
exactly the way it is supposed to be at this moment.

—ALCOHOLICS ANONYMOUS

Resisting WHAT IS enables you to convict the real or imagined perpetrators of your problems. You fear that if you choose acceptance, you will let those perpetrators off the hook. You will no longer have anything to blame on them—any way to prove how severely wronged you have been. The alternative—claiming responsibility for your life by accepting WHAT IS—feels much riskier, and thus causes you to feel more vulnerable. It may have felt like a benefit to not have to own your life. In Key Two, you claimed responsibility for your life as you began to realize it is costing you so much more to blame someone than you can possibly gain.

In the first three Keys, we highlighted how you may be resisting change, the flow of abundance, and even feeling your own feelings. If you take a step back right now to gain perspective, you may realize that you spend much of your life resisting. Each time you resist, you are in essence fighting with yourself and your life. This can be quite draining, tiring, and self-defeating. One of Belinda's clients, Lisa, had a huge "aha" moment when she recognized the source of her working 20 hours a day and feeling inadequate in the effort. "Words do not really express what I want right now, except to say thank you for listening and offering your thoughts. I took them to heart. Our conversation made me realize that I have still been fighting . . . everyone, everything, my career, but mostly ME. So the first thought this morning was "STOP FIGHTING MYSELF!" What a relief Lisa felt when she identified that she was holding on so tight to a picture she had of how her life and financial situation "should" be. She was fighting hard against the WHAT IS instead of creating and living into a more positive WHAT IS in her life. Next thing she did was plan a vacation and start enjoying her life again with a new sense of peace for her path.

The novelist Henry Miller said, "Life moves on, whether we act as cowards or heroes. Life has no other discipline to impose, if we would but realize it, than to accept life unquestioningly. Everything we shut our eyes to, everything we run away from, everything we deny, denigrate or despise, serves to defeat us in the end. What seems nasty, painful, evil, can become a source of beauty, joy and strength, if faced with an open mind. Every moment is a golden one for him who has the vision to recognize it as such."

Adding Meaning

The 'facts' of life carry no more weight than
the meaning you attach to them.

—MARY MANIN MORRISSEY

When it comes to accepting the WHAT IS of your current financial situation, what comes up for you? Is it disappointment? Regret? Relief? Millions of people have become avoiders, ignoring the reality, and fooling themselves into complacency. A new "ostrich" mentality emerged where burying your head in the sand seemed better than facing the reality. It may feel too painful for you to face the true WHAT IS, especially as you then may have to do something about it. Oftentimes, people imbue the current financial situation with meaning. Their coping strategy has organized the meaning of their life around what has befallen them. If you can relate to this, you don't want to accept WHAT IS because of the meaning you are placing on the good, the bad, and the ugly of your current situation.

The kicker here is that you are the one who is creating the meaning. There is no deus ex machina of meaning that descends upon you and sanctifies your WHAT IS, giving you the excuse to ignore it. If you actually saw WHAT IS for purely and simply WHAT IS, you wouldn't have so much trouble accepting it.

The reason why you may not be able to accept the literal WHAT IS, is because of the meaning you assign to it. You are, in effect, making your bed and then lying in it, as you sentence or condemn yourself in order to avoid facing the simple reality. Few people actually accept their current financial situation with pure joy and happiness. Even when the financial situation is positive, the majority of people condemn it as not being enough, making it more and more difficult to accept WHAT IS. If someone accepts WHAT IS, and the meaning they give it is that they are inadequate, then by accepting, they think they are proving that they *are* in fact inadequate.

When you react the next time with the same meaning that you have been assigning to that circumstance or situation, instead ask yourself, "What am I having this mean? What else could it mean?" And then again and again, "What else could it mean," until you begin to recognize that there could be positive meanings in your current WHAT IS.

Downward Spiral

Cia's client, John, an IT project manager, came to her after he was passed over for a promotion he was expecting, and was struggling with his resulting feelings and reactions. When he didn't get the promotion, lots of feelings naturally arose for John—anger, frustration, fear (of keeping his current job), and disappointment (a form of sadness). The feelings were based on the meaning he was assigning, as he concluded his boss was out to get him, lying to him, or because he was late two days the previous week.

The mind often goes into a downward spiral, similar to the domino effect, when something unpleasant occurs. It starts spinning stories and imparts meaning, which is actually only projection. It is probably rare that the spiral of your stories is positive. Be sure to ask yourself, "What are the facts here?" In John's case, the actual reality is simply that John was passed over for a promotion. Yet, if this was you, you may also find yourself creating a self-fulfilling prophecy by providing evidence that you are right in the meaning you have assigned.

To continue the story, John was then surly towards his boss because of his projection about his boss's reasons. His boss reacted with hostility, because of John's surliness. John gets to say, "See. I was right! She *is* out to get me." Yet what did that really serve?

You naturally act based on the meaning you put into your stories, and often wind up sabotaging yourself in the process. In the meantime, so much energy is getting wasted on projection and on spinning your stories that you lose your ability to be present to your life. The simple answer—accepting WHAT IS!

In John's case, he didn't ask why he was not given the promotion or ask more about the situation. What other reasons could there have been for John not getting the promotion? As a start, maybe they are reorganizing and going to give him the whole region, or give him more money but are not currently able to promote him. Unfortunately, John didn't go there. Nor do most people.

It may feel too painful to accept the WHAT IS of your financial situation. Yet if you don't do so and fail to truly accept, you are giving yourself a back door to taking responsibility, which may wind up perpetuating dysfunction.

A client of Belinda's, Patricia, was 55 years old when the stock market plunged in 2008 and her investments dropped over 40%. She let her emotions get the better of her and she sold over 70% of her assets at the depressed price. Then, within the next year, Patricia kept her money in cash, thus missing the rally. She compounded her shameful self-talk by not trusting herself to sell before the market plummeted, as she had now associated with this new shame on missing the rally. All of this blocked her from taking advantage of the upturn because she had already locked in her losses out of panic. In Patricia's case, it was a matter of separating out the reality of the situation and recognizing that she did the best she could with the information that she had. Belinda and Patricia worked on her self-forgiveness and accepting WHAT IS, so she could once again make smart unemotional decisions with her investments and other assets.

Complaining—Just Don't Do It

If you don't like something, change it. If you can't change it,
change your attitude. Don't complain.

—Maya Angelou

Complaining is a verbal demonstration of resisting WHAT IS. Beyond *playing the victim*, as described in Key Two, complaining is a way of expressing and furthering your dissatisfaction, thus immersing yourself in more negativity. You are then attracting more of what you don't want. Think of it like a huge lit billboard similar to those in Times Square in New York City. You are basically broadcasting in neon lights that you don't have the life you want—and choosing to focus on it.

As you complain more and more about money, or your lack thereof, you may slip into feelings of poverty and scarcity. These feelings are then fueled by pervasive negative messaging about the economy in the media or from your friends and family. The momentum picks up as you then (consciously or unconsciously) want to be right and thus look for evidence to substantiate your complaints and scarcity. This is a very dangerous downward spiral and breeds more complaining, scarcity, and feelings of poverty.

This is your wake-up call to heighten your awareness of your complaining and stop immediately. Instead, practice *verbal hygiene*. The mind tends to believe what the ears hear. The ears hear not only what others say but, more importantly, they hear what *you* say. Your words make quite an impression on your mind.

When we would rather complain about something than
do something about it we are in big trouble.

—Anne Wilson Schaef

ACCEPT WHAT IS

4

Uncommitted complaining is complaining in its worst form. This occurs when you are complaining and not at all committed to finding a solution. You can catch yourself in uncommitted complaining once you realize you are (a) complaining and (b) to someone that can't do anything about the situation. Bringing awareness to this behavior allows you to take the first step by honestly asking yourself if you are more committed to the problem or the solution. As you gain perspective on the truth of the answer, the next actions to take will become surprisingly clear.

As you begin to practice changing the way you think, what you say will also begin to change. It can work the other way around as well. Watch what comes out of your mouth and be sure it is something positive. This will help accelerate the process of changing your outlook on the world.

Will Bowen, author of *A Complaint Free World: How to Stop Complaining and Start Enjoying the Life You Always Wanted*, encourages you to wear a purple bracelet as a reminder to eliminate your complaining. Each time you complain, you shift the bracelet to the other wrist. The 21-Day Challenge requires that you not complain, and therefore not move your bracelet to the other wrist, for 21 consecutive days. This sounds simple yet it is not so easy! Bowen notes people complain an average of 20–30 times per day, so to go to zero complaints for 21 days is essentially eliminating 420–630 complaints from your life. Take the journey from Unconscious Incompetence to Unconscious Competence around complaining through Bowen's process.

Take a moment now to imagine your life without complaining. Do you already feel more at peace? Are you now closer to accepting WHAT IS, when you are not focusing on what isn't?

Where Cia lives in Costa Rica is cattle country, and the fences stretch for miles. They don't look like fences though. They look like rows of trees. There is a tree in Costa Rica off of which you can chop a branch and stick it in the rich and fertile soil and it sprouts a tree. The farmers buy barbed wire and nail it to the young tree stake. As that tree stake widens into the size of a full grown tree, it absorbs that barbed wire, so that all that shows is the wire connecting those trees. That's an example of what we call "accepting what is." When you can truly absorb what life throws at you, you can use that to connect to others rather than to grow bitter, cynical, guarded, or to push away all that might be yours for the taking.

Expectations

Your problems lie in the gap between your expectations and WHAT IS. Expectations are loaded and set you up for disappointment. Whether your expectations are high or low, they are still a set-up. They give rise to the deadly *shoulds*. This does not mean that you don't get to dream dreams or set intentions. It is not your vision that you must give up. It is your frustration, resentment, and resistance to WHAT IS. It means you need to understand and accept what is current reality and what is not, and what are appropriate expectations for yourself and what are unrealistic expectations that you have layered on yourself based on the believed expectations of others.

What if you replaced expectations with acceptance? Says Cia, "Each day is like a blossom for me opened with the act of acceptance. In my early 20s, after my body was attacked by a couple of viruses and a bout of extreme low blood sugar, I developed CFIDS (chronic fatigue immune deficiency). That was before it had been identified as an illness when doctors dismissed it as strictly a mental condition. By my early 30s, the weakness and exhaustion took on the addition of pain, and I was diagnosed with fibromyalgia. In my 40s, the years of living with those maladies evolved into an autoimmune illness as well, and by my 50s, the inability to exercise caused osteoporosis and cardiac insufficiency. Hooray for me: I made it to 60! I truly do not believe I would have though, without the daily practice of accepting what is. I have been gifted with a great opportunity and reminder to practice that. I have lived my life to the fullest. I have lived as if my life depended on it. I noticed early on that when I would fight the pain or exhaustion, they would both become worse. When I accepted them, and the limitations of what I was able to do at any given moment, day, or month, I could relax into WHAT IS and place my focus on the tremendous amount I have to be grateful for. My illness has been my greatest teacher of this vitally important key."

ACCEPT WHAT IS

4

The Platform for Change—Acceptance

Acceptance of one's life has nothing to do with resignation;
it does not mean running away from the struggle. On the contrary,
it means accepting it as it comes, with all the handicaps of heredity,
of suffering, of psychological complexes and injustices.

—Paul Tournier

When we say to people, you have to accept WHAT IS before you can change, they may look at us like we are crazy. The types of responses we hear include: "Well, how can I change it if I'm accepting it?" "Why do I want to accept it if I want to change it?" "If I were accepting it, I wouldn't want to change it." "How can I accept it if I want to change it?" or "If I were accepting it, why would I want to change it?"

In this Key, acceptance is the platform for change. It is from acceptance that we create the real possibility for change in our lives. Think of it as a clearing, fountain, or *catalyst for change*—the spark that lights the engine. Without the spark, it is cold, stagnant, and stuck. The engine is the energy to move ahead. Or, think of it as the springboard or diving board. It launches us into the realm of all possibility.

During a particularly challenging time in Belinda's life, she would repeat the affirmation to herself "I love and accept myself exactly as I am." At first, it was uncomfortable and she didn't feel like it fit. "How could that be possible if I am not totally happy with my current situation?" she thought. Her overachiever side even tried to one-up each previous day by doing one extra affirmation each day. Once she got to repeating it 100 times in a day, she realized that it was not about the number of times she repeated the statement. It was about welcoming the new state of being into her always-driving-forward persona. As she repeated the body-centered statement each day, at a more manageable ten times per day, Belinda started to recognize that she could love and accept her inner self and own self-worth while embracing her current situation. It is this context that she still turns to now when she feels the resistance surface.

The WHAT IS of Your Financial Situation

It is now time for you to recognize and accept the WHAT IS of your current financial position. You often gain power as you gain clarity about your true state, especially when it comes to your finances. Your *Net Worth Statement* ("NWS") can be used to show you exactly what your financial situation is in black and white—real numbers. Your NWS provides you the means to list your assets (what you *own*) and your liabilities (what you *owe*) to show you your current net worth as of a given point in time (i.e., today, or as close to today as you can get statements for).

We suggest you use a current month-end, and re-do this exercise at least quarterly, to keep on top of your evolving situation. See Exercise B for an easy-to-use template with thorough instructions. (As a gift with the purchase of this book, you may go to www.SelfWorthBook.com for a complimentary downloadable version of this popular template.) Use what you just learned about recognizing the WHAT IS in your life to complete this exercise. Approach completion as another step along this sacred journey, and one that you can do without self-judgment or shame. When clients of Belinda's complete this step, they are often pleasantly surprised at the outcomes. Often they have been in a scarcity mindset for way too long, or have been too afraid to "face the music" of their own reality. They had actually mentally excluded many items (such as retirement savings, inheritance, home equity, etc.), which served to provide evidence for their scarcity. The truth, in fact, was actually much more abundant and such a relief!

A later step in Key Five will be to determine monthly how much money is coming in and going out (your Cash Flow Statement) as this serves as additional insight into the WHAT IS of your current situation.

Increasing Your Energy Levels

Acceptance is the freedom from resistance. Once you let go of resistance, you free up huge amounts of energy. This energy could otherwise go into changing the WHAT IS—or better yet—living in the present. By not accepting it, you always want it to be different. So, what you want to begin to do is to use acceptance to liberate that energy. As you liberate that energy, then the possibility of change becomes more real.

The other possibility that gets created is the possibility of living life more fully as you step into present reality. Acceptance increases your aliveness. It does not mean resignation. It is not giving up. It is not becoming resigned to the status quo. Feel the difference in your body. If you are resisting, you are creating another bottomless hole where you allow energy to waste and then the downward spiral begins. Resignation is a dead feeling, like you've just sacrificed some of your aliveness. Acceptance, on the other hand, carries with it a sensation of release, of freedom, of possibility. It clears the way to move forward along your path.

One of Belinda's clients was holding onto this belief: "I don't have what it takes to be happy and fulfilled." Dawn kept herself powerless, sad, and uninspired instead of accepting that she does have what it takes and it was just buried inside. Instead of always running to be someone else and to be someplace different, consider what it would be like to say "I'm there. I'm where I'm meant to be. This is my life!" said with huge enthusiasm and excitement, instead of the monotone "This is my life."

Dawn created a clearing into acceptance of herself and her life to realize that she had exactly what it would take for her to be happy and fulfilled. It just required her to first accept WHAT IS in her life. She then felt alive, energized, and vibrant. She brought a new excitement for her life that enabled her to breathe easier and live from her fully self-expressed creative spirit. At 43, what a gift Dawn opened up for herself.

Path to Peace

Acceptance brings peace. We're not talking about an apathetic peace. On the contrary, acceptance frees up the creativity and inspiration to create what it is you want from WHAT IS. If you don't accept the present reality, then you are at war with it and settling into a constant state of discomfort. Acceptance is the foundation from which to move forward. Once you accept WHAT IS, all the resources that went into fighting are now liberated for constructive change—to create the life you want.

Acceptance is an opening to WHAT IS. It is not about tomorrow—what you could or could not do, be, or have. It is about this moment. It is about embracing the real. Acceptance is an opening to the nature of things as they are. In that lies freedom because bondage is something we create for ourselves out of our struggle with WHAT IS. If you start today, right now, to accept WHAT IS in your financial life, how do you feel? What opens up for you to create?

Change Your Mind

We can't change WHAT IS in the moment, yet our beliefs and perspective on WHAT IS creates or causes our reality. Therefore, what we can change is our attitude about it. And in doing so, we plant the seeds for creating our future the way we want it to be. The Serenity Prayer at the beginning of this Key states this beautifully. We can open ourselves to the possibility of celebration now—of joy and relief in our process.

Accept your life and accept yourself exactly the way they are in this moment. It simply is WHAT IS. Neither worrying nor complaining will change it. Go ahead and try it now. See if you can get a feeling inside yourself of total acceptance. As you experience this acceptance, what is the feeling inside your body? Do you notice the increased aliveness and energy?

Moving On

> Let the months and years come, they can take nothing from me,
> they can take nothing more. I am so alone, and so without hope
> that I can confront them without fear. The life that has borne me
> through these years is still in my hands and my eyes. Whether I have
> subdued it, I know not. But so long as it is there it will seek its
> own way out, heedless of the will that is within me.

—ERICH MARIA REMARQUE

ACCEPT WHAT IS

4

Jane, a single mother of three small children, lost her job when her company when bankrupt. Along with her job, she saw her retirement savings go from $500,000 to nearly zero as the stock lost all its value with the bankruptcy. Despite extreme diligence in looking for a new job, Jane met with one closed door after another. In three months, she could no longer pay her mortgage, and in another six months she had lost her house. She asked Cia how she could accept that.

How is it possible for Jane to accept this situation? Jane was not willing. What were her choices? She lived tormented by her own anger towards her company, her circumstances, and herself. Her bitterness toward life erupted unbidden at difficult moments. Her choices were to stay this way, or to accept WHAT IS so she could move forward. Cia asked her what she wanted. She wanted her old life back. Cia said that was not possible, and instead asked, "Where are you willing to go from here? Being able to move on can only come from acceptance of WHAT IS."

Jane seemed to feel that acceptance was too high a price for her to pay if it meant saying that what happened was okay. So Cia told her she doesn't have to say that. What happened is definitely not okay. But what happened, happened. It is WHAT IS. Living from a place of resistance, anger, bitterness, and blame will not change what happened and will not help Jane. It only holds her back (as it might for you as well).

It is WHAT IS. Say it out loud and say it with a sigh, not of resignation but of release. Feel the tight muscles in your body that have been busy resisting WHAT IS let go. Really get it and mean it. That is acceptance.

As Jane accepted her situation, her energy was freed and channeled to find a more lucrative job—one that had eluded her when she was stuck in resistance. She is now rebuilding and is more appreciative of her life and what she has.

Through acceptance, you liberate energy that was previously tied up in resistance—and this creates great opportunity. Use this newfound energy and opportunity to become clear about what you want your life to look like and begin to create it.

EXERCISES

Exercise A: Getting a Handle on WHAT IS

Start by taking a look around you. What do you see? How would you describe your life? Notice the good things about it, as well as the things you don't like. Do this with as little judgment as possible as you experiment with one or more of the following options:

Option 1: Draw a picture of your life. How does it look to you the way it is now? It doesn't matter if you think you can't draw—it is the feelings, the colors you choose, and the energy behind it which count. Alternatively, you may make a collage by cutting and pasting images from magazines which represent your life the way it is now.

Option 2: If you are good at visualizing/creative imagination, you may choose to create a picture in your mind which symbolizes your life as it is now and how you feel about it.

Option 3: Make a list called "My Life" by writing WHAT IS in your life right now (the big, the little, the good, the bad, the ugly) in random order, using a stream of consciousness technique as things pop into your mind. Here are some categories to consider: Financial, Business/Career, Recreation/Fun/Travel, Health/Fitness, Relationships/Family, Personal/Spiritual, and Contribution/Making a difference. *Feel your feelings as you do it.* Say each of your WHAT IS items out loud and feel your feelings. If you do this periodically until it becomes a habit—an automatic taking stock or checking in—you can get a clear sense of the overview of your life as needed without writing it down. Whenever you feel like you don't have a handle on it, journal!

Examples:

- I hate my job but I like my new supervisor.
- I need a new car.
- I love my house except for the bathroom.
- I feel guilty when I spend money, especially when I'm not sure I can afford it.

- I have created $30,000 in credit card debt in the last 2 years.
- My friends want to go out every night and I'm going broke trying to keep up with them.
- We take one vacation per year and I am unhappy as I would like 2-3 vacations or trips per year.

Exercise B: Choose!

Step 1: Identify the things you are resisting or not accepting in your life.
Step 2: Make a list of the benefits you get from not accepting them.
Step 3: Make a list of the costs of not accepting them.
Step 4: Do the costs outweigh the current benefits? Once you are clear that they do, create a new body-centered statement that allows you to accept each item you were previously resisting. (See the examples in Body-Centered Statements at the end of this Key.)

Exercise C: The WHAT IS of Your Current Financial Position

The three parts of the triangle below symbolize the three steps of Inspiration, Empowerment, and Action. Keys One through Three were designed to offer Inspiration for your journey. Keys Four through Six are primarily dedicated to your Empowerment. As you begin to take ownership of the WHAT IS of your current financial situation, you are taking a big step in the direction of your personal Empowerment. Use this important exercise below to help you get real about WHAT IS when it comes to your finances.

OWNYOUR
MONEY.

Part I: Net Worth Statement Instructions:

In following the instructions below, use bank account statements, investment statements, appraisals on property, credit card statements, mortgage statements, and other available information supporting what you own and what you owe. The Net Worth Statement worksheet will give you a good idea of where your money is and how it is working. Please use your most recent statements as this will provide you with the most accurate information as of a current point in time.

4

ACCEPT WHAT IS

Assets (What you own)	
Cash and Liquid Assets	
Cash	Cash includes the money in your wallet, under your bed, in piggybanks, envelopes, or in jars!
CDs, other term deposits	Include terms and expiration date on the CDs. Money markets are included in the Investment Assets below.
Money owed to you	Estimate what you think might be due you in back tax refunds and personal loans.
Investment Assets	
Mutual Funds, REITs	A professionally managed pool of equities, bonds, notes, CDs, and/or indexes
Stocks	Equity holding directly in a publicly traded company
Bonds	Savings Bonds, Treasury, Municipal, Corporate

Real Estate Investments	Commercial or residential property held for investment
Business Interests/ Equity	Partnerships or interest in non-public firms
Variable Annuity	Contract whereby the issuer agrees to make payments in future based on your investments
Long-Term Assets	
Retirement Account (401K, 403(b), SEP)	Tax advantaged savings plans established to promote retirement savings
Cash value of life insurance	There may be a portion of your life insurance premium that holds a cash value
Pension plans and profit sharing	Retirement investments provided by an employer usually based on earnings
Other, inc. ESPP	Employee stock purchase plans
Property Assets	
Personal Residence	Please use recent appraisal or zillow.com to value this property, if available
Recreational/Vacation Property	Please use recent appraisal or zillow.com to value this property, if available
Cars	Please use Kelly Blue Book to value, if available
Recreational equipment	Boats, snowmobiles, etc. Review Craigslist or EBay

Household furnishings/equipment	Look at similar items selling on Craigslist or EBay
Collectibles	Art, stamps, coins, jewelry, appraisals or estimate based "like" sales
Liabilities (What you owe)	
Short-Term Debt	
Multiple accounts and credit cards list all separately:	
Charge/credit card	List each major and store credit card separately, so add lines if necessary
Line of credit/ overdraft	List Home Equity Line and other lines of credit separately, add lines if necessary
Personal debts owed	Any personal debt and interest payments that you are accumulating
Long-Term Debt	Most long-term debt is self-explanatory
Net Worth	Difference between Assets (what you own) and Liabilities (what you owe).

Part II: Net Worth Statement Worksheet

Date Prepared: _____

ASSETS (What you own)	Stmt Date	Balance	Actual % Rate	Notes
Cash and Liquid Assets				
Cash				
Checking/Savings Acct 1				
Checking/Savings Acct 2				
CDs, other deposits				
Money owed to you (include taxes)				
Other				

Investment Assets	Stmt Date	Balance	$ amt Invested	Diff	Notes
Mutual Funds					
Stocks, Exchange Traded Vehicles					
Bonds					
Real Estate Investments					
Business Interests/Equity					
Variable Annuity					
Other					
Long-Term Assets					
Retirement Account (401K, 403(b), SEP)					
Cash value of life insurance					
Pension plans and profit sharing					
Other, inc. ESPP					

Property Assets	Stmt Date	Appraised Value	$ amt Invested	Diff	City, State
Personal Residence (Home)					
Recreational property/ Vacation home(s)					
Cars					
Recreational equipment					
Hshld furnishings and equipment					
Collectibles (art, stamps, coins, jewelry)					
Other					
TOTAL ASSETS		$			

LIABILITIES (What you owe)	Stmt Date	Balance	Credit Line	Rate %	Min Monthly Payment
Short-Term Debt					
Multiple accounts and credit cards list all separately:					
Charge/credit card 1					
Charge/credit card 2					
Charge/credit card 3					
Charge/credit card 4					
Line of credit/overdraft 1					
Line of credit/overdraft 2					
Loans/lease (car, bank, etc.)					
Personal debts owed					
Unpaid bills (include parking tickets)					
Taxes (all taxes owed)					

4

ACCEPT WHAT IS

ACCEPT WHAT IS

4

Charitable donation pledges					
Other (family obligations, etc.)					
Long-Term Debt	Stmt Date	Balance	Monthly Payment	Rate %	Notes
Home mortgage					
Other mortgage loans					
Other- Student Loans					
TOTAL LIABILITIES		$			
NET WORTH		$			(TOTAL ASSETS minus TOTAL LIABILITIES)

Visualization and Conscious Breathing

Part I

Sit back and close your eyes. Take some deep breaths. As you picture your life the way it is now from the exercise(s) you have done above, allow yourself to get an overall feeling in your body. What do you feel? What does your life as a whole feel like to you? You might be able to sense the feeling in your whole body, or in one place. Is it like a big combination of feelings: some sadness, frustration, suffocation, anxiety, excitement, happiness mixed with some fear, sadness mixed with some anger, ropes tied around you, letting go and saying goodbye, a lonely pit in the center of your stomach, a scary place, joy, or playfulness? There are no right or wrong responses here. Notice what it is for *you*. Go ahead and take your time to fully get the feeling of your life and particularly your current financial position. Breathe with that feeling and really allow yourself to feel the impact of it. Notice that on some level, you may be living with that feeling all the time.

Part II

Next, we want you to accept your life and your feelings exactly the way they are right now. This is your moment—your unique step towards change right now.

Go ahead—see if you can get a feeling of acceptance (the platform for change) in your body. Use your breath to help you do it. If you are doing it correctly, it will feel like a kind of opening and a sense of relief. As you breathe, invite yourself to open to WHAT IS. Ask yourself, "How can I really open up to accept this exactly the way it is right now?" You might imagine your body and your very cells opening and expanding to this sense of acceptance. Let yourself take in that this is the way it is. Take your hands and hold them out as if you are holding your life in front of you. Say to yourself, "I am able to hold my life the way it is now. I am large enough to contain all of these various components of my life." Keep breathing, and as you breathe, imagine your being growing broader and larger. Ask yourself, "What would it be like to recognize that you are larger than your life circumstances?" The truth is that you are greater than the sum of all the parts that you call *your life*, and *within you lies the ability to sculpt it to your liking*. Give yourself some time to be with that.

Body-Centered Statements

1. This is WHAT IS. I get it. I own it.
2. As I breathe into and open up to WHAT IS, I experience freedom from resistance, struggle, and scarcity.
3. The energy that comes with my acceptance is already creating conscious change.

Journal Joggers

Use the following questions or thoughts to lead you into your journal entries for this Key.

- What in your life are you having trouble accepting right now?
- How might your resistance be causing a problem for you?
- What does the feeling of resistance feel like in your body? What does the feeling of acceptance feel like in your body? Which do you prefer?

ACCEPT WHAT IS

4

- Would you be willing to accept WHAT IS first and then choose where to go from there?

When you're in pitch blackness, all you can do is sit tight until your eyes get used to the dark.

—HARUKI MURAKAMI

4

ACCEPT WHAT IS

KEY FIVE

SET YOUR BOUNDARIES

Good fences make good neighbors.

—FOLK SAYING

While the power of choice in life is extremely important to mental, emotional, and financial well-being—so much so that Key Eight is devoted to it—you also live in a world where the number of possible choices you are confronted with in any given moment can be truly overwhelming. Healthy boundaries help you to set healthy limits, thereby building a sense of empowerment and a greater sense of who you are.

Boundaries in Relationship

Boundaries are also vital in relationships, and a fundamental attribute of healthy self-worth. A boundary symbolizes where my stuff ends and yours begins. Boundaries apply to both internal and external resources and deficits. In other words, we are talking about your psychological and emotional baggage, fears, and ways of being with money, as well as your possessions, assets, and liabilities. Your *stuff* includes the good, the bad, and the ugly. Sometimes

5

when you focus on your *stuff*, or more accurately perhaps your partner's *stuff*, you may see it in terms of defects rather than seeing the good and positive. Have you found yourself falling into a similar trap?

When you know your boundaries, you understand what is yours and what is not, whether it is an issue or an object. This helps prevent over-reaction, defensiveness, and taking things personally. It helps you become and remain clear. You are then able to stand your ground without becoming either aggressive or defensive. Your partner's projections or attacks bounce back on him or her as if confronted by a mirror. (See Key Eleven for suggestions on bringing this enhanced sense of boundaries to support your conversations with your partner about money.)

Impact of Confusion

When you are in a state of confusion, you err in money choices because you are too full of doubt and insecurity to make appropriate decisions. The result is that you make a decision by following someone else's suggestion, either consciously or unconsciously, without fully understanding it yourself or coming from your own integrity. When you do that, you unconsciously release yourself from responsibility. The consequences are likely to be blame of another or of yourself, and an increased (false) belief that you are not smart enough. You fuel your own insecurity.

Belinda's client, Pat, was a successful attorney with a growing legal practice, however she had consistently lived without boundaries or clarity when it came to money. When she first approached Belinda, she strongly believed she made, as she put it, "stupid money decisions." Pat lost an investment property in Boston, a three-family house, to foreclosure. One of the apartments was vacant for four months and Pat fell behind on the mortgage payments. By the time she rented it, she was unable to catch up. Pat held to the belief that she could not make intelligent decisions regarding money matters, thus creating a form of self-fulfilling prophecy. Each time she was on the edge of determining her boundary, she defaulted to a confused, helpless belief system and defined herself as a victim. Belinda helped her create a different reality for herself. She helped Pat see that she was making many other very wise choices in her life, but when she remained in the cloud of boundary-less confusion, that capacity got lost. Once she realized how she was living into this non-supportive belief and creating her own erroneous boundaries on her financial success, she was empowered to recognize the wise decisions she had and could make as she moved forward. Her entire outlook on money changed in that instant.

Once you begin to create clearer boundaries for yourself, the risk of falling back into that lack of clarity may inspire you to become more discerning in your financial interactions as well as in events and relationships. Setting boundaries, financially and ethically, does not have to limit you from great investments or require a great deal of time. In fact, the clearer you are about your boundaries and criteria, the easier and faster you will be able to make decisions.

"Yes" and "No" as Human Rights

One 'no' averts a thousand evils.

—Indian proverb

Cia was very shy when she was young and had no real sense of self-worth. She was such a people-pleaser that she developed what she calls a "chameleon personality," taking on the characteristics of whomever she was with, in an effort to fit in and win approval. Doing so is precisely the opposite of having boundaries. At the time, Cia thought that having no boundaries was a *good* thing. "Yes" became her first response, even if it didn't really work in her life. She thought that being so open to everyone, so flexible, and so giving were positive qualities. Sometimes these can be positive virtues, yet Cia had taken it to such an extreme that she really had lost any idea of who she truly was. She had spent so many years trying to please others and finding a way to fit in within a world where she was quite uncomfortable. It wasn't until late in life, when she learned about boundaries, that establishing hers enabled her to discover, honor, and use her own unique gifts. Instead of feeling shame at being "different," she was able to use that uniqueness to help others break out of their own shell.

Cia tells the story of the first time she stood up to a friend and said "no" and how terrifying it was for her to do that. "I loved the quote by Jules Renard. 'The only man who is really free is one who can turn down an invitation to dinner without giving an excuse.' It made me realize how far away I was from being free. Not only could I not conceive of saying 'no' and not giving a reason, I had never really gotten as far as saying 'no.' It simply hadn't occurred to me to ever stop and ask myself what it was that *I* wanted to do. I was the girl who never refused anybody anything. I vowed to try it. The next time a friend asked me to do something with her, instead of my usual automatic knee-jerk 'yes,' I said, 'please give me a day to think about it.' That was a huge step. 'Thinking about it' meant checking in with my body for the answer—asking myself what it was that I actually wanted. It was a new concept and a new experience. I saw my friend the next day and I told her that I didn't want to join her. I was literally trembling; it was so hard to get the two-letter word out of my mouth. But she took it fine. Sometime later she complimented me on being a good role model for setting boundaries, and so did other friends I had begun to practice with. I was astounded. Not only had I helped myself, I had benefited others as well." It no longer takes Cia a day to know what she wants. After years of practice, she can get in touch with her inner knowing, i.e., her body wisdom, and give an answer almost immediately. If she needs a moment to feel it through, she asks for it, and now she counsels clients to be able to do the same.

Ninon de L'Enclos said, "Every action we take, everything we do, is either a victory or defeat in the struggle to become what we want to be." Every time we say "yes" when we mean "no," it is a defeat. Every time we sell ourselves short by compromising who we are, we are violating our own boundaries. And every time we stand up for who we truly are and what we truly want, we are celebrating a victory in the life-long journey to know ourselves.

You have basic human rights. You have the right to say "yes," and the right to say "no." The appropriate utilization of these rights is boundary-setting in a nutshell. Where does your sense of self come from? How do you know to which rights you are entitled? How do you know where *you* end and others begin?

In a healthy upbringing, you develop healthy boundaries early in life. Your mother supports your sense of self first, through mirroring and gradually through the individuation process. *No* and *yes* are some of the earliest words for most toddlers, and come with a budding sense of personal power and the right to assert preferences. If the mirroring and individuation were absent, incomplete, or thwarted, or if your boundaries were violated by those people whose responsibility lay in helping you develop them, your sense of rights and your parameters may be murky or confused. If this is the case, it is time to really educate and train yourself through experiment and practice. Work with the exercises at the end of the Key and affirm your rights on a daily basis.

A Powerful Two-Letter Word

Practice saying *no*—a lot. If that is a scary thought, you may have a people-pleaser or caretaker personality. You derive your self-esteem, and your related self-worth, from pleasing others. Are you willing to experiment with finding your self-esteem from a more reliable source—within yourself?

Recently one of Belinda's clients, Bob, a restaurant manager, declared, "No is not an option." His voice was filled with resignation, regret, and sadness though. Every time he said "yes" and added one more thing to his never-ending to-do list, Bob stressed himself out more and some of his priority items were not getting done as a result. Although we appreciate his high level of client service, teaching Bob how to expand his vocabulary to also proudly say "No," "Not now," or "Yes, and . . ." was quite an *aha* moment for him.

If you never say *no*, how good is your *yes*? We find it is easier to trust you when you say *yes*, if we know that you will also say *no* when that is what you mean. Your *yes* then becomes more powerful and meaningful, and you won't take on the resignation, as Bob did, of feeling stepped on or that his own priorities didn't matter.

Here are three sample circumstances for Bob to use his new expanded vocabulary:

- When something is requested of Bob that he simply cannot take on, *no* is an acceptable response, without a full explanation of why.
- When something is requested of Bob that by doing in that moment would disrupt his schedule and previous list of things to get done by a certain time, he can now say "No, *not now*. Instead, how about I do that for you by 5 p.m. today?" What a relief.
- When something is requested of Bob that he somewhat agrees with but does not want to complete exactly as requested, he can now say, "*Yes* we can do that, *and* how about we also do this as well?"

It is actually a gift to others when you say *no* because not only are you setting an example they can use in their own lives, they know they can trust that you mean it when you say *yes*. Grasp the concept of what we call *conscious selfishness*. Putting yourself first fills you up with so much more to give to others. Eliminate the words *duty* and *obligation* from your mental and spoken vocabulary. Once you have freed yourself from the tyranny of the *shoulds*, you will find that you need never experience resentment again. Where there was resentment, you will be sowing the seeds of genuine generosity, caring, and joy.

A healthy boundary does not interfere with your ability to love, experience compassion, or attend to the feelings and needs of others. Nor does it have to interfere with your ability to save, spend, or earn money. A boundary is not a *wall*. On the contrary, it serves as an opening. As it supports your wholeness and your worthiness, you can be you more fully.

Once you have a healthy boundary of your own, you are teaching yourself to honor the boundaries of others. Then your love and presence ceases to have strings attached.

Mother and Daughter Boundaries

When Katie came to see Cia as a client, she was having endless problems with her mother. She was virtually obsessed with the way her mother was "ruining her life." Katie accused her mother of having no boundaries and Katie was correct. Her mother was attempting to live her life through Katie: demanding daily contact, nagging Katie about the way she managed everything (especially her money) and even dropping by unannounced with some plan or gift she expected Katie and her kids to enjoy and be happy about. She had comments on Katie's appearance, behavior, home, and finances. Katie wanted to know how she could convince her mother that she needed to practice better boundaries. "You can't," said Cia. "That is not in the realm of what you can control. What you can do is learn to practice boundary setting yourself."

The concept was very difficult and even frightening for Katie. Saying a direct and clear "no" to her mother was something she had never done. Instead, she had learned to come up with more creative and elaborate excuses each time. Her behavior toward her mother had become passive-aggressive, without her even realizing it. The excuses were less respectful to her mother as well as to herself than a straightforward and truthful answer would have been. As soon as Katie began to practice setting actual boundaries, she discovered an interesting fact—that she had virtually no sense of self-worth. As much as she hadn't been willing to admit it to herself, she had defined herself by and through her mother's standards. Even in her rebellion against some of those standards, she was, in fact, defining herself through her mother based on her extreme opposition. Katie had been so focused on her mother's lack of boundaries that she was blinded to her own. As she gradually developed the strength to stand up to her mother, her own sense of self-worth grew by leaps and bounds. Katie could choose to address her appearance, finances, and other areas because she wanted to rather than in reaction to what her mother wanted. In Katie's case, the good news was that, in the end, she and her mother actually became great friends.

Time and Boundaries

One of the complaints we hear most frequently is that there is simply not enough time—that you wish there were more hours in a day or days in a week. Have you ever said that? Do you find that your time feels scarce? Stop and think about it. What would that get you, really, other than more exhausted with more things to do? Time itself is an illusion—a perception. What is needed is not more time, but a change in the way you view time itself.

Consider the touting of "labor saving" devices. In the '50s, things like washing machines were supposed to get women out of the kitchen so they would have more free time. As the computer became popular, predictions were made that we would have more time on our hands than we would know what to do with, and there was talk of a four-day workweek becoming the norm. That logic was faulty. The opposite occurred. Why? While this may be an over-simplification, human nature includes an element of wanting to keep up with others. If everyone else is doing more things faster, you may feel as though you must do so as well. Ironically, you too may have thus become a slave to your own "labor-saving" devices. Most people feel as if they are working eight-day workweeks rather than four. There is little or no time to recreate. Cell phones and computers—now often synonymous— can summon you at any time. And, without strong boundaries, you may feel compelled to answer just because it is ringing, singing, or whatever else you have it programmed to do. That is not freedom but the lack thereof.

Jeff Davidson, the author of *Breathing Space,* says, "The faster we are able to travel or to gain new information, the greater our expectations regarding what we can and what needs to be accomplished in our lives. We all seem to do more . . . A day is still twenty-four hours, but it seems to shrink in the face of more to do or greater expectations about what has to be done." This then results in greater stress in your life, and thus, ironically, greater *inefficiency*. What can you do about it? Slow down.

You have become conditioned to believe that the more you have to do, the faster you need to move. The truth is it works just the opposite of that. Oftentimes, the slower you move the more time you have. Try it! Remember time is relative and it is in the eye of the beholder. Set a timer to meditate for seven minutes. Do nothing and think nothing—just be. See how long that seven minutes feels. What if your life were a form of meditation in action? What if, in every moment, you were aware of what is around you and what is within you? Not only would you truly accomplish more of real value, what you were accomplishing would be so much more satisfying because it would be a reflection of who you are.

Belinda does an interesting experiment with her clients. She asks, "Instead of five days to complete your work, what if you only had one day?

What would you do in that day? List the items now." Then they reflect together and notice that those items listed are actually the priority items that her client could slow down and focus on now for maximum results. Interestingly, an abundance of time is created. Time is not money! Time is time and money is money. Dump the conditioning that tells you otherwise, and gain back control of your own technology as part of the process.

Money Boundaries = A Spending Plan

So, how do you set boundaries around the use of your money? There is freedom in making decisions ahead of time and then spending in line with your priorities. You may feel that *budget* is a four-letter word. It's not—it's six actually—nor should it be treated as something to stay away from or avoid. Even the term "budget" may signify to you limitation, lack of freedom, and self-sacrifice.

What would it be like to turn that around and look at a budget as a stairway to financial freedom? Your budget is your boundary. A boundary is not a prison wall. It is a framework you choose to protect and support you. Try calling your budget a *Savings and Spending Plan* (a "S&S Plan") so that you see it as a plan or a ticket to what you want instead of as a restriction. A S&S Plan helps you to consciously direct where you want your money to go so it aligns with your priorities and intentions. Healthy boundaries support you to be all of who you are. They help you honor and actualize your financial goals.

Creating your Savings and Spending Plan can be a relatively simple task. We say simple, yet not so easy, unless you follow these four basic steps to get started:

1. *Estimate: Where do you think your money is going?*

Cash Flow is your Income (what you make) reduced by your Expenses (what you spend), to equal your Net (positive or negative) Cash Flow. You will need to consider both the money you make (what comes in) and what you are spending (what goes out). You can use the template provided in Exercise B in this Key: Estimate, Actual, and Planned Cash Flow, or register at www.SelfWorthBook.com for a downloadable version of this easy-to-use budget template.

2. Next, you'll need to track your actual income and expenses. No more estimates!

Continue using the template provided in Exercise B. Start by tracking your actual income. If you are employed, review your paystubs, noting both pretax and post-tax income. If you are self-employed, include the net income from your business as income on the template. As an additional tip, be sure to track your business income (monies received for services or products) and expenses (monies spent on behalf of your business) in a separate bank account. Monthly, or as needed, transfer an amount that approximates the net of your income and expenses into your personal account, with consideration for the upcoming obligations of the business. Also, be sure to look at your bank statement so you can include any additional monies you may receive, for instance from your family or other inconsistent secondary sources of income.

Next, you also need to include monies paid on your or your family's behalf. For example, Belinda was working with a couple who hadn't been tracking the monies received from the wife's parents for their children's private school. Due to the economic downturn, the grandparents could no longer pay their portion, and the family had never considered saving additional money to be able to cover that expense if need be. (Tracking this income separately would have highlighted this money received.)

Two of the key things they addressed together were, first, how Belinda could help them create or find the money in their current lifestyle, and second, to see if they could afford to keep their children in private school by taking on the expense themselves.

Here's how you can track your actual expenses: look at your bank statement, actual credit card bills, and save your cash receipts. To make this process work, yes, you do have to open your bills and statements—and read them! Although this may seem silly at first, this is one of the biggest obstacles for people to set appropriate boundaries to secure their and their family's financial future.

Be sure you include the details of where your cash spending is going. This is the number one mistake that people make in this process. Further, if you use ATM withdrawals, be sure to also allocate that line item into the category where you spent the cash withdrawn. If you do use a lot of cash, then keep a small notebook with you—like from the movie *Dragnet*—where you write down your purchases. (For men, you can take a sheet of colored 8 ½ x 11 paper and turn it on its side. From bottom to top, cut the paper into four pieces, so each slip is almost three inches. Label each of the four pieces for the four weeks of the month and put the upcoming week into your wallet. Use that to keep track of all cash and non-receipt expenses.)

For those more technologically savvy, there are new applications available for smartphones that allow you to input entries at the time of the transaction. Whatever technique you use, the important part is that you use it and use it consistently, especially during this initial tracking stage. Using the 80/20 rule, inputting only 80% (not 100%) of the transactions could yield you only 20% of the impact possible from the information gathered through this system.

A student in one of Belinda's workshops mentioned she would stop on the way home from work or on the weekend to "pick a few things up" at stores such as Target or T.J.Maxx. Belinda asked her how much she thought she was spending on those items per month. She estimated $200 and could not recall the details of most of her purchases. When she did this exercise, she was shocked at how much she was actually spending. It was over $1,000 a month. Wow, the small items sure did add up! With this new awareness, she was able to start saving almost the entire $1,000 previously spent on miscellaneous unimportant items. That immediately made a huge difference for her, and her bank account.

Start simply by completing the rest of the worksheet in Exercise B in this Key. You can also take an additional step and use free money management websites (suggestions provided at www.SelfWorthBook.com) or a more extensive paid option such as the QuickBooks or Quicken software programs. Although the template provides for one month at a time, we have found that you may need to additionally track three, six, or even 12 months to realize a more accurate picture of your financial condition.

5

SET YOUR BOUNDARIES

3. Balancing Income and Expenses

So, how do your Income and Expenses balance? Once you have followed the suggestions above, were you surprised, or even shocked, at the results? Are you making more than you are spending, or spending more than you are making? Is your net Cash Flow over 10–20% of your income so you can be saving and building a financial cushion? It may not be. Don't worry, though—there is hope for you to continue building your worth and your wealth as you read this book.

This honest look at your situation can provide a new perspective for you. When our clients go through this process and then review the results of their Cash Flow, it is amazing how many areas appear where you can spend less without sacrificing your lifestyle. If you have a partner, be sure to involve them so you have two people on the case.

As a general rule of thumb, you can compare your actual spending to the following ratios: 50% on needs, 30% on wants, and 20% on savings. When you first review the comparison of income to expenses, you may notice that your savings is much lower and even negative (if the needs and wants total exceeds the total income). As you begin to gain awareness and put your choices in perspective, you will begin to intentionally increase your savings apportionment.

Remember: Cash Flow is your Income (what you make) reduced by your Expenses (what you spend), to equal your Net (positive or negative) Cash Flow. For more positive Cash Flow, you have two choices: decrease your expenses and (often overlooked) increase your income.

4. Setting a Savings and Spending Plan (a Budget)

Once you are fully aware of where your money is actually going from these first three steps, you can create your own Savings and Spending Plan, by completing the final column in the template provided in Exercise B. To do this, review your estimate and your actual amounts by line item and determine the Planned amounts using three criteria: (1) what you want the amount to be, (2) what you are committed to achieve, and (3) what could be realistic yet optimistic or aggressive targets (especially for discretionary items, such as purchases of clothing or food). If you are married or in a long-term committed relationship where you share many expenses, involving your partner at this stage of the process is essential. Without it, your success is doomed; with it, your success is in your combined power of implementation.

We have worked with clients who were afraid of budgets and never managed their money before, so they were able to start with a simple envelope system. Here's how this works: You keep an envelope containing a set amount of cash allotted for a certain category of spending, and then every time you take money out, you write on the envelope how much you spent and what it was for. When you run out of cash in a given envelope, you know that you have reached your category spending limit! This envelope approach could be used as a group of envelopes each marked for different purposes.

If you would like some assistance with tracking your finances, finding the key areas that you may be unknowingly wasting money, or creating your own Spending and Saving Plan, you may contact Belinda's office through www.OwnYourMoney.com to help you get started.

The Path to Clarity

Until you know where your boundaries are, i.e., where your limits are, it is very hard to be clear, confident, or directed. You will have a tendency to believe what others tell you because you lack a true sense of who you are and where you stand. You may experience a sense of paralysis and inability to make decisions, as will be further explored in Key Eight. You may be experiencing a state of torment. Have you ever felt this way?

Not only is a decision more challenging to make while in this state of torment, you may even find yourself continuing to doubt the decisions that you have made. This provides fuel and evidence for more confusion.

If you are not clear about your boundaries, you are likely to take more or less than 100% responsibility for the results, as we discussed in Key Two on claiming responsibility. It's good to create or discover your own boundaries. They are different for each person. There is no right or wrong boundary as long as you are clear. If you are saying *no*, for example, when you want to be saying *yes*, or you are saying *yes* when you want to say *no*, you have a boundary problem. Whether you are "saying" it out loud, or through your purchases and decisions with your money, it has the same impact. Succumbing to the "It's only" factor, where you tell yourself that because "it's only" X dollars then you can spend on that purchase freely, and ignore your appropriate plan boundaries, also has the same impact. These boundary problems use up your aliveness and your energy. That energy can be harnessed for change and used for transforming your life.

Every time that you say *yes* when you don't mean it, you are giving a little piece of yourself away. You are chipping away at your psyche and actually reducing your own self-worth (and often your net worth as well). You are violating a boundary and that doesn't support your integrity. You are not creating wholeness or worthiness in your life, or with your finances, and you need *both* to transform yourself and your life.1 Instead, choose to powerfully set your boundaries and enjoy the freedom that comes from truly knowing your *no*s mean *no* and your *yesses* mean *yes*—with your financial decisions, your language, and your actions. You are who you are in all aspects of your life. You have the opportunity to support your authenticity and your integrity through your boundaries.

EXERCISES

Exercise A: Your Personal Rights and the Rights of Others

The clearer you are about your personal rights as an individual, the easier it will be for you to set your boundaries. Personal rights are innate, exist with freedom, and require no entitlement to earn them. This exercise will help you to identify and own your personal rights as well as the rights of others.

Part I: My Rights

Examples:

- I have the right to express my creativity.
- I have the right to be successful.
- I have the right to speak the way I feel and not hurt others.
- I have the right to ask for what I want, including a raise.
- I have the right to be wealthy.
- I have the right to embrace abundance.
- I have the right to be calm and peaceful when I manage and handle my money.

Now list 5–10 examples of personal rights that are meaningful to you.

Pick one of the rights you have written above and write it several more times, or say it out loud until it feels true and more familiar to you.

Part II: Others' Rights

Identify and list the rights that others have which are separate from your rights.

Examples:

- People have the right to express opinions that differ from mine without changing how I feel.
- Molly has the right to get angry with me without me changing my stand.

- Tom has the right to say no to me.
- People have the right to say no to my requests.
- My parents have the right to spend the money they have worked hard to save.

Now list 5–10 examples of the rights of others that are meaningful to you

Exercise B: Estimate, Actual, and Planned Cash Flow (Making A Budget)

Part I: Spending and Saving Plan Instructions:

Fill in the monthly numbers. Ensure you also estimate your spending for items paid only once a quarter (or year) so amounts capture a monthly apportionment of the full year of payments. Your cash flow information gives us a look at what is happening over a period of time (weekly, monthly, and annually). Please change captions for line items necessary to capture all of your information. You want to have the numbers agree with your true current story, so once you think you are finished, review the net total. Is that how it actually works out each month? Review and estimate what may be missing (hint: think cash).

This line-by line instruction section will give more detail, but it does not provide information for every line item.

Income Sources	
Gross Salary (you and spouse)	Salaries - Use your gross pay, as taxes, insurance, and other deductions will be separately included below.
Interest and Dividends	Interest and dividend payments made by investments (paid out so that you receive cash in hand).

Capital Gains	Capital gains from assets and mutual funds paid out, so that you receive cash in hand.
Rental Income	Rental payments you receive from properties that you own.
Other	Self employment income, Child Support, Alimony, Pension, Social Security
Taxes (Combined for both spouses)	*Most of these usually are deductions on your paycheck*
Expenses	*Choices we make spending money are actually investment opportunities.*
Home	
Rent/Mortgage	Include only your mortgage payment less taxes and insurance payments
2nd Mortgage	2nd home or 2nd mortgage on primary residence
Property tax	Include all properties. Part of a mortgage payment? Please back it out.
Home maintenance (repairs, cleaner)	Estimate what you think you will pay in a year
Home renovations/ improvements (1-time)	Include appliances, furniture, curtains, linens, and all home-related purchases.
Utilities	*Generally self-explanatory. If you pay these for tenants, please include here*

5

SET YOUR BOUNDARIES

Insurance	*May be deductions on you paycheck*
Renters/Home insurance	If this is part of your monthly mortgage, please subtract it out of your payment.
Transportation	
Parking/parking tickets	Include monthly parking for home, work, meters and parking tickets
Car Maintenance	Include oil changes, new tires, any repair related expenses you expect
Car loan/lease	If you have a loan or lease, it should be noted on the Asset/Liability page
Food	*Generally self-explanatory. It is important to separate food eaten outside and inside the home.*
Entertainment	
Movies, clubs, bars, etc.	Include movie rental fees as well
Vacations	Include flights, hotels, event tickets and other vacation related expenses
Personal Care	
Health expenses (doctor visits, Rx, HSA)	Co-pays and co insurance. Do not include if you are reimbursed.
Education/conferences	Adult related classes, text books
Hobbies, toys, books, magazines	Purchases for the entire family, adults and children. Include subscriptions.

SET YOUR BOUNDARIES

5

Children	
Child support payment	Include any auto payments from your paycheck.
Child care	Include any auto payments from your paycheck.
School tuition/room & board/books/ supplies	Include any direct deposits from your paycheck, auto investment plans, and deposits.
Miscellaneous	
Cash uncategorized	Include all ATM withdrawals at first based on the bank statement review. Then allocate the amounts to the appropriate expense category. Once complete, this line item will be $0.
Credit card servicing expenses	These payments should equal the sum of the Minimum Monthly Payments on the Net Worth Liability section.
Credit card additional payments (monthly payments beyond the minimum)	The sum total of the credit card servicing and credit card additional payments should equal the total amount paid to the credit card company relating to past charges.
Loan payments (student, other)	These payments should equal the Minimum Monthly Payments in the Net Worth Liability section
Gym/health club, professional associations	Include all membership dues paid in the respective month. (If an annual charge, then allocate for your S&S plan.)
Fees	Bank fees, late payment fees (be honest please)

Gifts (including holiday, birthday)	Include gifts for others (not toys, clothes, etc. for your family)
Pets	Includes pet food, veterinarian bills, pet toys, collars, pet health insurance, day care, boarding
Small Business expenses	Include small business expenses such as your website, administrative support, design, advertising, marketing, and coaching. Please separate personal and business activity.
Net Cash Flow-Subtotal	*Subtotal difference between cash flowing in and cash flowing out.*
Retirement Planning/Savings	*May be deductions on you paycheck*
Retirement Account (401K, 403(b), SEP, IRA)	Usually employer-established, pre-tax, and you make the investment decisions.
IRA	Transfer/deposit of after-tax dollars. Ex: Roth IRA.
Automated Savings	Amount directly deposited into a savings/ investment account each month.
Net Cash Flow Total	*Total difference between cash flowing in and cash flowing out.*

Part II: Spending and Saving Plan Worksheet

Date Prepared: _____

In terms of finances, making a savings and spending plan (budget) and following it are very concrete ways of setting boundaries. We highly recommend that you take the opportunity to use the form* below as is, or as an example, to help you set boundaries around your own spending patterns. The first steps toward creating a budget are to estimate where you believe your money is going and then to track what you are actually spending.

Once you have done this for a few months, you can consciously choose where you want the money to go, based on what is realistic, and set limits in each category.

Actual Month: _____

OWNYOUR
MONEY.

**Use Estimate +
ACTUAL One Month**

	Estimate	Actual	Savings and Spending Plan
Income Sources	Monthly	Monthly	Monthly
Gross Salary (you and spouse)			
Bonuses (you and spouse)			
Interest and Dividends			
Other (Gifts, Rental Income, etc.)			
Gross Income			
Taxes (federal, state, employment, etc.)			

SET YOUR BOUNDARIES

5

After-tax income			

Expenses

Home

Rent/Mortgage and 2nd Mortgage			
Property tax			
Condo or association dues			
Home maintenance (repairs, cleaner)			
Home renovations/improvements (1-time)			

Utilities

Phone (land line and wireless)			
Cable, Internet, DSL			
Gas/oil, water, electricity			

Insurance

Disability insurance			
Life insurance			
Health insurance (premiums only)			
Dental insurance			
Car insurance			
Renters/homeowners insurance			

Transportation

Gas			
Parking/parking tickets			
Tolls, subways, taxis			
Car maintenance			
Car loan/lease			

Food

Breakfast/lunch/dinner outside home			
Groceries			

Entertainment

Movies, clubs, bars, etc.			
Alcohol and/or tobacco products			
Vacations			

Personal Care

Clothes			
Health expenses (doctor visits, Rx, HSA)			
Salons, spas, hair cuts			
Personal care products			
Laundry/dry cleaning			
Education/conferences			
Hobbies, toys, books, magazines			

Children

Child support payment			
Child care			
School tuition/room & board/ books/ supplies			
Activities (sports, band, art)			
Clothing			
Allowance			
College funding			

Miscellaneous

Cash uncategorized (should be $0 and allocate)			
Credit card servicing (minimums only)			
Credit card additional payments (monthly payments beyond the minimum)			
Loan payments (student, other)			

5

SET YOUR BOUNDARIES

Gym/health club, professional associations			
Fees			
Gifts (including holiday, birthday)			
Pets			
Donations to charity/tithing			
Electronics/computer			
Supplies (home office, paper, pens)			
Small-business expenses			
Other (sundries, small miscellaneous)			
Total Expenses			

Net Cash Flow- Subtotal			
Retirement Planning/Savings			
Retirement account (401K, 403(b), SEP)			
IRA (after-tax, ex: Roth IRA)			
Automated savings			
Total Savings			

Net Cash Flow Total			

* You may register at www.SelfWorthBook.com to receive a downloadable version of this template so you can re-use it, benefit from the formulas, and create a new habit with this as a monthly resource.

Visualization—The Bubble Experience

Stand in a comfortable, yet erect, position, feet shoulder-width apart, knees slightly bent, head high, belly soft and expanding as you breathe. Imagine that you can sense an energy field extending out from your body, projecting like a giant soap bubble around you. Next, imagine that the bubble is your boundary, that you have a right to that boundary, and that it is perfect for you. It is not a wall, as it is permeable, yet you can control what passes through it. Imagine that you can play with how large or small that bubble gets. Experiment with what feels just right, what feels familiar and what feels comfortable. What, in other words, is your boundary? There is no right or wrong; there is simply your experience of your own energy space.

Now practice imagining that bubble when you are with another person. The other person doesn't need to know that you are doing this exercise. Simply notice what your comfort zone is. How much space do you want for your bubble? You might even imagine that this person has his or her own bubble and that there may be a place where these bubbles meet. See if you can notice in the space between the two of you, your sense of where that happens. Where does your friend's energy field end, and yours begin, or vice versa? Remember, you are just playing with your perceptions. There is no right or wrong way to do this exercise. What we hope is that you will get a sense of your entitlement. You own your own boundary, however you perceive it. It is a safe place for you to be. It weighs nothing and it does not get in the way, yet it is tremendously powerful.

Continue to observe how you adjust your boundaries in different settings and in different areas of your life. Without judging, take a gentle attitude of curiosity as your awareness increases.

Conscious Breathing

Breathing in, I calm body and mind. Breathing out, I smile. Dwelling in the present moment, I know this is the only moment.

—Thich Nhat Hahn

Remove any heavy or constricting clothing. Lie down flat on a firm but soft surface, such as a carpeted floor. If need be, use a small flat pillow under your head and/or a thicker one under your knees.

Become familiar with the boundaries of your breath to see if you can expand your boundaries. Experiment with touch to begin. Feel your collarbones. Try running your hands along the full length of them, as well as gently tapping them with your fingers. This will enliven this part of your anatomy, helping bring your awareness there. Do the same with the sternum. Gently explore the xiphoid process (i.e., the sensitive spot at the base of the sternum) and notice its connection to the diaphragm muscle as you breathe in. Explore each of your ribs, noticing that some parts are too deep to feel with your touch. However, you can use your imagination and your breath to feel them.

Notice the expansion and contraction of the ribcage as you breathe. Notice how the ribcage mirrors the shape of the lungs, with the largest ribs where the lungs are the biggest lower in the body. This important large bottom part of the lungs is often neglected by the habit of shallow breathing, as you may not allow your breath in enough to nearly reach the lung's capacity. Put your hands on your belly. If you are one of those people who do not love their bellies, take this opportunity to send it some love. Often prized tight belly muscles tend to restrict the capacity for deep breathing. If your belly is round and soft, celebrate it. Experiment with just how much breath you can take in by allowing your belly to get as large as you can when you breathe in and allowing your ribs to expand as much as they can. Your ribs are meant to expand and contract with the movement of the diaphragm, however often many people think of them as fixed.

As you breathe deeply and more deeply, imagine that you are expanding your boundary—your capacity to take in breath. The word for breath in Latin is "spiritus", the same root from which we derive the word "spirit." Imagine that you are expanding your boundary so that your spirit may more fully inhabit your body. Imagine that you bring this sense of presence and capacity to your entire life, and especially your experiences with money. Imagine the abundance that follows. Enjoy for as long as it is comfortable.

Body-Centered Statements

1. I do _____ (pick a situation) from choice, not from duty or resentment.

2. Honoring my boundaries frees up energy inside me, allowing me and everyone around me to experience joy, compassion, and love.
3. I embrace my new Savings and Spending Plan and follow it with ease.
4. The most loving person arises when I put myself first.

Journal Joggers

Use the following questions to lead you into your journal entries for this Key.

- What would be a direct and positive way of expressing my needs, desires, or limits (my boundaries) in this situation?
- What would I have to give up or change in order to assert my boundaries?
- What are some other, more direct ways I can get or replace what I would give up?
- Why have I resisted creating and living by a Savings and Spending Plan before, and what has changed within me now to welcome the process?
- What small steps can I take to incorporate these changes in my life?

Whatever games are played with us, we must play no games with ourselves.

—Ralph Waldo Emerson

TRANSFORM YOUR SELF-TALK

Man is made by his belief. As he believes, so he is.
—THE BHAGAVAD-GITA

Does it seem to you that what you have and what you want are very different? If so, it is critical to find out what has created this gap. What is it in your programming that has set it up this way? The primary culprit is generally your limiting beliefs: your "B.S." (belief systems). This Key will help you discover what they are, where they come from, and how to transform them into new ones. Unconscious beliefs trickle down and become the thoughts that fill our mind. These thoughts are what we call *self-talk*.

Most of us give more thought to the programs we want in our computers than to the programs we run in our mind. Do you direct your thoughts or do you let them direct you? Your thoughts stem from the programming you have. Let's explore how those thoughts manifest as self-talk which can run your life (if you are unaware of it) and what you can do about it.

Self-talk is the result of your belief systems, as they weave themselves into the stories or the voices that you hear in your head. Notice what you say to yourself as you consider decisions about affluence and your underlying worthiness. Some of the self-talk may be supportive. Unfortunately, most of it is not. In addition, it has a pervasive tendency to be repetitive. Although you practiced transforming some of your individual B.S. earlier in this book, it is essential that you address your self-talk as a whole to effectively move forward.

If you find that, when you listen, you can hear this self-talk broadcasting in your head, you are not alone. Everyone has an inner dialogue going on that is generally not supportive and often extremely hard to quiet. This self-talk is known by many names. Some of the more common are the inner critic, the narrator in your head, your "story", your "act", or your "game." Even the most apparently self-confident and successful people are often inundated with harmful messages.

The person reading this at the moment, the part of you that's attentive and specifically attending to this, might be saying, "Oh yes—yes that makes sense." But notice if there is some little voice inside you saying something quite the contrary, perhaps, "No that doesn't make sense at all." Or, "I'm bored—why don't I get up and get something to eat?" That's self talk. It goes on inside of you all the time, and some of it is conflicting. It's only harmful when you are unaware of it and thus fail to exercise the all-important choice you have over what you think. Becoming aware of your self-talk, and your various personae, is the beginning of *synthesis*, which is to say integrity or wholeness, as in being a whole person. You have lots of different parts inside yourself. You may assume that there is such a thing as a unified "I," yet if you really introspect deeply, there is no such thing, while at the same time you can be as whole as the sum of your diverse parts. Try it now.

Identifying self-talk, and all the different aspects of you, is the first step. We call these various voices *personae*, from the Greek word for mask, as they do mask your authentic self. Sometimes when clients do begin the process of identifying their various personae, they become concerned that they have multiple-personality disorder! That is not the case at all. You have different facets, including the child part of yourself, at different ages. We like to say, "You have to separate in order to integrate." Becoming aware of your patterns of self-talk, and the different aspects of yourself who are agreeing with them, is liberating. The awareness helps you to no longer be a victim of those voices. See the examples within Strategy Four for help with identifying some of your personae specific to your relationship with money.

Where Our Messages Come From

It is hard to fight an enemy who has outposts in your head.

—SALLY KEMPTON

Your self-talk is likely a collection of messages you originally received from outside yourself and adopted as your own over time. Your self-talk may have allowed you to cope and manage at some point in your life. The truth is it may no longer be serving you. This is an excellent time to review the messages you give yourself and discover which no longer serve you so you can change them to support yourself more fully.

Sometimes in doing this work, you can become aware of the original source of your self-talk. When Cia did these exercises, suddenly, in the tyrannical voice of her own self-talk, she very clearly heard her father's voice saying exactly those things she had internalized and come to assume were a part of her. Once you realize the source is not original to you, it may be less compelling.

Childhood Messages

When it comes to money, parents are our major influence. How they behave with money, how they talk about money, how they relate to each other on the subject, and how they relate to you about money—virtually every habit that they have—becomes your model. You may go one of two ways with it. You may go to the opposite extreme, which is still a form of being under the tyranny of that belief, or you may consciously or unconsciously take on the same behavior. So in effect, you are often either *matching* (modeling the same behavior) or *mirroring* (creating the opposite). What messages did you get from your parents about money? Consider how this is directly influencing what you are telling yourself now.

6

TRANSFORM YOUR SELF-TALK

Belinda's father used to say, "Turn out the lights. We don't have stock in Con Edison." She took this to mean that they needed to shut off the lights as they couldn't afford to pay a big electric bill and couldn't afford to purchase stock, as if that would help their situation. When Belinda got older, she noticed that they, ironically, did own stock in the Con Edison electric company! When she asked him about it, he said "Well, I needed something to encourage you to keep the bill down." Parents often create stories and mantras that, although sometimes only subtly negative, lead to non-supportive behavior later in life. Be sure to do Exercise B at the end of this Key related to listing your childhood money messages and how they relate to your current relationship to money.

In this Key, we will explore what you would *like* those messages to be. To start though, we will need to identify what they are and where they came from. What programming do you use to keep yourself in line and bring yourself down?

Without being aware of it, you have adopted identities based on concepts of who you expect yourself to be and how you expect yourself to act, as well as how you think others want you to be and act. Those expectations may have originated from your parents, peers, jobs, religion, or society. After a while, you internalize them and treat them as though they are valid demands from an authentic part of you.

Common Messages

Self-talk is always with you, coloring the way you view life, putting words into other people's mouths, or distorting the meanings of what they say. You are constantly on the lookout for reasons to reinforce and validate your perspective—your self-talk. So you become a filter for life, taking in only that which agrees with your own preconception. Does any of the following money self-talk sound familiar?

Get a good job.
I don't deserve to make what I could earn.
Make X amount of money.

Don't ask my boss for a raise.

I'm just not good with money.

It feels like everyone has more than me.

It's dangerous to put all my eggs in one basket.

Try harder.

Why can't I be like _____?

I'd better buy this because it's a bargain and on sale.

I can't buy anything because I can't afford it.

Save more.

It's no use to save because I can't do it anyway.

I don't deserve to have a lot of money.

I'll never have enough, no matter how much I make.

I'll never do well, so why try?

Work hard.

Succeed.

Don't succeed.

I never succeed at or finish what I start.

Don't take chances.

I can't earn more than my parents did.

Have more than others do.

Don't have more than others do.

I will never amount to anything.

I can't do that.

It's not the right time.

I'm crazy to want that.

Everyone has his or her own lists and often the beliefs can be one or both sides of the same coin, such as "Succeed" and "Don't Succeed." The list can seem endless. What is on your self-talk list? (It might be helpful to refer back to the beliefs identified in Key One as foundational to your understanding of your self-talk, then complete Exercise A at the end of this Key.)

6

TRANSFORM YOUR SELF-TALK

Pervasiveness of Negative Messages

In one study, researchers put tape recorders on a group of school children and recorded everything that was said to them as they went through their day. It was all processed by computers and analyzed. They found that 80% of the messages were negative. You likely grew up with mostly negative messages too. Therefore, they are so familiar to you that you don't even notice that you're doing it to yourself. Your self-talk is often like water is to a fish. It has become so pervasive that you cannot imagine there is an alternative.

The significant "take away" from all this: Negative messages will not help you move forward in designing the life you want—financially or otherwise. They do not work. You may unknowingly have convinced yourself that they do, usually because they are the kinds of messages your parents gave you when they wanted you to improve your behavior. You learned this technique and now use it on yourself. Check it out. Are you getting the results you want? If not, are you willing to consider that all this beating yourself up won't get you where you want to go, and that you don't deserve it? As any good trainer of animals or humans knows, we respond better to the carrot (rewards) than the stick (punishment).

Subtle Self-Talk

In some cases, it may be a challenge simply to identify your belief systems and related self-talk. Although the self-talk may sometimes seem like a loudspeaker in your head, other times it may be more like background elevator music that you have grown accustomed to hearing. There are layers of self-talk—loud and blaring, along with the subtle, buried, and not always self-evident messages. Self-talk may be like an undercurrent, not visible but deeply powerful nevertheless. Until you do enough work identifying the more obvious self-talk, it may be a challenge to begin to observe the undercurrents and the belief systems they stem from.

Some examples of thoughts or belief systems that may be hard to recognize include:

- The sacrifice or the change isn't worth it.
- Why should I do anything differently if I am going to get the same result?
- You don't understand my situation.
- Once I achieve the level of success I am aiming for, I will lose all of my friends.
- I'm not clear on my value in the marketplace so I'd better not charge what I'm worth for my services. If I do, they will think I'm a fraud.
- I've already lost my one big chance so I might as well give up.

Can you see how these are simply re-creations of experiences you have had in the past that you have since absorbed into your systems as reality? You let your past live in your present and shape your future. It is time to step into your NOW and unwrap your PRESENT.

Mindfulness and Personal Awareness

A thoroughly good relationship with ourselves results in being still, which doesn't mean we don't run and jump and dance about. It means there's no compulsiveness. We don't overwork, overeat, oversmoke, overseduce. In short, we begin to stop causing harm.

—PEMA CHODRON

Use the practice of *mindfulness* to become aware of your self-talk, your programming, your core beliefs, and your filters. Mindfulness is simply the practice of applying a witness-consciousness to observing your mind. You don't need to judge or criticize. Simply notice. That awareness will set you free. It gives you the option of opening to a much wider perspective.

Mindfulness and self-observation are very powerful tools. They can help through your *Self-Worth to Net Worth* journey. Mindfulness with your money is essential along the way—from each dollar you spend to each time you have a belief about money. (Consider how powerful this mindfulness technique could be in supporting your new Saving and Spending Plan developed in Key Five.) As you increase your awareness, you will embrace your worthiness, as you will realize that you and your authentic self are what is true, and the stress is actually a circumstance that you have simply created.

Be gentle on yourself as well. This is the work of a lifetime and it is important to note that you don't get it once and you're done. It is a continual deepening and improving process, much like the practice of yoga.

Seven Strategies for Transforming Your Self-Talk

Through the exercises in Key One, you began to articulate your belief systems around money. Your self-talk is the voice and fabric of your belief systems. This talk is usually negative and non-supportive. However, with a perspective change and a conscious shift, self-talk can actually become supportive! Even though you may not have a direct impact on financial markets, you *do* have 100% impact on how you talk to yourself about your money and your capacity for abundance.

As you recognize the impact that your non-supportive self-talk has been having on your life, you are empowering yourself to transform it. Think about a recent time when you told yourself how terrible you are with money, either overall or because of a particular action you took. Allow yourself to feel right now exactly how you felt at that time. How would you rate it on a scale from one to ten, with one representing it has little negative charge and ten it has significant negative charge for you? Consider the one over-arching belief you had at the time that contributed to that feeling. Consider each of these strategies and determine for yourself which one, or which combination of the six, works the best for you to create your personal shift.

Strategy One: Unearthing Your Belief Systems

One way to unearth your belief systems is to recognize that a belief system is like an over-arching thought. This primal belief creates more thoughts—which later create even more thoughts! All of these beliefs ultimately inform virtually every thought you are thinking. If you adopt a practice of watching what you think (mindfulness, as described above), you are likely to catch yourself having a thought that doesn't serve you. This is a good time to trace it by following your thoughts backwards. What thought did it stem from? And before that? And before that? And what belief system is that ultimately related to? Does that B.S. still serve you?

Strategy Two: Creating Your Antidotes (or Affirmations)

After making a list of your non-supportive self-talk, related to both your overall life and your financial life, write an antidote for each statement with a new supportive statement. Remember the discussion of antidotes in Key One? An antidote is a statement that, when you say it out loud, will give you a bodily felt sense of empowerment, compared to the disempowerment of the statement you want to change. At first, when you create this new statement, it may feel unfamiliar, uncomfortable, and even a little scary or incorrect. That's completely normal. That is generally a sign that you are onto something—perhaps the next stage of your growth.

Repeat the antidote over to yourself each day. Doing so in the mirror will give you additional feedback. Notice if each time you say it, it begins to feel more real, possible, or true, and if you begin to visually embody it. When you select the antidote statement, pick something that feels like a bit of a stretch but not so much so that you roll your eyes in complete disbelief and think to yourself, "Yeah, right—like I could ever believe that!" (Review Appendix I at the end of the book on Body-Centered Statements and apply this to your antidotes.)

Strategy Three: Release the Thought

Byron Katie, an American speaker and author, teaches a method of self-inquiry known as "The Work of Byron Katie" or simply as "The Work" (www.thework.com). Katie's method is an excellent example of how questioning your assumptions/thoughts/beliefs can bring dramatic results very quickly. The method consists of identifying your stressful thoughts, then answering four questions and doing what she calls a "turnaround," which is a way of experiencing the opposite of what you believe.

The four questions:

1. Is it true?
2. Can you absolutely know that it's true?

TRANSFORM YOUR SELF-TALK

6

3. How do you react, what happens, when you believe that thought?
4. Who would you be without the thought?

Katie suggests that, especially for beginners, The Work is more potent if the stressful thought points the finger of blame outward. Further, when you are judging someone else, you are actually describing yourself. Thus, for the purposes of including stressful thoughts specifically related to money for inclusion in this book, Katie suggested using stressful thoughts such as:

- I'm angry at my boss because he's unfair.
- I'm disappointed at my wife because she spends too much money.
- I'm angry at my bills because they're hard to handle.
- I'm scared at the economy because it's making my job harder.
- I'm upset with money because I'm not good at it.

Here is how Katie presents her questions, phrased as if you were answering them now, and how we worked with a client to apply the process to a common stressful belief.

Belief: "I'm angry at my parents because they didn't teach me to be good with money." (In order to apply the four questions, we're going to shorten the belief to "My parents didn't teach me to be good with money.")

1. Is it true?
    A: Yes. (The answer to the first question is either a simple "yes" or a simple "no." If you find yourself explaining, justifying, or defending, you are not doing The Work.)
2. Can you absolutely know that it's true? (Take this question in. Contemplate it.)
    A: No.
    Our commentary: Actually, by believing it is true, you are projecting a whole past in which you are not good enough and a future in which you are a victim. If you stay fully present in this very moment, can you really know what your parents taught you, or even that you aren't good with money? Take a deep look. You're

not good with money—compared to what? Compared to whom? Can you absolutely know?

3. How do you react, what happens, when you believe that thought? (Be specific in your answers. How do you treat yourself? How do you treat your partner, your boss, or your employees?)

    A: I feel scared. I blame my parents. I get furious at them. Then I take it out on my husband. I see my father's inadequacies in him. I shut off emotionally. I feel not good enough. I sometimes feel like a total moron. Every time I bring in or create more money in my life, I seem to just need more. I feel terrified that we will lose our house. I see myself as a bag lady on the streets. Enough feels unattainable and I keep feeling like a failure.

    Our commentary: For most people, feeling inadequate with money causes some combination of stress, fear, frustration, and self-blame. Unpleasant images and bodily sensations occur. Notice what they are. Do you tense up, for example, as you consider this now?

4. Who would you be without the thought?

    A: Gee, if I didn't believe that thought, I'd feel much less stress. I'd certainly feel more open to my parents and probably to my husband too. Definitely to my husband too. I wouldn't be stuck in resentment. I'd feel like an adult, free to learn whatever I need to learn about managing money. Wow! I would feel a lot less anxious, and more confident. I wouldn't feel chained to the need to make more money all the time. I could be grateful for what I have and enjoy my life more. I could imagine that perhaps there is a place where I could be abundant, with more than enough, not always needing more and more. I am already smiling!

    Our commentary: When you have deeply answered this question, you will understand that it's not your situation that is causing your stress—it's your *thoughts* about your situation. If you didn't even have the capability of thinking "I'm not good with money," wouldn't you be fine? Note that believing you need more money doesn't help you. If you don't question your belief and it doesn't change as a result, no matter how much money you have, it will never be enough. Imagine yourself evicted from your home and all your credit taken away because you have nothing. You are sitting on the curb of your neighbor's lawn, looking at your old house. In that moment, you no longer have to pay the mortgage. Surprisingly, you feel free. Right in that very moment you are OK. Would you notice the sky and the ground, or the breeze and the flowers?

You have a right to be happy. Your peace and happiness are not conditional upon what you have, but they are conditioned by your thoughts.

After completing the four questions, turn the thought around. Turnarounds can be to the self, the other, and the opposite. It is important to stick to the words of the original statement, and important to find at least three specific, genuine examples for each turnaround.

Using our example, one turnaround could be "I didn't teach me to be good with money." How can THAT be true? Find at least three specific, genuine examples of how this turnaround is true in your life, right here, right now. Another turnaround could be "I didn't teach my parents to be good with money." A third could be "My parents did teach me to be good with money." How do you experience that as true, even if you had the most irresponsible, improvident parents? You may find additional turnarounds as well. For each turnaround, find at least three specific, genuine examples of how it is true in your life.

Other release techniques, such as the Sedona Method and the Emotional Freedom Technique ("EFT"), can be instrumental to transforming non-supportive self-talk. Specifically around money, Dr. Joe Vitale's *Attract Money Now* and Margaret Lynch's *Secret of Intentional Wealth* programs are helpful resources to fast-track your wealth creation through using EFT.

Strategy Four: Address the Conflict

Where do your voices come from? Are they the embodied or incorporated voices of a parent or other authority figure that you heard at some point in your life and adopted? You may have a character that sort of sits on each of your shoulders, like the cartoon image of a devil and an angel, telling you what to do. Or the conflicting voices may take on very different forms. Here are some examples of the conflicts that occur around money and success:

- Let's spend on this. No, we have to save.
- I deserve it. No, we can't afford it.
- It's important to live for today and have fun. No, we have to focus on saving for tomorrow and behaving responsibly.
- I can put this off. No, I have to do this right now.
- I will rent my apartment/home and be free from the responsibility. No, it's better to buy and feel grown-up.

Give a name and image to each "party" to the conflict. Feel the feelings each side feels. Create a conversation between them. There are two ways to do this. You can actually move back and forth from one chair to another speaking to the imagined image of the other part in the other chair. When you sit in each chair, take an extra moment to get into the feelings and emotions of that part of yourself. Or you can use a written dialogue, with one hand writing for one part of yourself and the other hand writing for the other part.

In either case, the dialogue may start out as heated and confrontational. As you proceed with it, you are likely to find that the parts of yourself can arrive at a greater commonality or compromise. After all, each of them is doing and saying what it believes is best for the whole of you. If you find you have more than two conflicting voices, this exercise can be adapted to accommodate each of them.

Strategy Five: "Friend" Your Personae

Internal conflict, such as those illustrated above, creates stress and exhaustion in your being, thus robbing you of the energy and motivation to move forward in your life. Growing your net worth is often self-sabotaged when you are suffering from this inner self-worth conflict. When you find yourself plagued by a troublesome thought, belief, or character trait, often the harder you try to drive it away, the more persistent it is. Take the opposite approach. Become familiar with it. Befriend it perhaps.

Your persona serves as a defense system stemming from a belief. Usually

TRANSFORM YOUR SELF-TALK

6

it is developed early in life as a way of protecting yourself. Unfortunately, it gets cemented in. A persona is just a façade, no matter how much we have come to associate ourselves with it. If we can have compassion for that persona, by understanding that it was there originally to help us, it will be much easier to identify and make friends with it.

As you discover your "friends," give them names as you did in Strategy Three. Some examples include: Ms. Perfectionist, Superman/woman, Mom, Busybody, Mr. Worry-Wart, Money-Meanie, and so on. How has your attitude toward them changed? That attitude or character trait has its own persona, and as such is a part of you. You don't have to hate it to release it. In fact, it works better if you don't. By understanding its true nature, it loses its hold on you. Take a lighthearted view of this personality trait. Appreciate that its intention has been to serve you even if that is no longer working. The sooner you are able to embrace this as a part of you, the sooner you will be able to facilitate its transformation.

Once you are aware of these characters/caricatures/voices that no longer serve you, you can send them away on vacation, put them up on a shelf in a closet, switch the channel as on a radio station, or however you want to turn them all off in a friendly way. You might try thanking them for working so hard to keep you in line all this time. After all, the part of you creating that self-talk believed it was acting in your best interest.

Eventually, as you are thinking or talking and a negative message arises, you will be able to drop it and replace it with a positive message, or simply replace it with the act of being present in the moment—with awareness. This is freedom.

Exercise A – Part II at the end of this Key will help you identify some of your personae specifically related to your relationship with money.

Strategy Six: Disarm the Words of Your Self-Talk

Consider the voice and actual words that your non-supportive self-talk uses. What is the voice that your self-talk speaks to you in? Does it sound stern, angry, judgmental, ashamed, or embarrassed, for example? Does it sound like a family member, such as your mother or father? Most of the voices are quite serious and judgmental. Now, it is time to let go of the energetic hold that this self-talk has had on you. Take that one over-arching belief and say it while laughing. Yes, say a few words of it and then start laughing out loud in the middle, and then finish the sentence. Do that at least five times. Then say it with a high-pitched Mickey Mouse voice. (Out loud is again best.) If you find yourself starting to giggle or laugh, you are releasing the hold that the negative words and the related belief have on you. Keep repeating this process until the words are just words without any charge to them.

Strategy Seven: Magnetism—Self-Talk and the Attraction Factor

Imagination is more important than knowledge.
—ALBERT EINSTEIN

The feelings in the body are where you actualize things. This leads into a deeper discussion of one of the primary manifestation principles: *You get what you focus on.* That is where you put your energy. If you focus on the negative, then that is what will keep showing up in your life. Early on, we discussed the mind as a *reality filter.* At any given moment in time, you are only aware of a minute portion of potential reality. You are constantly selectively screening. This process, unconscious as it is, is based on your belief systems. You select according to your beliefs. There is a great deal available to you at any given moment in time, but you will be unaware of it, if it is not part of the narrow lens or reality filter of your beliefs that condition the way you see the world. Your self-talk is a clue to your reality filter, and therefore to what you believe and to what keeps showing up. This strategy will help you alter what you focus on and thus what you see and attract to you.

How would you like things to be in your life? How would you like your financial picture to look? Are you willing to believe that is possible? Are you willing to widen your vision to take in other possibilities you might never have imagined, like the shaman who was viewing Columbus' ships?

Use the feelings in your body to help you do this. These feelings are energy (emotion = energy in motion) and therefore are magnetic. Imagine that you can use these feelings, along with your beliefs, to magnetize things to you in a very kinesthetic way.

We use the word *visualize* in the broadest sense. Use your senses along with the visual. Picture what it is you want, using your whole body—your emotions and all your senses. You must know what you want in order to create it in your life. As you "visualize" your desires, imagine drawing to you that which you really want. Get the feeling in your body of what it will be like the moment you receive what you want. Feel into what it will be like having it. For this to work, you will have to first release any negative messages that stand in your way, such as "You are not worthy of it," "It will be taken away from you," or "This can never work." Going for what you want will tend to flush up any remaining negative self-talk, as if you are peeling away layers of an onion. You will need to reapply the strategy or strategies that work for you and choose to let these additional non-supportive beliefs go. As the saying goes, "At each level, a new devil."

As we mentioned earlier, the brain cannot tell the difference between something imagined vividly with full details and the actual experience itself. The experience IS in the brain. The same parts of the brain light up in the same way under magnetic resonance imaging whether you are thinking of a thing or doing/having it. Athletes who are unable to practice have been shown to do as well or almost as well as their counterparts by practicing in full detail in their imaginations first. What about you? Are you willing to engage in the "willing suspension of disbelief" long enough to create the life and financial abundance you want visibly and tangibly in your mind? Try it and see what happens.

Your belief system is going to create your feelings, as we discussed above in Strategy One. The feeling lives in the body and that makes it very alive and very vibrant, which is why it becomes such a powerful manifestation tool. To exercise this strategy now, try on the belief system that you are wealthy. Notice the *feeling* sensation that arises from that, and invite it to increase as you connect with the feeling of what it is like to be rich. You are actually magnetizing wealth to you through the process of stepping into the reality you choose.

Reassessing Your Non-Supportive Self-Talk

Once you have reviewed and tested each of the *Seven Strategies for Transforming Your Self-Talk*, now it is time to re-assess the power that your non-supportive self-talk has on you. On the same scale from one to ten, with one representing little negative charge and ten identifying significant negative charge, how would you rate the charge that the non-supportive self-talk has on you now? Are you pleasantly surprised at how much lower your number is as compared to when you started? Be sure to complete the exercises at the end of this Key to further your transformation process. Both Cia and Belinda use these methods in their coaching programs, so refer to the back of the book for their contact information if you want additional support with implementing these steps and eliminating any negative self-talk from your daily life. What a relief it will be to be free!

There is more to us than we know. If we can be made to see it, perhaps the rest of our lives we will be unwilling to settle for less.

—KURT HAHN, *GERMAN EDUCATOR AND PHILOSOPHER*

While your self-talk may have done you a lot of harm in the past, the good news is that you can make choices to use it in ways that better serve you. A powerful truth, and one we wish people were taught early in life, is that you have choice over your thoughts. Knowing this, and with the application of mindful awareness, you can train your thoughts to serve you. As you make them into your friends rather than your enemies, you can live in harmony with the various voices, and parts of yourself, that exist. With this new harmony, true self-worth and peace of mind now become possible.

6

TRANSFORM YOUR SELF-TALK

EXERCISES

Exercise A: Changing Your Self-Talk

Part I: Your Common Self-Talk

Make a list of your most common self-talk phrases, such as, "Well, you messed up again, didn't you?" or "Can't you ever get anything right?" or "If you'd only try harder!" or "Don't inconvenience anyone or make them angry." Do all these voices seem to come from the same source? If not, break the list into the separate voices you can identify inside yourself and give each a name.

Part II: Your Money Personae

Recognize how your self-talk contributes to creating your money personae. Make a list of your Money Personae and describe them. Here are some examples to help you identify yours:

Controller; Spendthrift; Princess; I have to work so hard to keep up; Yuppie; Hippie; Money is beneath me; Ms. Jealous; Tightwad; I can't be overdrawn since I still have checks; I will always be provided for; It is my duty to provide for others; Easy come and easy go; Manager; Impulsive; I always have to take care of myself; Beggar; Ms. Well-off; Ms. Super-competent; Workaholic; Poor me; I am a much better person for valuing non-material things so I won't make too much money; Independent; Caretaker/helper; Underpaid and overworked; Ostrich—If I ignore it then it will go away; Victim; Helpless; Have to do it all; Just one step behind; Cleopatra—Queen of Denial; Always one step behind; etc.

Were some of these familiar? After you make your list, play with your personae. Take a lighthearted approach. You don't have to "get rid" of them. Consider assigning them new, more helpful roles. It is when you are not aware of them that they take a high toll on your life.

For each one, note how that particular persona both serves you and also gets in your way. Some of your personae may be designed to work well and win you approval. Some may get you into trouble. Some may win you attention, either positive or negative. Consider the impact in your own life.

My personae:

How it (they) have served me:

How it (they) gave gotten in my way:

The impact on my life has been:

I am now choosing to be this new way with money:

Notes on exercise:

Exercise B: Childhood Money Messages

Use the table below to make a list of your childhood money messages and how they relate to your current relationship to money.

Here are some examples of childhood money messages many people have received:

- Money doesn't grow on trees.
- We can't afford it.
- We don't have enough money for that.
- Don't worry about tracking where your money is going. We'll just go make more.
- You have to work really hard to earn it.
- Money is a struggle.
- There is never enough.
- Women aren't good with money.
- Marry money.
- Money is wrong to spend or enjoy.
- Rich people are snobs.
- You can have love or money—not both.
- Money is something someone else takes care of.

- Money is something you will get if you are good.
- Money is the root of all evil.
- Money separates people.
- What I have takes away from someone else.
- Money is a taboo subject.

In column 1, list the money messages that you heard growing up. These could have come from your parents, grandparents, other family, school, environment, and so on. Childhood messages often come from your immediate parents, yet the influence is much broader.

In column 2, reflect on your current relationship to money. List how you see these money messages contribute to your current self-talk.

Column 1 Childhood Money Message	Column 2 Reflection in Current Self-Talk

Once you have completed your list, sit back and feel the impact—the weight—of this conditioning and the effect it has had on your life and in creating the belief systems which get in your way.

Exercise C: Limiting Labels

We often use self-applied labels which limit our images of ourselves. In this exercise, work to identify the labels you want to keep and which ones you would like to change. Of course, you may notice an overlap between some of these and your common self-talk. However it is worth exploring the labels themselves. Calling yourself names is not nice!

Make a list of the limiting labels you tend to attach to yourself (frantic, flustered, poor planner, fat, stupid, silly, disorganized, dumb, broke, incompetent, and so on).

Next, make a list of the expansive and inspiring labels you would like to use to replace the old labels (free, focused, fit, competent, smart, confident, caring, empowered, energetic, abundant, and so on).

Now, consciously recognize which labels are the "authentic you", which ones support you, and then choose the ones you *want* to continue to use to describe yourself.

Visualization – Removing Limiting Beliefs Around Money (or Anything Else)

As with all our visualization exercises, start by breathing deeply and feeling the feelings in your body. Now, visualize a fertile field. Imagine that it has just been plowed. The rich, dark rolling earth is ready to be seeded. You are about to plant the seeds of your creativity—the seeds of how you want your life to look. But there are a few obstacles in the way. This field has some stones in it. (These are your limiting beliefs.) It is up to you to remove them. Maybe there are lots of little ones or just one big one.

Trust your imagination to see the obstacles that are in your way. These are the beliefs that no longer serve you in regard to self-worth or net worth. You are about to remove them from your field. Feel the weight of the stones of each unwanted belief you are removing. Are they heavy? Do you need to use a tool or get someone else to help you? Or can you find the strength inside yourself to move that stone? Go ahead and use whatever means are necessary for you to clear your field and remove these obstacles. Once you

6

TRANSFORM YOUR SELF-TALK

have removed these stones—your limiting beliefs—your fertile field is ready for planting. Plant your seeds, plant your visions, and plant anything you want to see grow in your life. When you feel complete, allow yourself to transition slowly back to your awareness of present reality. (Note: if you find it easier to listen to the instructions, this is one of the exercises on Cia's CD, *Manifesting Abundance: Consciously Creating the Life You Want*, available through www.live-life.com.)

Conscious Breathing – Release the Burden of Unwanted Conditioning

Review your conditioning and limiting beliefs from the earlier exercises and get a sense of how it affects you. Feel the weight of it in your body and realize that you have been burdened with this weight for a long time. Get yourself into a comfortable position. You may want to start with a safe-space visualization (see Appendix I). Loosen any tight clothing and begin taking very deep breaths slowly and fully.

With each exhalation, imagine the weight of all this unwanted conditioning begin to leave your body. If breathing alone doesn't release it completely, shake it out. Let some sounds out with it to boost your sense of release. With each inhalation, begin to imagine that you are filling yourself with beliefs that serve you—with positive messages and affirmations of your own value and self-worth. Feel your energy now. Is it a little freer? Lighter? All of that freed up energy can now go into creating your entire life the way you want it to be.

Body-Centered Statements

1. I feel _____ and _____
   _____.
2. I am large enough to contain both.
3. Thank you, dear inner critic (or name you have chosen), for your tireless efforts on my behalf. Your services are no longer required.

4. I appreciate all my unique qualities, and at this moment especially

_____.

Journal Joggers

Use the following questions to lead you into your journal entries for this Key.

1. What am I telling myself that keeps me upset regarding how I feel about myself or my financial situation?
2. Why do I think I need to tell myself these things?
3. Am I willing to say good-bye to my former money personae?
4. What does my new way of being with money look, sound, and feel like?
5. How will this shift open me up to real worthiness?

Whether you think you can, or that you can't, you are usually right.

—HENRY FORD

KEY SEVEN

LEARNING
TO LOVE YOURSELF

I do not care what others say and think about me. But there is one man's opinion which I very much value, and that is the opinion of James Garfield. Others I need not think about. I can get away from them, but I have to be with him all the time. He is with me when I rise up and when I lie down; when I eat and talk; when I go out and come in. It makes a great difference whether he thinks well of me or not.

—PRESIDENT JAMES GARFIELD

There is no more direct path to happiness, worthiness, and abundance than learning to love yourself. Without self-love, none of these other Keys will be of any value to you. Without self-love, you will quickly sabotage any gains, any headway that you can make. Self-love is expressed through self-care and self-care means that you will lovingly do the things that will serve you—making the choices that are in your best interests and that support you.

As we stated in Key Two, there is nothing you need to do to deserve money. It is your birthright. Who you are sitting here today is amazing and wonderful and you deserve all the best, no less so than anyone else. Are you willing to own that? To claim that birthright? To fully visualize/feel your right to abundance and your capacity for it inside yourself? Step into it. Imagine/experience that you have it right now at this moment.

Cia has seen more lives transformed by this particular Key than any other. She believes so much in the importance of this principal that she recorded an audio CD entitled, *Learning to Love Yourself*, to help listeners truly absorb the exercises and body-centered statements needed to make self-love a reality in their lives. Over and over, Cia observes and reports where a lack of self-love and self-worth is evidenced in a related pervasive lack of both happiness and true abundance.

"For many people, including myself," says Cia, "there may have been a lack of unconditional love, nurturing, and mirroring early in life. For people who have had a deficit in that department, the journey to true self-love is not an easy one because there is no model for it. It involves truly starting from scratch to develop a sense of what it is." The exercises in this Key, plus those available in Cia's audio CD, can help you through this process, even if and especially if you too are starting from scratch to get a sense of what unconditional love feels like.

Don't forget: The universe is an abundant place, rich and giving to those who are willing to believe and trust in that fact. You are a part of that—a part of all that is, *and* all that is available to you as you tap into it.

Perhaps you have blocked yourself from that flow with some self-blame that has caused you to feel separate or undeserving. In earlier Keys, we discussed the importance of and process of replacing negative messages. It is time to unwind the downward spiral of self-blame or criticism that is keeping you separate from the joy, abundance, and prosperity you deserve.

What are you angry or disappointed with yourself about in regard to money? Notice how this creates a vicious cycle. Example: You're angry at yourself for not giving yourself a break. So, actually, you're not giving yourself a break for not giving yourself a break. Then you'll be angry with *that*, and so on. Perhaps you're angry at yourself for spending too much. Do you try to make yourself feel better by spending some more? The result? You're miserable! The antidote: breaking the cycle.

How Do You Change?

You change with love, forgiveness, and acceptance. Love yourself for not giving yourself a break. Love yourself for spending too much. Love yourself for doing something stupid. Love yourself for all of who you are and for all that you have done. If you can't forgive yourself, forgive yourself for not forgiving yourself until you can. Start where you can and begin to unwind the spiral.

"How can I love myself for botching up my financial life (in small and big ways)?" you may ask. That question comes from confusing love and forgiveness with condoning the behavior. You are afraid that by loving yourself you will condone it and therefore do it more. When you were brought up, you may have been scolded for doing something wrong. Unconsciously you believed, and may continue to believe, that the only way you can train yourself is to scold yourself. Trainers of animals and humans have found that to be just plain incorrect. Has it worked for you so far? Have you changed your habits by scolding yourself? Love and compassion will bring quicker and more positive dramatic changes.

"But I just can't love myself for doing something wrong!" you protest. We realize that it is not easy at first. It is, however, a habit you can cultivate. Sometimes it helps to look upon the part of yourself that made the mistake, as a small child. After all, the small child who once was you still exists in some part of yourself. Would you criticize or blame a child for acting on an impulse or making a mistake? She/he was just doing what felt right at the time, right? Could you lovingly point out to the child that the results of that action did not serve her? Could you love her for having the impulse that was the best way she knew to take care of herself at the time? Could you lovingly instruct her on other alternatives that might serve her better? Try it. It will change your life and up your quotient of joy and success immeasurably.

Another way of looking at practicing learning to love yourself is to ask yourself if you would forgive someone else for similar wrongs—the same things you hold against yourself? Most often the answer is "yes." You may be blaming yourself for something you would never think of holding

7

LEARNING TO LOVE YOURSELF

against anyone else. If you would blame someone else, would you blame a child? No? Well then, how about forgiving the child in you as a start?

Spending to Fill a Void

Within the body you are wearing now, inside the bones and beating in the heart, lives the one you have been searching for so long. But you must stop moving and shake hands. The meeting doesn't happen without your presence, your participation.

—ROBERT K. HALL

If you are about to make yourself feel better by overspending, stop and ask yourself what is it that you are REALLY trying to get. What is really the trigger? What is the need you are really trying to fill? What is it you are in reaction to? You are somehow trying to feel better about yourself or a circumstance.

Think of the last time that you went shopping because you felt particularly emotional, lonely, or were struggling with some negative feelings. This is often humorously known as *retail therapy*. With some distance and perspective, can you see now how the shopping was in reaction to the feelings you were having? Once you can recognize what your triggers are, then you can begin to find other ways to fill those voids for yourself. This will increase both your inner self-love account and your bank account!

Are you willing to consider that you can feel better by taking a pause and giving yourself some much-needed love? As a start, before you make any purchase, whether in a store or on the Internet, ask yourself two questions: "Do I need this?" and "Do I need this now?" Answers to both need to be emphatically "YES" to support a current purchase. Otherwise, stop the process and reconsider buying the item tomorrow or another point in the future.

No matter what the problem you are struggling with, a big part of the solution is in loving yourself. When you shop to fill an emotional void, the emotional void usually comes from not feeling loved enough from the outside, which is tied to not loving yourself enough from the inside. Picture this on a billboard: When the emotional void is in loving yourself, you can *never* buy enough to fill it. Whether your purchase is another nice pair of jeans, a fourth nice dinner out this week, or the new piece of furniture or appliance, it is *not* going to make you feel better for more than a few seconds. What is it that YOU buy when you are looking to fill your emotional void? And what does that really symbolize for you?

> *You can never get enough of what you don't **really** need.*
> —DR. APRIL BENSON

Mandy—Shopping Leads to Guilt

Belinda coached a client, Mandy, who would go on spending binges for her kids and then beat herself up about it and obsess about her inability to handle money and credit cards. When she started to work with Belinda, Mandy felt like this was the only way she knew how to be. Eventually, she discovered that there were other options for how she could view herself and her spending habits.

Mandy began to understand that new thought choices could give her the ability to create the outcomes that she wanted. She then started choosing actions that better supported her. Mandy recognized that *spending is a choice*, so she set herself up for success. Switching tracks for Mandy meant that she would either (1) leave her credit cards at home, or (2) pre-determine an amount that she was comfortable spending and wouldn't feel guilty about. If the amount was over $100, she also added a step to consult and gain agreement with her husband, thus providing Mandy the ability to speak her commitment and ensure a better partnership with her husband around money.

Wealth From the Inside Out

True wealth is not something that you can buy yourself into or find outside of yourself. This *Self-Worth To Net Worth* journey blends the inner and the outer work to help you understand that wealth and worth start inside.

Create a short list now of the things you can think, do, or create that bring you joy, validation, and freedom—often what you may be seeking from shopping. Here are a few items to consider for your list: reading a funny joke, talking with a great friend, smelling a fresh flower, holding a child's hand, laughing out loud, and writing in your journal. As you remove shopping to fill the void, allow these positive simple steps to serve as replacement activities. Consult and employ that list as often as necessary to remind yourself of your alternate go-to behaviors that bring you back to your own beauty, authenticity, and sources of joy.

Allow yourself to occasionally give yourself little things too—within reason that is. That will help you nourish the need while not breaking the bank, so to speak. Even when you feel completely broke, buy yourself something small like a flower, so that you don't drown in the feeling of deprivation and poverty consciousness, which makes the cycle worse.

Discovering Your Real Needs

What is it that you really need? Could it be that you want to feel valued, listened to, seen, or loved, for instance? Once you identify your real needs, you can begin to appreciate that this current need has become so strong and persistent in you because it likely comes from the little child in you, and especially the part of your little child who never had her/his needs fully met in that particular way. Sit down with that child who is still alive in you and let the child know that she/he is okay; that she/he made it through, and that you are living proof of that. Then give that child what she needs—authentically, not in more "stuff" that can be purchased.

Paul and Ruby came to see Cia seeking help in their relationship. They were battling constantly, and both quite unhappy in the relationship. Their struggle was negatively impacting their financial situation too. Cia watched patiently for a while to observe the dynamic as their usual war was waged in front of her on their first session. It was not the details of the discussion she was listening for. Rather, she was noticing body language, tone, the general dynamic, stressors and coping strategies. Coping strategies are like the well-known "fight or flight response"—what one does when under pressure. Actually there are four "f" words—fight, flee, freeze, or faint. Often when Cia works with couples, she notices that one member of the couple acts the role of the aggressor and the other may counteract/defend (flight), exhibit avoidance behavior or threaten to leave (flee), get emotionally paralyzed and unable to respond (freeze), or crumble under the stress (faint). What she noticed was that Ruby and Paul were truly well matched in their coping strategies. They were both defensive counter-attackers and so honed in their practice of this strategy that there was no one clear aggressor.

Once she called a "time out," Cia was able to get each one of them to share with the other what it was about their childhood that had been such a threat to them or hurt them so badly. As Paul and Ruby told their stories to each other, they both began to cry and to see each other in a new light. Most importantly, each one was able to recognize in himself or herself where all this defensiveness came from. Neither one had received unconditional love. Neither one had felt truly valued and so each one projected onto their partner that he or she was not valuing them either. The truth was that neither one truly valued themselves.

Cia continued to see each of them privately, as well as together, as they made progress through their childhood wounds and built a core sense of self-worth within themselves. Having done so, they were no longer quick to defend/counter-attack and therefore were able to diffuse their partner and find out what was really wrong. As they each deepened their own sense of self-worth, they learned to support each other and that resulted in dramatic gains in their net worth as well. The energy that had previously been wasted on competing against each other could now be used to forge a powerful and loving team.

Sourcing the Resistance

You may have a huge amount of resistance to loving yourself and to a sense of your own "deservability." Why is it so hard for you to love yourself and to allow yourself all the goodness that is your natural birthright? Where does all this resistance come from? Some of it is cultural. Religions, in their eagerness to glorify God, have often gone overboard in an effort to portray both humanity and wealth as essentially flawed. Religions often encourage vows of poverty, for example. Moreover, religions are often misinterpreted and misunderstood. These teachings, including their misunderstandings, seep into your consciousness early in life, leaving you with an unconscious belief system that money is bad. A common misquotation, for example, is that "money is the root of all evil." But the passage is this: "For the *love of money is the root of all evil:* which while some coveted after, they have erred from the faith, and pierced themselves through with many sorrows." (1 Timothy 6:10; The King James Bible) Reading it this way, if you focus on, attach to, or "love" money itself for its own sake, you will get stuck and may create a life of challenge and deprivation. In contrast, remember our emphasis on *affluence* as flow, and our encouragement to focus on what it is you truly want, so that money itself is only a part of the process.

Concepts like original sin or the seven deadly sins give ammunition to the idea that you should disown parts of yourself. Society has had reason to fear the extremes of the darker or more passionate energies. However, by learning to repress these energies, you deny the wholeness of your being, and often eliminate a large measure of your own aliveness and creativity. If you think there are dark, hidden, monstrous places inside yourself that you cannot expose to the light, you can never be whole. It takes a huge amount of what otherwise would be used as creative energy to hide and fear that you will be discovered or "found out."

The thing you fear most has no power. Your fear of it is what has the power. Facing the truth really will set you free.

—OPRAH WINFREY

In Belinda's case, when she was in her early 30s, she spent energy and focus on making sure other people didn't see her experience her lack of self-love. Yet when she asked herself, "What is it that I don't want others to know about me? What am I hiding or covering up?" she opened herself up to actually experience self-worth. Ask yourself similar questions and then sit quietly and listen to your own answers. For each response you discover, take baby steps to love yourself for that aspect of yourself and share each item with someone. As you do both of these steps, you will be amazed at how your worthiness begins to immediately expand. Ending this hiding brings great relief.

At the source of the cover-up is often shame or guilt. These are very strong emotions, especially when it comes to money, and are wrapped in self-judgment, making the feelings even more debilitating. These are some of the darker emotions, and often result in a resistance to getting help with money issues. Belinda worked with a client, Brittany, who had taken out a credit card in college and accumulated nearly $10,000 in debt before she graduated. Ten years later, she was still paying that off and feeling ashamed of her prior lack of responsibility. Each month, when she wrote a check to the credit card company, she shamed herself for her past behavior and then often went out and spent more to ease her guilty feelings. That one poor decision she made in college continued to haunt her for years as she held onto self-judgment and blame. Once Belinda helped her to realize how she was shaming herself again and again, Brittany could then begin to love herself for the past decision and acknowledge that she did the best she knew how to at the time. This recognition then allowed her to stop impulsively spending, generate an extra $600/month in savings, and have the debt paid off in less than two years. Each time she wrote a check, she felt empowered in creating her new financial future instead of living into more shame and guilt.

Recognizing Your Nourishment Barriers

A *nourishment barrier* is a psychological block to taking in emotional and other forms of nourishment. It is particularly common in people who did not receive much of the kind of nourishment they needed in childhood. Do you have trouble receiving compliments and/or appreciation? If so, you may be experiencing a form of a nourishment barrier. This can interfere with your success levels in life. Not only with developing a healthy sense of self-worth, but with increasing your net worth as well. Blocking an incoming flow of money is not unlike blocking appreciation—it may be hard for you to accept that you deserve it. By encountering these barriers in a conscious way, you can begin to break through the barrier and tear it down, allowing in more appreciation in both material and emotional forms.

In the exercises at the end of the Key, you will be asked to choose at least one body-centered statement that will help you fill yourself with love and/or acceptance regarding self-worth and net worth issues, and say it out loud to yourself. You will have the chance to notice how you are feeling as you say it. Notice any statements that invoke an uncomfortable bodily response, no matter how subtle, within you. That is a sign that you are encountering some resistance—thus highlighting a possible nourishment barrier. When you are done, tune in to how you are feeling and, where the feelings are pleasant, imagine what it would be like to feel that way all the time! You can through self-love.

Financial Anorexia

Financial anorexia, as we call it, is a form of a nourishment barrier. In the case of financial anorexia, you are prone to deprive yourself financially and deny yourself the luxuries (or even sometimes the necessities) that money can buy. The questions below serve as examples of this condition. A resistance to the flow of abundance and money can be a symptom of a larger resistance to the flow of life, breath and all good things. Is there even efforting in the way you breathe? Do you hold your breath instead of allowing and opening to the flow—the affluence of life?

Notice your breathing in this moment. (See *Conscious Breathing* at the end of this Key for more on releasing your blocks and embracing abundance with your breathing.) Is it deep or shallow? Not taking a deep full breath is a form of starving yourself just as living in scarcity is a form of starving yourself, i.e., financial anorexia.

Do you ever find yourself:

- Not feeling worthy of wealth, a promotion, or commanding your value in the marketplace?

- Hiding the fact that you have money if you do?
- Living in scarcity, such as refusing to buy yourself a bouquet of flowers, a meal out, a massage, or other items that support your self-care and well-being?
- Trying to appear wealthy and healthy on the outside, yet inwardly feeling ashamed, embarrassed, or guilty about an action you took with your money?
- Craving shopping as a cure for your inner unfulfilled needs?

While *anorexia nervosa* is an eating disorder characterized by refusal to maintain a healthy body weight and an obsessive fear of gaining weight due to a distorted self-image, *financial anorexia* involves an inner starvation of joy and prosperity. Many suffer from this syndrome, yet so many have become so accustomed to living in scarcity that the possibility of claiming true wealth and abundance—essentially your Self-Worth *and* your Net Worth—can be frightening.

Breathing in Abundance

What if you could imagine that for every inhale you could feel yourself expand, get larger, create a sense of space inside yourself to take in all the abundance that the universe has to offer. Ask yourself, "How can I do this with less effort? How can I do this in a way that is kind and gentle, with more ease, and just a little bit freer, easier, or lighter?"

Can you trust, as you breathe, that you will be able to create what you need? Give up the old messages. Use each exhalation to release them. You no longer have to work hard for everything. You no longer have to struggle and hold on for dear life. Keep checking in with your feelings to see if you are feeling more in alignment. Gently, lovingly, and slowly. Trust your inner wisdom. Plug into the flow and you will be amazed at how much you can accomplish with this new sense of ease. Breathe deeply. What does that feel like? Willingness gets so much easier as you breathe into the abundance and affluence on the other side.

As you progress through the Keys in this book, you will find yourself

7

LEARNING TO LOVE YOURSELF

able to shift from a financially anorexic or scarcity state to one of *exquisite sufficiency*, where you recognize you have what you need and you have the power to create the *enough* in your life.

Acceptance As a Step Towards Love

Sometimes, the resistance to the word *love* is so strong that, for some people, it helps to start with the concept of *acceptance*. If that is easier for you, begin with acceptance. Be willing to hold yourself, your feelings, your finances, and everything about yourself with complete unconditional acceptance. If that resonates more strongly for you right now, just mentally replace the word love with the word acceptance.

Six Steps to Loving Yourself

So, how do you learn to love yourself? Good question.

It's likely not easy for you to learn to love yourself, especially when you may have spent most of your lifetime not truly loving yourself. In addition, you probably have very little role modeling for what self-love looks like. You may even have had very little experience of what being loved unconditionally feels like! Sad, but true. If that is the case for you, as it is for many, then you have to start from scratch to teach yourself the feeling of what it is to be loved unconditionally. How do you do that? By loving yourself more and more, little by little.

Step One: Allow Love

Have you ever loved anyone or anything? If you have, then you know what love feels like. Take a moment and get the feeling of that love, the feeling of what it is to love someone. Create that feeling inside yourself right now. Once you've done that, direct the love into yourself. Give it to *you*. Put your hand over your heart and imagine feeling love, like warmth or rays of light streaming into you. Create a circuit, send it out and let yourself take it in. Feel what it feels like to receive unconditional love. Drink it up. Absorb it into the cells of your being.

Step Two: Understand You Are Enough, Regardless of Your Money Issues

You are the only one who can truly give yourself the message that you are enough just as you are. You are complete. You are lovable. You deserve success, wealth, and abundance. Once you absorb these truths, a greater sense of self-worth and deservability will begin to emerge. Once it manifests, you will attract like-minded people to you. As you become radiant with your own sense of lovability, you'll be a magnet for love from others as well as a magnet for an improved financial state. Otherwise, even if you enter a relationship with the kind of person who would really appreciate you for who you are or start the career of your dreams, you will sabotage the relationship or the career because you don't feel you are worth it in some aspect.

As Belinda realized from her transformed self-talk that she did in fact deserve to be loved and accepted exactly as she was, she was amazed how her inner satisfaction and joy transformed and grew. Then somewhat unintended positive consequences started to occur. On a personal note, the quality and depth of her relationships improved. She had become more present once she was no longer trying to keep them from seeing how much she didn't like herself. It was quite a relief for her, and actually for everyone in her life. Belinda became a magnet for love and then a magnet for money too.

From a financial perspective, she had been uncertain about which new job she would choose and how she could maximize her worth in the marketplace. Once she loved herself at this greater level, and grew her own self-worth, she was then able to see clearly which one of the four offers she truly wanted and then negotiate a higher salary, a signing bonus, and stock options into her compensation package. Cha-ching! (Two important notes: First, on the outside, everyone thought she "had everything handled" the entire time and already loved herself. She knew the truth though and it was eating her up inside, as she knew she often felt like a "fraud" or inauthentic. Second, this was a process for Belinda. The recognition was an important "a-ha" moment and initiated the healing. It did not all happen overnight. It may be the same for you, or healing may happen in the instant you begin to love yourself.)

Let's say you get a bonus check for $50,000 and you are so used to not having a savings account and a financial future to count on, that you squander the money by lending it to friends who won't pay it back, take a trip and pay too much for it, and so on. Remember this: you deserve to be loved and you deserve solid financial security—not for who you are, not even for what you are, but simply for the fact that *that you are*. And you deserve to have abundance in your life—start living today from that new powerful belief.

Step Three: Recognize You Deserve Affluence, Inside and Out

Do you believe that you deserve your desired level of internal and external wealth? One business owner Belinda worked with, Peter, shared that he would create really successful businesses, and yet with each business, something unusual occurred which caused the business to fail. At the core of these results was Peter's inability to believe in himself, trust himself, and know that he was worth having that level of success. Have you ever considered starting a business, but are afraid of outcomes similar to Peter's? This Key is then especially important to your transformation.

Step Four: Love Yourself Now

You may tend to have it backwards when you think if only he/she/they would love and value you, *then* you would begin to love and value yourself. If you could just get that one more/next relationship, raise, new client or promotion, make that next milestone, break that nasty habit, or even lose those 20 extra pounds, *then* you could start loving and caring for yourself. *Then* you will be worthy.

The truth is that it works the other way around! Love yourself now, just the way you are, and you will be much more likely to attract that promotion, gain that new client, make that milestone, kick that habit, lose the weight, or find that special person. The radiant, centered quality that comes from loving yourself will attract others, and you will no longer need to seek love, approval, acknowledgment, or a raise from others in order to validate yourself.

This is the source of the self-worth and net worth mix-up. When you put those external drivers at the source of your worthiness, then you give them power over you. You become victim to your circumstances instead of the source of creating the life you want. As you learn to love yourself, you create a solid foundation for your self-worth to develop. On that solid groundwork, you can then determine the strategies, create the habits, and follow through on the actions that will lead you to a related enhanced net worth. Say out loud now, "My Self-Worth Leads To My Net Worth!" (If you would like a $1 Million Bill with this affirmation, contact Belinda's organization at www.OwnYourMoney.com and request one (or many) for yourself.)

Step Five: Become Whole

When you accept yourself and your feelings as they are, you become whole. The refusal to love and accept yourself fully splits you off from yourself. You wind up working against yourself in spite of your best intentions, and that disowned part of your being has no chance to heal or to integrate. This self-rejection then becomes a self-created block to your growth, vitality, happiness, and wealth. In contrast, once you achieve a level of self-love and acceptance, you increase your capacity to feel deeply, as you allow feelings to flow through you, rather than blocking them. You also increase your capacity for wealth as you allow abundance to flow through you rather than blocking it.

Step Six: Live in Appreciation

Self-rejection can be healed with the gentleness of love. Remember, you are letting go here of some very old patterns. There is often grief associated with letting go, even when you are letting go of something unpleasant. It can be painful or scary to let go of the familiar in favor of the unknown. Be patient and gentle with yourself. Live in appreciation and generosity and that's what you get back. Drop a pebble of appreciation or give away something into the pond and watch the ripples roll. As you focus on what you do have, versus what you don't have, you will be amazed at how wealthy you begin to feel and how your self-worth begins to grow. Your self-worth creates your net worth and not the other way around.

LEARNING TO LOVE YOURSELF

7

True Self-Love

There is nothing that you can buy in any store to make you truly happy—you must love and accept yourself first and foremost. The rest will be the icing on the cake.

Your sense of self-worth, or lack thereof, forms the basis of how you create your life. Your level of self-love, value, and worth influences all of your choices and decisions and thus shapes the life you live for better or worse. Often this creates a vicious circle—or a positive one. If you see ugliness and lack in your life, it will reinforce a lack of self-worth. If you see beauty and affluence around you, it is likely to reinforce a belief in your own value and worth.

Nathaniel Brandon, author of *How to Raise Your Self-Esteem*, refers to what he calls "the principle of reciprocal causation." Brandon explains that "behaviors that generate good self-esteem are also expressions of good self-esteem." And vice-versa. Manifesting abundance and consciously creating the life you want is both a cause and effect of a healthy sense of self-worth. Thus you may begin to see how directly self-worth feeds into net-worth, which in turn tends to reinforce your self-worth as you more fully manifest your power in the world.

True self-love and self-worth is experienced and lived at a core level. It is deeper than simple self-esteem. It touches the very essence of your being. Fundamentally, it does not need a reason. You have the right to love yourself, not for what you have accomplished or who you are, not even for what you are, but at the deepest and most fundamental level, simply for That You Are. The very fact of your existence is reason enough to bask in the unconditional and universal love that surrounds you and is your birth-right. Fill yourself up to the brim with this love and you will find that it will overflow and touch all who surround you—creating ripples of happiness and abundance in your wake.

EXERCISES

Exercise A

Part I: Loving Yourself Unconditionally

This exercise is a test of how easy or difficult it is for you to love yourself unconditionally right now. Say the words, "I love myself unconditionally" out loud. (As a reminder, if using the term *love* feels like too much of a stretch, you can replace the word with *accept* and begin there with the process.)

Take a few deep, slow breaths, close your eyes or say it to yourself in the mirror. Repeat it over and over, trying different ways of saying it. Say it slowly enough so that you can pause in between the words to feel the feelings in your body. Say it with enthusiasm. You may feel awkward, distracted, agitated, or notice some physical discomfort. Listen for any little voice which may be chiming in with contradictions. It may say something like, "Are You Kidding? This is so dumb. No way."

What do you notice? Whatever comes up for you is fine. It is an indication of where you are right now in your own process. When you finally feel a sense of inner peace, you will know that you have really been able to take in that gift of love from yourself.

Part II: Loving Your Financial State Unconditionally

Repeat the exercise using the phrase "I love my financial state unconditionally." (Your financial state encompasses all of the aspects covered in Keys Four and Five with the current WHAT IS of the financial and business/career aspects of your life.)

Theoretically, the first part of the exercise (Part I above) would have covered everything about yourself and your life. However, many people find that even when they are OK with loving themselves, they compartmentalize their finances and then find it difficult to specifically love and accept their financial state unconditionally. Remember, as described in Key Four on "Accept What Is," that loving it unconditionally will not prevent you from changing it—it will actually make it easier to do so.

Exercise B

Part I: What Stands in the Way

Having done the above exercise, there may still be some withholds—some excuse you have for refusing to love yourself fully. If so, this exercise can be powerfully transformative and we suggest you do this in a serious and heartfelt manner while deeply introspecting. Perhaps it would help you to meditate with some sweetly sad music as you check inside for any blocks which are still in the way between you and loving yourself unconditionally. Make a list below of whatever stands in the way between you and loving yourself by filling in the blank with as many things as come to mind, or perhaps there is only one.

If it weren't for _____, I would love myself.

Part II: Loving Yourself for What Stands in the Way

There is a tremendous amount of power in actually loving yourself for (not in spite of) the very same things that have been causing you to withhold love from yourself. For example, if your previous list said, "*If it weren't for* being twenty pounds overweight, I would love myself," now write, "*I love myself for* being twenty pounds overweight!" If you wrote "If it weren't for having blown my big opportunity, I would love myself," now it is time to write "I love myself for having blown my big opportunity."

You may protest vehemently, and say that you are absolutely unwilling to love yourself for the things that you have been so passionately holding against yourself. You may say that if you love yourself for them, then you won't change. None of this is true. Loving yourself for these things will free up the energy which will make it easier to change them. Go ahead and fill in the blank with the items from your list on the previous page and feel your feelings. Feel your resistance and do it anyway! (If you absolutely can't bring yourself to love yourself for your "sin," then love yourself for not loving yourself for _____!) If you can honestly and truly do this and feel it, it will transform your life.

I love myself for _____.

Good luck with the list!

Exercise C: Writing a Letter of Appreciation

For a powerful healing experience, write *yourself* a letter of appreciation! Start simply by making a list of things you appreciate about yourself. Some suggestions include appreciating your body for supporting you to do all the things you love; your mind and its uniqueness, including the way you think, reason, visualize, etc.; your feelings and capacity to feel, including your passions; your spirituality; your personality traits and actions such as kindness and generosity; your creativity; your potential; your aliveness; and finally just appreciate yourself for being you. Then write it in the form of a love letter to yourself. Mail it to yourself (really), or give it to a friend and ask her or him to mail it to you at a time you might really need to be reminded of your unique qualities (or to be kind to yourself). Whenever you need a boost, read it to yourself out loud.

Note: If you need more work on this Key, we recommend The Learning to Love Yourself Workbook *by Gay Hendricks, from which some of these exercises were derived as well as the* Learning to Love Yourself *CD by Cia Ricco, which contains similar exercises spoken in a soothing voice, along with affirmations, music, and more, and is available through her website: www. Live-Life.com.*

Visualization – An Experience of Self-Love

This exercise is particularly important if you have never been the recipient of truly unconditional love in your life. In that case, you will need to start from scratch to get a sense of what unconditional love feels like.

Start by taking some deep breaths and feeling the feelings in your body. Now imagine someone that you know that you love beyond a shadow of a doubt. If you can't feel this for a person, you may imagine an animal, or even a place, a thing, or an activity. The key is to get a feeling in your body of what this love feels like. See this object of your love vividly and in detail and, as you do so, notice what this love feels like inside you. Where do you feel it in your body? What are the sensations? Does it feel warm? Does it have a color, shape, texture, sound, word, or gesture associated with it? Let the feeling of love begin to increase and expand inside you. Let yourself be filled to overflowing with this feeling of love.

Now take that feeling of love and direct it toward yourself. Instead of focusing on the original object of your love, love yourself in the same way. You can do this by replacing the original image of your love with an image of you. Or, just take that love and turn it back into yourself. Make that outpouring of love an *in-pouring*, instead, by turning the flow inward and pouring the love back into yourself. Alternatively, you might visualize it as taking a spotlight that has been shining the light of your love outwards, and turning it around to shine that light back into yourself. Really allow yourself to fill yourself up. Bask in the feeling. If you lose the feeling, go back to the original object of your love and do it again. Relax your mind and trust your body to do the work of loving and really absorbing that love. When you get a sensation of self-love, take the time to bask in the sensation.

Was it easier to generate a feeling of love for someone or something outside yourself than it was to love yourself? If you have trouble with this exercise, you may choose to start by using an image of your child self instead of an image of yourself as you are now. Remind yourself that this child still exists inside of you and deserves your love. Once you are able to fully love the child within you, you may find it easier to give yourself, as you are now, the same kind of unconditional love.

Do this exercise daily until it becomes easier. It is not only healing, but serves as a diagnostic tool to help you notice any resistance you are still carrying to loving yourself. You may notice that there is something for which you have not yet fully forgiven yourself. If that is the case, what better time than now to do the much-needed work of self-forgiveness? There really is no other time you can act to complete this important process of self-forgiveness, self-acceptance, and self-love. Your worthiness is counting on it.

Conscious Breathing

Similarly to the breathing exercise in Key Five, you may wish to do this exercise lying down in a comfortable position, perhaps with a pillow under your knees and a small one under your head. Loosen any constricting clothing.

What does self-love look and feel like to you? Cia says for her, it is like rays of the sun. It might be a golden glow, a bubble of some color, or a sensation. Once you get the feeling/image clearly, breathe as slowly and deeply as you possibly can. With each in-breath, fill your belly with this image/sensation, extending it first before your chest and imagine that the bigger you can expand your chest, the more self-love you can take in.

This is also a good opportunity to send some love to your body specifically. If there are parts of your body that you have neglected to love, chances are those are parts that are shut down, and not getting a lot of movement or oxygen. One at a time for any parts of you that you have a hard time loving, imagine that you are breathing directly into that body part and, along with the breath, sending that body part a message of appreciation. You may owe it an apology for having disowned it!

Use your exhales to breathe out and release fully anything that has been standing in the way between you and loving yourself. Those things will be fresh in your mind if you have done Exercise B above.

Body Centered Statements

As discussed in the part of this Key entitled *Recognizing Your Nourishment Barriers*, now is your chance to select at least one statement for yourself that will help you fill yourself with love and/or acceptance regarding your self-worth and net worth issues. We suggest starting with a list of the statements that are the most meaningful to you and saying them out loud. Notice if any generate resistance or show signs of your nourishment barrier appearing.

You may want to say your statements to yourself in the mirror as well. This will give you visual feedback regarding whether you are resisting or embodying the statement. Another effective technique for you might be to record your statements, slowly, into a recorder, so that you can relax and focus on your feelings as you hear them. Or use one of our CD products, especially Cia's CD, *Learning to Love Yourself*, to support your process.

7

LEARNING TO LOVE YOURSELF

Here are several examples to get you started:

- I am completely surrounded and supported by universal abundance.
- I am uniquely valuable and deserve to be paid well for the value I deliver.
- I deserve to have what I want.
- I am deeply valued and appreciated.
- All the abundance I have been searching for is here within me or is within my reach.
- My very nature is part of the flow of affluence so there is no need to search for it, struggle for it, or work at it.
- I did the best I knew how, forgive myself for any mistakes, and am ready to move on.
- I trust myself and make smart decisions with money.
- I love and accept myself, my feelings, and my financial state exactly as they are.
- I love myself exactly the way I am—not for who I am, not for what I am, simply for THAT I am.
- I understand that the love for myself is the greatest possession I will ever have.
- Loving myself provides the power for transformation. I am willing to love myself now.

Now write some body-centered statements that are perfect for you.

Journal Joggers

Consider the following questions and directions to lead you into your journal entries for this Key.

Think of someone who you have recently done something loving for or someone who you have recently said something loving to. What would it take to get you to say or do something similar for yourself? Are you any less deserving of this care and attention?

What is the source of your love for someone or something? Identify the characteristics in your loved ones that you love about them. Now turn to yourself. Where can you source your love for yourself from? Make an extensive list.

If you have trouble believing in your own deservedness, write a letter to your own inner child. Upon completion, see if a place of compassion has opened within you.

To love oneself is the beginning of a life-long romance.

—OSCAR WILDE

7

LEARNING TO LOVE YOURSELF

HARNESS THE POWER
OF CHOICE

*Until one is committed, there is hesitancy, the chance
to draw back, always ineffectiveness. Concerning all acts of initiative
(and creation), there is one elementary truth the ignorance of which kills
countless ideas and splendid plans: that the moment one definitely commits
oneself, the providence moves too. A whole stream of events issues from the
decision, raising in one's favor all manner of unforeseen incidents, meetings
and material assistance, which no man could have dreamt would have come
his way. I have learned a deep respect for one of Goethe's couplets:
"Whatever you can do, or dream you can, begin it. / Boldness
has genius, power, and magic in it!"*

—MOUNTAINEER W.H. MURRAY

Choice is not only a basic human right, it is a necessity. If you take away all choice, you would be an automaton with zero sense of personal self-worth. Many studies show a direct correlati-on between the amount of freedom of choice a person has and his or her well-being. As people become elderly or infirm and have fewer choices permitted them, their

HARNESS THE POWER OF CHOICE

well-being can be compromised as much by the diminishing of choice as by their age or infirmity.

Do you ever catch yourself using the phrase "I have (or had) no choice"? Think harder before you utter those words. They send a message to your body which is unhealthy. You might not *like* the options, i.e., your choice might be more of a dilemma; however, it is important to hold onto the fact that you have a choice. Even if one of the choices is to die, you have a choice. If someone is holding a gun to your head and telling you to do something, you still have a choice. Forcing yourself to become aware of how many choices you actually do have increases your sense of empowerment (choice = power) and along with it, increases your sense of self-worth.

You can't begin to *have* what you want until you *know* what you want. Money is a tool that supports you to be whom and what you are, and to create the life you want for yourself as a *reflection* of who you are. Being clear about what you want helps you grow a sense of your true identity— helps you to understand who you are. Do you know who you are? Do you know what you want? Actually, identifying what it is you want in life helps you to create a clear sense of who you are. What is the dream or vision you have for your life that makes having money a priority? What is your INSPIRATION? Remind yourself of the Inspiration developed in Key One, and then use this opportunity to dream bigger. Remember, it is not, as many claim, that people dream too big, it is that people dream too small and then make choices based on playing small. Then they get their small results and believe that is all that is available for them. Choose to own your choices and not be owned by them.

If you have had little practice with loving yourself, you may also have had very little practice with choosing what you want in life because you didn't know you had that right. If this is the case, you are suffering from what we call *atrophied wanting muscles*. The muscle, or *capacity*, atrophies when you feel helpless and hopeless. Even if you haven't allowed yourself to use it in a while, it is still there waiting to be strengthened. A strengthened ability to choose is an outgrowth of self-worth and self-love.

Cia says, "My birth son, unlike myself, grew up having lots of choices from an early age. (He was an only child growing up so it was easier.)

When there was a family decision to be made, he was a part of it. Of course I encouraged him to think and feel through his choices and to be able to express his reasons clearly for making them. If the reasons were sound and clear, he was more likely to get his way. Thus he built his 'choice muscle' at an early age. It didn't make for a docile, easy-to-raise child who would conform to everything, but it has surely made for a man who knows what he wants and does not hesitate when a choice is in front of him. He has had lots of practice." How can you engage yourself (or your children) in actively exercising your own choice muscles more frequently to provide and create choosing as a practice or a discipline?

Many people fail to make conscious choices that will truly serve them because, at some level, they don't believe they deserve the good they could create by harnessing the power of choice. Some don't choose because they don't believe they can possibly achieve or hold onto what they choose. Perhaps they (or you) have been disappointed with decisions you have made in the past and have learned to distrust your own decision-making capacity, thus abdicating your power in the world.

Four Major Obstacles to Choosing

Here are four major obstacles that may impede your ability to make conscious choices and move in the direction you deeply desire.

1. *Fear of Choice*

> *You gain strength, courage, and confidence by every experience in which you really stop to look fear in the face.*
>
> —ELEANOR ROOSEVELT

Have you ever been so afraid to choose that you got stuck? That is what we call *decision-making by default*. You have made a decision by not making one. The more you do this, the more you weaken your decision-making muscle—your ability to trust yourself with a decision.

There are numerous belief systems that may cause you to abdicate your ability to harness the power of choice in your life. Most originate early in life through unfortunate experiences or messages which were given to you. Generally they are unconscious. Some examples are:

- Believing you don't deserve to have what you want
- Believing that you don't have a right to outdo someone else (such as a parent, sibling, spouse, friends, etc.)
- Believing that by having what you want, you will be depriving someone else of having what they want (This is an especially ironic one, as governments literally burn and manufacture more money every year.)
- Fear that if you allow yourself to want, you won't get it anyway
- Fear that whatever you get will be taken away from you
- Fear that if you get it, it will result in unhappiness (for you or someone else)
- Fear of failure
- Fear of success

In order to learn the most important lessons of life,
one must each day surmount a fear.

—Ralph Waldo Emerson

2. Perfectionist syndrome

Are you owned by your choices, so afraid to make the wrong decision that you make no decision at all, especially regarding your financial and related matters? You may be stuck in inaction, allowing the choices to be made by default around you, unwilling to take responsibility for actually making any. Perfectionism is rampant in our society and perfectionists are the worst procrastinators—thus contributing to a significant extent of people avoiding any financial action at all. Be honest with yourself. Are you putting your life (financial or otherwise) on hold because you fear it can never live up to your (or someone else's) expectations? If so, begin to unwind that by purposely complimenting yourself every time you stop short of "perfection," which of course you can never achieve anyway. Pat yourself on the back for messing up, caring less, making mistakes, and simply letting yourself BE. See below for the additional impacts of perfectionism and the *Be More Model* to help you move through this obstacle to choosing.

3. *Life and Death Mentality*

Paralysis around decision-making may be related to the fear of death, loss, or finality. If you have a hard time making decisions, notice that you may be imbuing those decisions with a life-and-death quality. Somehow you feel the wrong decision equals death—is *irrevocable*, in other words. It is true, in one sense, that when you make a decision there is change, and thus you die to the old. To live, you must die. Essentially, each moment you die to the moment before it. Embrace the unknown—this is the adventure of life. Take a chance! If what you have is not working for you, you really don't have much to lose, and everything to gain, by trying a new course of action.

4. *Black and White/Right or Wrong*

We often tend to come from a black and white, wrong or right way of looking at things. The fear of making a *wrong* decision may stop you in your tracks. Both paths may be valid choices in their own way. You may need to take a leap of faith and trust that neither decision is wrong or irrevocable. Either decision moves you forward. A sailing ship, in order to reach its destination, has to move one direction and then another with the wind in order to finally reach its goal on the horizon.

What are your reasons? What holds you back from choosing—and choosing powerfully?

Perfectionism and Procrastination

As we just mentioned above, perfectionism can serve as a clear block to choosing. Although oftentimes well intentioned to create an amazing product, perfectionism causes all manner of unhappiness and ills. Somewhere along the way, you may have unconsciously absorbed the message that you had to be perfect in order to be loved or successful. You may believe that your self-worth and/or your net worth require it. In attempting to be perfect, you have likely over-complicated your life. People seem to pride themselves on how busy they are, as if there would be something wrong with them if they were not. Taking on more than what is truly comfortable may result in fatigue (studies show that the majority of North Americans are sleep deprived), health challenges, unhappiness, and a feeling of never being enough because you just can't fit it all in. Instead of enhancing your sense of self-worth, all you have taken on may be eroding it.

An additional side effect of perfectionism is that it most often leads to procrastination. This is true because, knowing that you can't get it perfect and fearing the consequences, you put off taking any action at all. This, again, leads to a lowered sense of self-worth and winds up affecting your net worth as well. You may not pay your bills, for example, because you don't want to do it until you have the time to properly balance your checkbook. In the meantime though, your bills are late. Try on the motto that Belinda, a recovering perfectionist herself, created: "Done is better than perfect."

Perfectionism is a key cause of avoiding choice, especially when it comes to having to make a choice to actively better manage your money. You may be so scared of making a wrong decision, for example with where to invest or what financial advisor to use, that you'd rather not make any decision at all. Clients often approach Belinda for help when they have $20,000 or even $100,000 in their liquid low-interest bank accounts and are petrified that they will do the wrong thing with it. Her assistance is often holding their hand through assessing their current needs, finding better higher-interest places for a portion of the funds, and finding a trusted financial advisor to safeguard and invest the remainder.

Just as we recommend taking small steps to move yourself in the direction of your dreams, here too you can start by taking smaller steps to get into action. Here is the 3-phase *Be More Model* to help you create your step-by-step shift:

1. Avoid Less – Think More
2. Think Less – Do More
3. Do Less – Be More

Just as when you learned to love yourself, and that there may be areas where you need to accept yourself first, so too here you may need to use a gradual approach to get to the point where you realize a more active role in your finances and move toward a peaceful self-worth position—and soon a more peaceful net worth position too.

Here is a visual diagram of the shift, to ultimately allow yourself to Be More!:

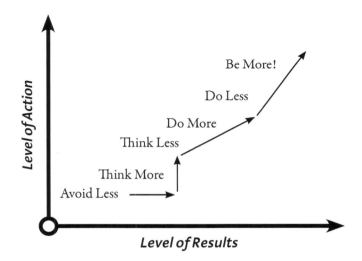

As you move along the continuum to avoid less of the seemingly fearful or scary things in your life, you will allow yourself to move to an enhanced ability to actually live in the moment—being yourself in all your glory. Choose to enjoy yourself as a human *being* of life rather than being caught in only the human *doing*.

The Under-Simplification Syndrome

People are sometimes criticized for over-simplifying something. Yet we find that is not actually a problem at all. The concern is how almost everyone *over-complicates* their life. They have more stuff than they need. They buy more food than they can eat. They over-stress about the level of effort that a task is actually going to take, and then have a great excuse why they didn't do it. Even something like creating a Saving and Spending Plan in Key Five is usually not completed as many over-complicate the steps and never actually track a dime. Do you ever find yourself over-complicating something and making it harder than it needs to be, so much so that it holds you back from taking any action at all? You are not alone, yet you now have a new perspective on your behavior. So tomorrow, instead of doing the same thing again, recognize your pattern and instead find the aspects you can *under*-complicate, i.e., simplify, instead.

Learning to simplify and under-complicate will create huge benefits in your life. You will get more of what is important to you done as you will spend less mental and emotional energy avoiding it. You will have more time as you won't need to shop as much for stuff you don't really need anyway. You will be able to spend less money on your lifestyle and save more money, thus taking the steps you need to better provide for your financial future and then feel better about it. This simplification will also fast-track your path to financial freedom, as your passive income (income earned without working) will exceed your living expenses faster, since you will have less living expenses and more money saved.

Review all aspects of your life for areas where you could simplify and under-complicate your current life situation. Start today with one area, and then build momentum as you enjoy the opening you are creating.

Strengthening Your Wanting and Choice Muscles

So, you may have given up wanting and given up the power of choosing what you want. When that happened, stagnation, resignation, and a sense of hopelessness set in. Sound familiar?

There have been innumerable psychological studies shown about what hopelessness does to rats and to human beings. Hopelessness or a sense of powerlessness leads to disease, apathy and even death. These studies demonstrate, over and over again, that the transformative power for rats and other laboratory animals, as well as human beings is (drum roll please) . . . choice! Psychologists say that in order to be psychologically healthy, we need to have a sense of control over our environment. What we are talking about with control is nothing more than the power of choice.

If you don't know where you are going, any road will take you there.
—Lao Tzu

If you don't know where you are going,
or what you want, no road will take you there.
—Belinda Rosenblum

There was an interesting psychological experiment conducted in a nursing home. Residents were doing poorly and the mortality rate was high. A psychologist was invited in and changed just one thing. The residents were given a choice of what they watched on television. Almost immediately, there was a marked improvement in the health and general well-being of the residents, and the mortality rate declined.

How strong is your *choice* muscle? If you are not used to making affirmative choices in your life, begin to exercise your choice muscle. It really is just like strengthening a muscle. The more you practice, the more natural it will feel for you to make choices consciously—and innately recognizing that you have a right to want and expect things will feel more natural as well. They may not always be attainable, but you have a right to want them. You have a right to choose your life, to choose your way, to choose your path, to choose your destiny.

As you go through life, notice what it is that you are attracted to—what you want. In order to do this, you first have to give yourself permission to want. Don't confuse this *wanting* with *having* to have it. Notice that the wanting in itself can be a good feeling—a form of creativity. What would it take for you to believe that wanting is not wasted energy, nor does it have to lead to disappointment, if the wanting is process-oriented, rather than goal-oriented? See the wanting itself as planting seeds of your expansion—as broadening your vision. Noticing what it is you truly want (not just because it is the latest thing to have or what you *should* want), teaches you something about yourself.

8

HARNESS THE POWER OF CHOICE

Choice as Sacred

People talk about surrendering to God or to the universe. Instead of surrendering, consider this an interactive process, not a giving up. You are not separate from the universe so what you want may be what the universe wants. What if you are the vehicle through which God/Goddess gets to enjoy His/Her own creation? What if it were a "sin" NOT to experience pleasure in life—quite the opposite of how most of us go through life. Try on this new context for choosing to be happy and wealthy in your life as if it were a sacred duty.

Sure, things happen. Sometimes it feels like we don't have much choice. When unexpected events occur, such as a sudden layoff or other unpleasant surprise, we can let them sweep us off our feet and knock us over (feeling we have no choice or control), *or* we can attend to our reactions. Always remember there is choice involved. That is empowerment.

Getting in Fiscal Shape

Physical fitness and fiscal fitness are quite similar—and both involve an initial choice. If you want to lose weight, you have to eat better and get off the couch to work out. To improve your financial health, you need to spend better and take action to protect yourself and invest wisely. Taking action may be a bit uncomfortable at first, yet you quickly realize that the resulting increased energy, health, and strength are worth the effort and sacrifice to you. Look at all of these similarities:

What works to get in physical shape:	What works to get in fiscal shape:
Use a food journal to get conscious about what you are eating.	Track your money to get conscious about where you are spending your money.

8

HARNESS THE POWER OF CHOICE

Eat better and work out.	Spend better and enjoy the money-making opportunities all around you.
Accountability works. Consider hiring a personal trainer.	Accountability works. Consider hiring a financial coach—like a personal trainer for you and your money.
Motivation helps. If you have a teeny-weenie-yellow-polka dot bikini to fit into by a certain date, you are more likely to be inspired to take the steps to get into shape.	Motivation helps. If you have a vacation, home, or wedding to save for, you are more likely to be inspired to take the steps to save.
Support systems work. Weight Watchers and Jenny Craig have created multi-million dollar businesses through building communities of encouragement and accountability.	Building a dream team of the key advisors to support your financial success is helpful to realizing your intentions. Creating a community of like-minded "owners" also supports your ongoing process.
Consistent discipline and strategies work.	Consistent discipline and strategies work through automation, especially automated savings programs.

You have to make a clear choice to get fit—financially and emotionally. We encourage you to make the choice *today*.

Choosing BOTH

One of the largest words in the English language has only three letters— AND. The reason this word is so big is that it creates space for all to be. A by-product of linear thinking is that we think in terms of either/or. The word BUT implies limitation. Replace it with AND then notice the space open up to hold unlimited possibilities. You shift from the *either/or* to understand *both* is possible instead.

For example, you may be telling yourself "I really want to travel and do fun things but I feel an obligation to save for my financial future." Notice the difference if you change that to, "I really want to travel and do fun things in my life AND I want to save for my financial future." What creative ideas burst forth to make both possible? Perhaps new ways of bringing in more income? Less expensive travel alternatives? Not lending money to people who won't pay you back in short order? Other opportunities to save? When you realize that you don't have to live in the world of BUT—you can have BOTH—your choices get easier.

Decisions Every Minute

If you need to strengthen your decision-making capacity, begin by noticing the myriad of decisions you make every minute without even realizing it. Then begin to affirm yourself for even the small decisions you make. As you receive the acknowledgement from yourself, the bigger decisions will begin to get easier. Generally, the act of making a decision and how you make it is more important than the choice itself. It moves you forward in life.

When Cia was a little girl she experienced her first panic attack when her teacher read Robert Frost's Poem *The Road Not Taken*. The poem seems to indicate that once you pick a certain road, then that decision is irrevocable and you will never come back to that juncture again. Cia became terrified of making a decision for fear she would be choosing the wrong path. Once she realized that in life she was faced with a myriad of decisions in every moment and there is no way to stand still—she realized she could simply proceed. She let go of the belief in a *right* or *wrong* choice—as that belief would hold her back and keep her stuck at that crossroads.

Learning to see all possible choices in front of you contributes to your creativity, and that creativity is likely to dramatically increase your net worth. Generally those who have made fortunes are people who have come up with new ideas, however simple and obvious the idea may seem in retrospect, or even slight improvements on current ideas. These creative thinkers started by finding ways to expand the choices available to them. Such people are said to be those who think *out of the box*. The box, of course, is your self-imposed limiting beliefs, which we have also referred to as your comfort zone. If you live in a box that, by virtue of a poor sense of self-worth and empowerment, seems impossibly small to you, please remember that your ultimate choice, the power that no one can take away from you, is the choice over your own thoughts. It is the choice to think outside of your self-created box that will set you free.

In the movie *The Matrix*, people, who were virtual automatons, bought into *the box* or what appeared to be reality. It took a great leap of faith to step outside of that limiting reality into a realm of all possibility. The film is an analogy of what eastern religions have been telling us all along, and now quantum physics has been proving—there are an infinite number of options if we had but the eyes to see them. And, what the eyes see, the mind must first believe.

Five Strategies for Decision-Making

Typing your strategy for decision-making will provide you a powerful tool to consciously make decisions in your life—both personally and professionally. Consider these five strategies and determine your primary and secondary methods for making decisions in your life. When Belinda was deciding to retain her city apartment as a rental property or sell it, she referred to each of these strategies and they became essential in her final decision to keep the property. Similarly, consider using all of the below for decisions which are of high importance to you. Your strategy of choice may differ depending on what you are making a decision on. Consider what different strategies you commonly use for different kinds of decisions.

1. Gut Level

We are all familiar with this kind of decision making. It's the first impulse, trust your instincts, go with your gut, fly-by-the-seat-of-your-pants kind of decision-making. There's nothing wrong with it, but on any significant decision, we don't recommend using this alone.

2. *Analytical*

This is the second most common form of decision-making. We all know this one, too. It's the weighing of the pros and cons approach to making choices. Make a list of the pros in each situation, and make a list of the cons. Assign a value to each item on the list, as they may not be equal in value. For example, on the pros put a number from one to ten with ten being the most important. On the cons, put a number from −1 to −10 with −10 being the most important on the negative scale. Do the pluses of making this decision outweigh the minuses?

3. *Heart-centered*

We have all heard the expressions "follow your heart" and "follow your passion." This method involves listening to the inner directives of your heart or your passion—your own secret yearnings. What excites you is often a valid way to make a decision. As you make a decision, especially using this approach, you can begin by taking small steps to move closer to a definitive choice. This is called *leaning into* the decision. As you lean into it, open to the response in your heart and intuition in determining if you are getting closer to, or farther away from your joy and abundance.

4. *Body-centered*

This method involves the tool of visualization. Appendix I will give you some clues on how to use your bodily-felt sense and vision for making decisions. First, establish your "baseline" by checking how you are feeling in your body right now. Once you have made a mental note of that, go through a detailed visualization of what making a certain decision will involve. Imagine how you will feel as you make the decision and as you experience the consequences of that decision. What will your life be like in the immediate future and down the road?

Extend your visualizations far into the future (say 5, 10, 20, and 30 years ahead) as you imagine the impact this decision might have. During this

8

HARNESS THE POWER OF CHOICE

visualization, check in with the feelings in your body. When you are clear about how your body reacts to this decision, take some deep breaths, release the feeling, and go back to your baseline to prepare to start the process over again with the alternate decision or decisions. When you have visualized all the applicable courses of events, and noted your bodily response to each, you will be in a good position to decide just what it is that your body is telling you about these decisions. You can then make the actual decision powerfully, and you know your body feels good in that choice.

5. Purpose-Guided

When your decisions are out of alignment with your Life Purpose, you are not living up to your full potential or claiming your full measure of joy as a human being. Coming from your purpose empowers you and creates a dynamic alignment of body, mind, and spirit. You will literally feel the power in your body as you move through life knowing that you are in tune with your reason for being.

The key to making decisions from your life purpose is to first clarify and appreciate your own Life Purpose. Complete Exercise B now to reveal your own Life Purpose, with an in-depth example using Cia's purpose. Allow this new understanding to help guide your decisions.

One important note for you: Your Life Purpose does not necessarily equate to what you do for a living. Sometimes making this revelation can help you determine if what you are doing for a living is in alignment with what you believe you were meant to be, do, and have during this lifetime.

One of Belinda's jobs, prior to starting Own Your Money LLC, had been directing the accounting and finance division of a $300 million business that manufactured x-ray screening machines for baggage handling. When she started there, it was shortly after the tragedy on September 11, 2001 and the products produced were necessary to protect and save lives around the world. Belinda's work was constantly engaging, exciting, and new, as the organization faced challenges with extreme accelerated growth. She was able to be the problem-solver, the creative thinker, and the relationship builder.

After almost four years though, the nature of her work shifted to the monotony of "closing the books" and facilitating the basic accounting

8

HARNESS THE POWER OF CHOICE

process each month. This new expectation of her work created a dull routine that was mind-numbing and seemed to suck the life out of her. It was not until a deep introspection, direct coaching, and several personal and professional workshops on both life and money, that she came to discover her own Life Purpose: *To inspire ownership and action for financial success to create a truly rich life—for her and for you.* It was within a week after that epiphany that she founded Own Your Money LLC.

If you know your purpose in life, you can use it as a yardstick to measure your decisions. For each decision, take a moment to consider to what extent your decision is in keeping with your purpose. In choosing among two or three decisions, which brings you closer to your purpose?

See Exercise C in this Key to further explore which one of these strategies most resonates with you and how our new techniques can support your decision-making processes from this moment on.

Deciding to *Own Your Money*

Now is the time to make the decision to truly *own your money*. This is the opportunity to make the bold move toward real fiscal responsibility. You may have never made this choice. Perhaps you have never even thought about making this choice. In fact, unconsciously you may have been making the opposite choice. It is now time for your wake-up call. There is much more in your control than you may have allowed yourself to realize. *RIGHT NOW* is the best and only time you can take action. Make the bold move *now* of choosing to step into a greater level of fiscal responsibility in your life.

Facing the decision-making moment flushes up the unconscious material so that it becomes conscious. This moment of consciousness may be the turning point that opens the door to your own treasure trove of internal and external resources for creating the life you want. By not making this fundamental decision, you have been holding the key and not using it to access the possibilities in your life. To use a Buddhist analogy, you have been a beggar suffering needlessly day in and day out who has a diamond in his pocket without realizing what it is.

Making the decision to *own your money* is a simple—yet often not so easy—move. It means finally letting go, once and for all, of the renter described in Key Two, and actively choosing to have power over your money, instead of allowing your money to have more power over you.

How do you make decisions about money? Do you do it by default, leaving it for the last minute until it is made for you? Are you the researcher type who feels that you always need more information before you can act? Are you the impulsive type, who, in the desire to avoid the feelings around the process, grab at the first thing that presents itself, like going for the bright, shiny object? Do you suffer from paralysis, inaction, avoidance, or procrastination? What is your own unique process? Understanding your decision-making process with money is key to growing your net worth and improving your financial situation.

Increasing Your Aliveness

Decisions are such a vital part of your aliveness, your creativity, your *you-ness*. Decisions are the rudder with which you navigate the waters of life. Your power as a human being comes from your decision-making capacity. Don't give up this precious birthright out of fear. Fear and power are not contradictions. Courage is not the absence of fear. As we began to explore in Key One, you can feel the fear and do it anyway. When in doubt about whether something is right for you in life, use aliveness as a yardstick. If that thing, person, or situation increases your aliveness, you are on the right track. (If you're not sure, try vividly imagining it and check the reaction in your system.) If, on the other hand, some part of you shuts down around it, head the other way.

The Choice No One Can Take Away

Victor Frankel, the Nazi concentration camp survivor turned philosopher, and author of *Man's Search for Meaning*, makes an eloquent case for the power of choosing our attitudes. He discovered that when everything else was taken away from a person—when apparently there were no choices left to be made—there was one choice that could never be taken away. This was *the choice of one's attitude*. Frankel noticed that those who recognized and acted on this fact were able to survive through sheer force of will, while those who clung to their (albeit understandable) view of themselves as victims, perished. The difference was one of choice—those who harnessed the power of that choice, not only maintained a sense of dignity against all odds, but were, indeed, far more likely to survive.

Where in your life do you cling to the victim position? Although this may feel hard to admit to yourself and accept now, it will be a giant step forward in your transformation. Consider this: clinging to your story, your belief, and your old baggage is what has imprisoned you. Are you willing to let it go? You have the power of choice yourself to do that—right now.

Are you waiting for a miracle? The only miracle is you. It begins when you empower yourself by stepping into choice—choosing to create your life the way you want it to be. To wait for something to come from outside you is to *dis*empower yourself. Give yourself the miracle you've been waiting for. Give yourself you. Each time you make a conscious decision, you further empower yourself.

8

HARNESS THE POWER OF CHOICE

EXERCISES

Exercise A: What You Want

With your newly expanded power to choose, make an expanded list of what *you* want. Include what you want from this book as well.

Do it spontaneously and see what arises. Mix the little and big in random order as they leap to mind. Start each item on the list with the words "I want." Say each out loud.

Start to enjoy and bask in your newly harnessed power to choose.

I want _____

I want _____

I want _____

I want _____

I want _____

I want _____

I want _____

I want _____

I want _____

Exercise B: Uncovering Your Life Purpose

Write your life's purpose. Do it as an "I AM" statement, in the present tense positive. Use this format:

"I am a _____, _____, and _____ (woman, man, person, spirit, being [pick the one that resonates]) who_____

_____."

To help you do this, start with four lists:

1. A list of adjectives which describe you in a way that helps you feel your most expansive. Check that they are true and an expression of who you are and always have been.

8

HARNESS THE POWER OF CHOICE

2. A list of the activities which you find the most uplifting and inspiring.
3. The way in which you interface with the world.
4. The ways in which you give back.

Here is Cia's purpose as an example:

Part one: **I am a** passionate, unique, daring, and creative woman. *(Cia picked four out of a long list of adjectives asking herself, if it were not for this, would she no longer be her?)*

Part two: Who **sings** *(She picked an activity that truly inspires her)*

Part three: the **praises of life** in all its glory *(a way she interfaces with the world)*

Part four: and **teaches others to do the same**. *(the way in which she gives back)*

So, Cia's purpose statement reads, "I am a passionate, unique, daring, and creative woman who sings the praises of life in all its glory and teaches others to do the same."

A purpose is not something you create. It is something you discover. You were born with it. Similar to Michelangelo's remark in Key One about chipping away the stone to find the sculpture hidden within, you are chipping away layers of conditioning, trauma, resistance, and belief systems to find out who you already are. If in doubt, ask yourself what you were like as a child. Can you find some of those qualities and delights still buried within you? Can you trace the thread that has been the continuity of that essence? You have found your Purpose.

Exercise C: Exercising the Five Strategies for Decision-Making

Refer to the Five Strategies for Decision-Making in this Key. Which of these strategies seems more familiar to you? Which would you like to start to implement more?

Experiment with some of the others. On major decisions, try using them all.

Visualization – Your Power to Magnetize

What if you truly believed you had the power to draw into yourself what it is you want? You now understand that you get what you focus on and you often have to believe it first to then see it. Now, equipped with that awareness, visualize yourself as a magnet. Again, when we say "visualize" it is more than just the sense of vision we want you to use. Get an actual sensation. Imagine a coil of energy at the very core of your being. See it in your mind's eye and feel it growing more potent. This is a part of you. This is creating a magnetic energy field around you to which you can see yourself drawing in what it is you want in life. This Key is called *Harness the POWER of Choice*. This is your chance to truly sense this power within you.

Conscious Breathing

Remember the power you generated in the Visualization exercise above. This time, with each in-breath, imagine breathing in abundance, aliveness, energy, wealth, pleasure, joy, play, sexuality or whatever it is that you want more of in your life. Allow yourself to get the actual feeling of being filled with the things you choose to imagine. With each out-breath loudly exclaim "YES!" extending your arms and fists up toward the ceiling. As you do so you are affirming for yourself your right to have whatever it is you have chosen to breathe in. (*Note*: Make your "Yessssss" a long one to prevent the exhale from becoming too rapid and hyperventilation occurring. Take your time with the exercise. If you feel lightheaded, enjoy it and gradually bring your breathing back to normal). Enjoy the feeling of saying "YES!" to that which you genuinely want.

Body-Centered Statements

1. I choose _____
   ___ and I feel joy whenever I think about it.
2. I trust in the flow of the universe, knowing that ultimately whatever

choice I make is not a matter of life and death, or of wealth or poverty, as it is a movement forward.

3.   I am strengthened and empowered by my choices.
4.   I choose to own my money.

Journal Joggers

Use the following questions to lead you into your journal entries for this Key.

What decision have you been hesitating to make—financial or otherwise? What is it costing you to sit on the fence? When do you want to make the decision by? What inspiration do you have for making a clear powerful decision?

Choose a financial situation that happened this week. What did you want the outcome to be from this situation? Did you help the situation move towards the outcome you desired? If not, what did you do to stop it? If the situation did turn out the way you wanted, was it because you helped it to move in that direction? Did you use a type of behavior that you can repeat in future situations?

Pick another situation that happened this week and caused you to react to someone's behavior. Were you able to accept the situation? What about the situation made you want to choose or reject it? Were you able to choose how you felt about the situation?

Our two greatest gifts are time and the freedom to choose—the power to direct our efforts in the use of that time.

—STEPHEN R. COVEY

KEY NINE

COMMIT AND FOLLOW THROUGH

Obstacles are things a person sees when he takes his eyes off his goal.
—E. Joseph Cossman

I t was ten years ago and Belinda was sitting at her dining room table about to burst into tears. She was feeling ashamed, embarrassed, and completely overwhelmed. When Belinda took over the family money management after her father had a stroke a few years before, she had no idea she would need 10 bank accounts to manage the cash flow. It was so much more challenging than she ever imagined, especially amidst the rest of her busy life. In addition, Belinda's corporate auditing role required her to be travelling to clients 4–5 days a week (often out of town), with a bit of down time on the weekends when she would visit her father at the nursing home. She had let the bills and statements pile up for her, her house, and her father. Belinda became especially agitated and afraid that she would inadvertently fall behind on payments for her house and risk losing her house or ruining her great credit. In her mind, she was risking her father being forced out of the nursing home and put on the street for non-payment. These fears had started to keep her

COMMIT AND FOLLOW THROUGH

up at night and had brought her to this fall day in October, unsure how she could possibly move forward.

In a moment of clarity, Belinda realized that she was bigger (mentally and emotionally) than these three huge stacks of mail and, although they towered over her when she sat down, that she could in fact stand up and reach out for help. She swallowed her pride, called her friend Annette, and said, "Annette, I need your help. I have let my mail pile up and now I am paralyzed on what to do. I am so embarrassed and afraid. Would you . . . be willing to come over this weekend and help me go through the mail and pay our bills?" There was silence on the line and Belinda held her breath. Annette enthusiastically replied, "Sure, no problem. I'd be happy to help you. How's Saturday 2 p.m.?" Again, silence on the line as Belinda was stunned. She mustered, "Uhhh . . . ok. That sounds good. See you Saturday." Annette said, "Great! Bye!" and the phone call was over.

It was in those few moments that Belinda realized that she could be financially independent while not doing it all herself, she was more powerful not less powerful asking for the help, and she could own her own money not feel owned by it. Now she affectionately calls herself a *recovering avoider* and has viscerally realized the importance of commitment and follow-through.

This Key is about taking what you have learned so far and supporting you to bring it out into the world. This will serve as the key action opportunity of our program.

This Key is, in effect, the culmination of the last eight. In Key One *Be Willing to Change* we spoke about INSPIRATION. Keys Five through Seven were intended to create your personal sense of EMPOWERMENT. Key Eight *Harness the Power of Choice* gave you important tips on DECISION making in your life. Here, we will discuss the powerful impact of making clear agreements with yourself and others, and the final step of Acting from that inspiration, sense of empowerment, and the decisions you have made in the last Key.

The I.D.E.A. system below (adapted from © Own Your Money LLC), visually represents one way the key concepts we have just mentioned work together.

the I.D.E.A. system™

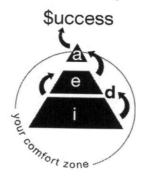

i = inspiration   d = decision   e = empowerment   a = action

Think of what we have covered as a triangle surrounded by a circle, with that circle representing your comfort zone (or your un-comfort zone). Here is a description of each stage:

Inspiration

The base of our triangle consists of INSPIRATION—your motivation and your full willingness to change. Inspiration creates motivation—while motivation helps fuel inspiration—and actually helps move you. The more grounded you are in a solid purposeful inspiration, the more intentional you will be about taking the risks and actions necessary to move you forward. This brings your whole being into alignment. Re-connect with your identified Inspirations and Intentions in Key One.

As a reminder, your inspiration cannot be laden with what you *should* want for yourself. Your true inspiration is a clear authentic representation of who you are and what you are creating in the world. It serves to ground all of your future activities.

Think about an activity in your life that you made a decision to do. Before you were able to make the decision, you were grounded, perhaps unconsciously, in an inspiration. We are now bringing a new awareness to

9

COMMIT AND FOLLOW THROUGH

your process and adding intentionality to it, so that your Action Process becomes smoother, smarter, and easier.

Decision

Once you make a decision, the universe conspires to make it happen.

—Ralph Waldo Emerson

After you are clear on your Inspiration, you then make a clear choice—a DECISION—to move your life in the direction you want. You created that decision through your transformation to claim responsibility, accept what is, and harness your power of choice. Although we have focused on your ability to make the decision to truly *own your money*, you can use this process and system for any major decision and action you want to be making in your life.

Remember the analogy from Key Two of the owner and the renter? The owner is in the powerful position of making clear and assertive decisions in life and following through on them—living smart and strong with her/his money. The renter goes along for the ride, blaming, complaining, and justifying why she doesn't have what she wants. At this stage in the I.D.E.A. system, you are making a decision to leave behind the renter mentality once and for all and instead opt in as the owner of your own life in general, and, very specifically, of your money.

Empowerment

That decision reinforces your sense of EMPOWERMENT. Empowerment is the place where you gather your internal resources and galvanize your energy into action, like priming the springboard or diving board for your high dive or for something that gives you a lift. Empowerment recognizes the combination of strengthening your boundaries so that you have enough internal energy, appreciating yourself through self-love, and being able to support that recognition through positive self-talk (Keys Five, Six, and Seven). Choose to view yourself, and live your life, from the authentic inside out rather than the outside in. It feels so much better. It is your time to appreciate your unique contribution to the world. Once you clarify who you are to yourself and to the world, you open yourself up to a greater sense of joy and fulfillment.

Action!

You can then use that sense of power to take the ACTION which will bring you your desired results. You commit yourself fully and you follow through. It's wonderful that we have all the Keys and yet, if we do not use them and take action, what is their real value? So notice whether, after you've worked through the previous Keys, you are now ready to make a commitment to yourself. One of the major reasons you may not have the results you want is because you haven't yet committed to and taken the actions to get the outcome you say you want.

Your decisions and actions don't have to be huge commitments. In fact, we would rather them not be, especially to start. We call these "baby steps for grown-ups." A series of small steps lead to big actions, which otherwise might feel overwhelming. Oftentimes, you may not take any steps, because completion feels so monumental that you just turn away and don't start at all. The power in the baby steps is that it makes large tasks very manageable. What big task is looming for you to handle in your life, and especially in your finances, where you could be employing the "baby steps for grown-ups" approach and then actually accomplish it?

Make small commitments in moving forward in the activities you need to do to upgrade your self-worth and net worth so that they feel manageable. Complete the exercises for each Key as a start. The idea is to gradually build your commitment-keeping muscle and strengthen your faith and your trust in yourself. For an extreme example, "I'm going to commit to putting my right foot in front of my left foot. Okay, I did that. Now I'm going to commit to putting my left foot in front of my right. Okay, I did that." Really get it down to the bare basics so that you can start building a sense of trust in yourself.

9

COMMIT AND FOLLOW THROUGH

Your Comfort Zone

Your COMFORT ZONE is represented by the circle in the diagram. This is an essential part of understanding how the I.D.E.A. system functions. These inspired decisions and empowered actions then serve to move you through and expand your Comfort Zone. Note in the diagram how "a" (for *action*) lifts through the circle representing your comfort zone to lead you to the success, financial and otherwise, available to you.

Each action you take creates a new behavior and soon a new way of being that includes this new action. For instance, if you are not used to paying your bills online, the first time you log in to your online account and send your first payment may feel scary and uncomfortable. You are motivated, though, as you know this will save you time and energy as an alternative to manually paying your bills. Your motivation moved you through the I.D.E.A. system to even log in the first time. By the second bill you pay successfully online, you are feeling more comfortable and even proud of yourself for moving through your fears and out of your comfort zone. After three months of paying your bills online, you may now be sharing your success with friends and calling vendors to see if you can pay their bills online too!

In studying the diagram, notice your areas of strength and weakness. If you notice that most of your challenges fall under inspiration/intention, for example, review Key One. For challenges with decisions, review Keys Two through Four as well as Eight. If your problem area lies with empowerment, review Keys Five–Seven. For difficulties with taking action, you are in the right place!

As we described in the previous Key Eight, your purpose in life, like our I.D.E.A. system triangle, actually has four parts to it: 1) who you are (your inspiration); 2) what you do with who you are (a decision); 3) the interface between you and others (where you bring your empowerment into action); and 4) how you take that out into the world and give back (your ultimate action).

Now is the time to galvanize yourself into Action. However, at this point, you may be wondering "How?" Or, you may be thinking of reasons why taking action may be a problem for you. This is a frequent response, as often people are conditioned to resist, since that would require change. You may then use reasons as stall tactics, which is really negative self-talk. The truth is that you can choose to have *reasons* why you can't do something or *results* of what you did. More reasons keep you more reasonable, and not getting what you want. They are often mutually exclusive, so, now knowing this, you can decide which you want—results or reasons. Just as in Key One, we highlighted that you may have found yourself choosing to be comfortable and unhappy rather than a little uncomfortable and truly happy. Now is your chance to be a little unreasonable and a little uncomfortable and truly happy and get the results you desire.

To ease this action process for you, we have an additional technique to support you. The A.C.T. technique is composed of the following three steps:

A. ADD STATURE TO YOUR SENSE OF SELF. This is about You. It expands on your sense of self and who you are.

C. CHOOSE A PASSIONATE POINT OF VIEW. This is how you demonstrate who you are, by showing up as passionate about what you do.

T. TAKE IT OUT INTO THE WORLD. This is about connecting with the larger community. How do you want to give back in a way that is in alignment with who you are and what you are passionate about?

Step One: "A"—ADD STATURE TO YOUR SENSE OF SELF

Little minds have little worries, big minds have no time for worries.
—Ralph Waldo Emerson

How big is your sense of self when measured against your problems? It is important that you, your dream, intention, and inspiration are bigger than your problems to avoid a sense of overwhelm or victimization. Are you willing to expand fully into your true sense of self? Are you willing to take ownership of your life and your money? When you keep yourself small, it often seems like everything is a problem because proportionately the problems outweigh your inspiration, motivation, and vision.

For example, if your inspiration, intention, and spending (or lack thereof) is based on the habitual, smaller version of you, you may want to create a façade to protect your own insecurity. You may have found yourself striving to "keep up with the Joneses." Yet in many cases, the Joneses can't even keep up paying for their own lifestyle, especially in challenging economic times. This façade may manifest itself as something as simple as wanting new clothes or a fancy car. Or your fear may get the better of you in other ways and you may hide your gifts, or focus excessively on safety—poor substitutes for the real confidence that comes from living your life fully. In either case, you are essentially feeding your insecurity, rather than expanding who you are and what you truly want in the full confidence of that knowing.

When you act from the scared "little you," choices you make are more likely to be short-term and may S.T.I.N.G. you down the road. S.T.I.N.G. is an anagram for "Short-Term Immediate Need Gratification." Practice learning and enjoying the art of delayed gratification. It is not the opposite of living in the moment—it is recognizing that desire can be pleasurable in itself once you train yourself to rise above the base instinct that says you need to get rid of the desire by fulfilling it immediately.

Step Two: "C"—CHOOSE A PASSIONATE POINT OF VIEW

The happiness of a man in this life does not consist in the absence but in the mastery of his passions.

—Alfred Lord Tennyson

How do you take your new-found security in your true sense of self, rather than a façade or bravado as a compensating mechanism, and embody it through your actions? Remember back to Key Six on "Transform Your Self Talk" that you have the capacity to change your thoughts and beliefs and *choose* the ones that serve you. We are suggesting that you choose to live more fully. You started by expanding your sense of self—adding stature and depth—and then embodying it. Now we ask you to connect with this expanded viewpoint in the world—connecting to your inspiration, dreams, goals, and passion. As you take these to a higher level, your passion will begin to stretch and become integral to how and who you are. Like the apt expression, "put your money where your mouth is," we are asking you to invest in your passions—in what you truly want in your life. Investment is not only in money. It is in time, focus, and the act of stepping into that vision. Genuinely living from that passion will enable you to be *irresistible* and bring your skills, products, and services to the world in a way that has people wanting whatever you are offering.

A helpful analogy is to consider life as a game that you are playing. (Note: This is not to be confused with game playing, such as where you are inauthentic by having someone jump through hoops or do something unnecessary to test them, which we do not condone.) Take a moment now to consider how big a game you are playing. Are you playing a game that is tiny, where everything that happens feels like the sky is falling and is more evidence why you can't have the life and money you want? Or are you playing at the level of a Gandhi, where he was willing to put his own life and well-being on the line for his country and for humanity? You are likely somewhere in the middle. Considering life as a game will provide you additional insights as to where you are on the spectrum, and how you can start to add stature to your sense of self to expand and grow yourself. Are you "on the field" (living your life filled with the passion, abundance, and joy you are meant to live) or "sitting on the sidelines" (allowing opportunities to pass you by as you avoid risk and play it safe)?

Step Three: "T"—TAKE IT OUT INTO THE WORLD

Once you notice your capacity to choose your point of view—to show up in the world as who you truly are—it is time to expand your paradigm even further. How do you connect with the larger community, which may start as small as your own family and/or grow as big as the global community itself? Keeping yourself small and not taking your gifts out into the world is doing both yourself and your community a huge disservice. To provide you two

9

COMMIT AND FOLLOW THROUGH

examples, this applies whether you are a single person and not sharing yourself with other possible single partners, or if you own a business and you are not promoting your services or products to your community. This may be quite a paradigm shift for you—to consider yourself selfish for staying small and being generous by bringing yourself and your gifts out in the world.

If you have a family, you might start with considering the impact that having money might have for your children's education or to care for your family. Taking it to even a higher level, how can you use money to enhance the community that you care about, and even help make the world a better place for all to enjoy?

It is important to have desires, a sense of purpose, and intentions at each level. When you only set intentions at a personal level you are playing small in your life. The risks that you are willing to take are likely to be correspondingly small. If you set your intentions only on a community or global level, they may seem so big and far off that you may not actually or emotionally connect with the intention. Creating intentions that move and inspire you at *each* of these three levels solves this challenge and brings more joy into your life, thus allowing you to go even deeper than the original three levels of inspiration discussed early in this *Self-Worth to Net Worth* journey.

Just as you connected with your Inspiration in Key One early and often, connect with your A.C.T. early and often. This is where you will require the commitment and follow-through. Read them out loud to yourself every day: "I **A**dd stature to my sense of self. I **C**hoose a passionate point of view. I **T**ake it out into the World." Do this in front of a mirror whenever you can. Observe your body language. Feel your feelings. Notice how you grow into it day-by-day until they become an extension of who you are. Please review Appendix I on Body-centered Statements to help you do this in a way that stretches and embodies your commitments.

Making and Keeping Agreements

Let's look at another vital "A" word—Agreement. If you are not keeping agreements in your life, your life is out of balance. It's dysfunctional. Your level of commitment and follow-through has a very direct bearing on whether or not your life is working. Check in honestly with yourself. Are you in integrity with yourself and others, or is there an area of your life where you are out of alignment? It may be something as simple as showing up on time. If your life is not working, there is a very strong likelihood that, if you are honest with yourself, you could trace it back to a broken agreement with yourself or another.

Do you keep your word, i.e., do what you say you are going to do, to yourself? To others? Often you may find yourself more likely to keep a commitment to others than to yourself. This is part of why coaching can be so valuable, as you have someone else who can support your progress and hold you accountable to what you say you want and will do. (If you are interested in coaching, refer to Cia's website at www.Live-Life.com for life coaching and Belinda's website www.OwnYourMoney.com for money management, mindset, and business coaching.)

Now, look at your level of commitment and follow-through when it comes to money. Where have you been in integrity and where have you been out of integrity? This is not an additional chance to be hard on yourself. It is another check-in of WHAT IS as it relates to your commitment to financial responsibilities. Being out of integrity with your finances can demonstrate itself by your breaking agreements with yourself or another whether in not taking actions that will support your prosperity or in spending more than you have, for example. The United States of America, along with many world economies, runs on significant debt (essentially out of integrity) and the system is set up for you to do the same. Much like the government, some people's debts actually outweigh their assets. That is a life out of balance, thus out of integrity and lacking in wholeness.

As you begin to notice your ability to take action and manifest (attract what you focus on) working in your life, your sense of inspiration, possibility, and potential can begin to grow. Remember you can use gratitude as a tool for noticing what it is you like and grow your clarity about what you want more of. Acknowledge yourself for everything you have created, even if some of it isn't positive, because you created it unconsciously. Just think—if you created all that unconsciously, what will you be able to do now that you are applying consciousness? Allow your mind and heart to expand to imagine what could be possible with this new consciousness about your life, your worth, and your wealth. If you can see what you have created in the past without judgment, you can further empower yourself to make that process of creation more conscious.

Clarifying Your Commitments

There is a certain sense of freedom awaiting you as you clarify your commitments. No longer do you have to get caught up in the default busyness of life, wondering what to be doing and where to be spending your time or money. Once you have gotten clear on what you want to be committed to in your life, and the related actions you want to be taking, you can relax into the path and alignment of your life.

If you are struggling connecting with that path and your commitments, consider meditation. Meditation is also a powerful way to gain clarity in your life. As you let the busyness of your mind fall away to the point that you can watch your thoughts as they arise, it will become clearer to you what percentage of your thoughts are serving you, and what kind of thoughts it is now time to release. Eventually you will be able to take the sitting practice of meditation into your day, through the practice of *mindfulness*, or keen awareness. You began this new practice in Key Six, and can now expand it to include mindfulness of your actions as well as your self-talk. This mindfulness can then be carried into your entire life, so you can become more mindful about your money, your time, your purpose, your path, and your actions.

Reclaiming the Meaning of *Commitment*

You may be so habituated to making commitments that you don't keep, that the meaning behind the word *commitment* has evaporated. If you're making agreements with yourself or others and not keeping them, you are actually eroding your trust in yourself. That's insidious and toxic. By so doing, you are disempowering yourself and hampering your ability to act. When you don't trust yourself, you just give up. You may consider a better approach to money management and then say to yourself, "What's the use? I'm not going to do any of this, so I might as well not even commit. The last three times I promised myself I was going to start tracking where my money goes, I did nothing. So it's no use."

So whatever you do, do not let yourself down. Build that faith in yourself. That faith is going to go a long way. Don't make promises to yourself that you won't keep. If you tell yourself, "I'm going to save money this month and not buy any clothes," and then you go out and buy yourself a blouse (even if it is on sale), you've broken a promise. And then the next time you say, "I'm not going to buy any clothes this month," a part of you says, "Yeah, right, I've heard that a million times." As you stop believing yourself, it snowballs. You lose more and more power over your sense of commitment. So be very careful what you tell yourself and other people. Start small. Practice. Practice really keeping your agreements. Make a tiny commitment to yourself and follow though. Be meticulous about keeping agreements with yourself and others.

If the agreements you have made are too much for you, acknowledge and tell the truth about that. Overwhelm comes from two sources: Either you are taking on too much all at once and your goals are unrealistic or you are taking on too many of the details. With this new understanding, how can you instead make agreements that are do-able and keep you out of overwhelm? If you are not keeping your agreements, you are not taking responsibility for yourself.

Key to Relationships

Making and keeping agreements is a very important tool in any relationship, including your relationship with yourself. The agreements you make and how you keep them are a measure of your integrity and the health of your relationship with yourself and others. Keeping agreements is a way of honoring yourself and the other people you care about. Even the way you handle an agreement with a stranger impacts your self-image. Are your actions reflective of your values? This is a very important question to live with. Once you make a commitment, take action. Take that step that

COMMIT AND FOLLOW THROUGH

9

brings you just a bit closer to what it is that you want and how you want your life to look and feel—to be all of who you want to be.

Throughout this book, you have been learning tools to have a more powerful conversation about money with your partner. The next step is an understanding of how essential it is that you follow through on the commitments that you have made to each other. With one of Belinda's client couples, Melissa and Jack, Jack was resisting sharing the financial responsibilities with Melissa because he did not trust her to stay on track and follow through with what she was promising she would do. In the past, he had asked her to write down what checks she had written from their shared account, and she did not complete this task consistently. Ironically, when he shared his lack of trust in her follow-through during a coaching session, she agreed with him and also did not trust herself to complete the task. Once Belinda could shed light on their mutual lack of trust in her ability to keep commitments, and removed her block in completing them in the first place, Melissa stepped up to be a new valuable member of their family's financial team and actually enjoyed helping to manage their family finances.

This situation is quite universal as one partner will often maintain all of the financial record-keeping. Having a family Chief Financial Officer ("CFO") of sorts is inherently not a problem, as long as the other partner continues to be involved and is an integral part of the family finance team. It does become a problem though when one partner does not trust the other or simply doesn't want to ask their partner to take on additional commitments. If you are in a relationship, consider how you can create a strong team together in completing the commitments. You can bring a *united front* so that all major decisions are made by the team and both members can feel confident and money smart.

Financial *independence* does not mean you have to do it alone; on the contrary, becoming a team brings you the connectedness you actually desire. And whether you have a partner or you are single, your *team* can include your accountant, financial advisor, coach (financial, business/career/ executive, life, clutter-clearing, or image consultant), banker, mortgage specialist, attorney (especially for estate planning/family law), realtor, or other key person you trust to assist you in making your important financial decisions. It is also supportive if you view your life partner, business partner if applicable, friends, and family on your team as well.

Take Inventory and Start Completing

Take an inventory of the agreements in your life, both spoken and unspoken. (See the exercises at the end of this Key.) Start with those agreements impacting your self-worth and your net worth. Highlight those items on the list that have not been kept. If nothing leaps to mind, ask yourself what areas of your life are not working. If you look honestly and closely at those areas (of your financial well-being) which are not working, you will find a broken agreement with yourself or another at the core of it.

Once you have your list of unkept agreements, write down the steps you will take in order to clean up these agreements, and commit to a date you will do them by. Decide how you want to remake the agreement if necessary, add any new commitments that will serve you, determine which you are sure you will keep, and only commit to those new agreements. If you've made a bad agreement that wasn't healthy for you, that's okay. You can change it. But changing it through conscious acknowledgment has a very different effect on your system than just ignoring it. Make amends, if appropriate, for your error in making the agreement.

Along with cleaning up unkept agreements, make a list of all of the bits and pieces in your life that are incomplete or anything else that needs to be completed in your life. Some may be projects you have been meaning to get to for years. Some may just be light bulbs you have meant to change. We realize this may be a long list. Each one of these things is holding important space in your life now.

Ask yourself, "Are these items really that important?" If they were, would you not have completed them by now? Is it time to let the *should* of completing them go, or to make an actual commitment to complete them? Cross off the ones that you are making a conscious choice to not complete (at least for the foreseeable future) and release the nagging *should* you feel when you see this project. Then, highlight three items to get started with and add dates for each by when you want the item actually completed by.

9

COMMIT AND FOLLOW THROUGH

Consider setting aside one full weekend day to complete these priority items. Although at first this may seem daunting, completions make space for the new and free up energy. They are one of the most powerful ways to open a space for manifestation. You *need* completions in order to move on. Moving through this seeming intimidating or frightening task of completing these items will remove the distractions of the incompletions so you can enjoy the huge relief and greater presence awaiting you.

Next, look at the areas of your life in which you feel stuck. Ask yourself what you need to complete in order to be able to freely embrace the new. It might mean clearing up an old grievance or debt. It might mean running your credit report or reconciling your bank balance. It might mean forgiving yourself or someone else. It might mean doing what you said you would do at work. It might mean cleaning your desk or closet to metaphorically and literally make space for the new.

Your heart knows exactly what's needed. When it's done, a door opens. Organize your life in such a way that everything around you reflects back to you who you are. In the next Key, we will further explore letting go as a form of completion and provide you tools for embracing the letting go process to achieve your completions and commitments.

Every moment is an opportunity to recommit. We're asking you to consciously and continuously recommit to being in integrity with yourself and your financial life. You are making commitments all the time. Make them as conscious as possible. Practice being aware. Engage your power and enjoy your new sense of peace arising as you honor your commitments. This is true freedom—and essential to your financial freedom!

9

COMMIT AND FOLLOW THROUGH

EXERCISES

Exercise A: Commitments and Agreements

Use the chart below to answer these questions:

1. What are the areas of my life, especially my financial life, which are not working? (Recall these areas addressed in the WHAT IS of your life: Financial, Business/Career, Recreation/Fun/Travel, Health/Fitness, Relationships/Family, Personal/Spiritual, and Contribution/Making a difference.)

2. What agreements with myself and others have not been kept in each of these areas?

3. Are you willing to step into integrity and create completion in order to get these areas of your life working and move on? If so, make a written commitment here to speak to the person or people you had an agreement with, whether written, verbally explicit, or implicit, and acknowledge that the agreement hasn't been kept. Include credit agreements as well as debit agreements (if someone owes *you* something). If the agreement was with yourself, commit to a ritual acknowledgement with yourself. You could write yourself a letter, perform a small ceremony, or meditate on the importance of building trust in yourself by keeping your agreements with yourself. Commit to a specific date or time by which you will make this acknowledgement.

4. For each un-kept agreement which you are acknowledging, indicate which course of action you choose: 1) Remake the agreement; 2) Modify the agreement (state how); or 3) Consciously break the agreement. (If you choose number 3, acknowledge to the applicable party or parties that you made the agreement in error, and you will not be able to keep it and still stay in integrity with yourself. Then find and agree upon an appropriate way to make amends or restitution.)

5. State clearly any new commitments you are willing to make with yourself or to others to get these areas of your life working better.

Areas of my life which are not working	Agreements which have not been kept (with self or others)	I will speak to _____ (name) by _____ (date)	I chose to: 1. Remake it 2. Modify it 3. Consciously break it	I commit to:

Exercise B

Part I: Using Back-planning

Refer back to Exercise C in Key One. What were the three most significant intentions/inspirations you selected?

1.
2.
3.

Have they changed? If so, replace them with new ones. If not, use those intentions to complete this exercise. Determine where you want to be with each intention 12 months from today. (We have used 12 months in this exercise and example. You can adjust to a time frame which feels more appropriate for that intention. Whether it is one month or five years, you can use this process.)

Write down the specific date twelve months from today and describe in vivid detail where you will be at that point in time. Connect with these visualizations and with your journaling about this state that you completed in the Journal Joggers section of Key One. Using the exercise format below will support your process.

Date 12-months from today: _____

Status 12-months from today for each Intention:

1.

2.

3.

Now turn around and think about where you will need to be at interim milestones between today and the date in twelve months. For instance, what is the state of completion at nine months? At six months? At three months? At one month? The state of each of these will drive the successful actualization of your desired twelve-month intention. Frequently, people never get started because they can't jump directly from today to twelve months from today. By using this approach, you create your milestones along the way and live into them, starting with the end in mind.

Interim Steps Required To Realize Your Intentions

Using the following suggested time frames (or creating your own), write a series of interim intentions for each of your one-year intentions:

1. 9-months:
    6-months:
    3-months:
    1-month:
2. 9-months:
    6-months:
    3-months:
    1-month:
3. 9-months:

COMMIT AND FOLLOW THROUGH

9

6-months:
3-months:
1-month:

For example, if you would like to have $3,300 saved in 12 months (and today is 1/1/12), then your bank-planning could look like this:

12-month goal (1/1/13): Save $3,300 additional in the bank. Celebrate achieved goal!

9-months (10/1/12): Have $2,400 in new bank account. Continue tracking Cash Flow and staying aware of where money flowing each month.

6-months (7/1/12): Have $1,800 in new bank account. Re-do Cash Flow exercise in Key Five and review for additional possibilities of saving. Re-listen or re-read products purchased.

3-months (4/1/12): Have $600 in new bank account. Update the Cash Flow exercise in Key Five and review for additional amounts of money that can be made or saved each month. Go to www.OwnYourMoneyStore.com for additional resources to help support your spending better and saving more efforts through focused, directed, and easy-to-implement high-payoff tips.

1-month (2/1/12): Open a separate bank account to accumulate your savings. Maximize your interest rate using an on-line bank. Complete the Cash Flow exercise in Key Five and find another $300 that you can be keeping each month (whether from increasing your income or decreasing your expenses). Make the calls necessary or put the additional tracking/controls into place to make the $300 saving per month a reality.

Part II: Stepping Stones

Using what you have come up with in the above exercise, we would now like you to make it a body-centered experience. Take a number of blank sheets of plain paper (recycled with the blank side up is fine). Put the date and a short note about where you will be on the furthest one (12 months for example) and then do the same for each of your interim dates. Now lay them out in front of you as a pathway of stepping stones. Slowly and deliberately walk the path, pausing on each piece of paper and doing a full-bodied visualization to imagine where you are and how it feels to be there.

Really allowing yourself to feel the feelings in your body helps make this real and to fruition. Once you reach your final intention, stand powerfully in the full sensation of being there. Allow yourself to celebrate ownership of that accomplishment.

Exercise C: Determining Your Unconscious Agreements

Now it is time to take a look at any unconscious agreements in your life which keep you stuck in old patterns which no longer serve your worth, your wealth, or your dreams.

Write a list of any *unconscious* agreements you have in your life, particularly pertaining to your self-worth and net worth.

Some examples: Do you have an unconscious agreement with a parent, whether that parent is living or not, that you will not outdo them in some way—whether it's how much money you make, or how you manage that income? Do you have an unconscious agreement with someone to make yourself less than they are, or to give in to someone else's will or point of view? Did you have a certain role in your family of origin that you keep replaying in your life? Are you down-playing or avoiding success from an unconscious belief that you will otherwise lose your friends? Maybe you have an unconscious agreement with someone you work with or someone at home to keep messing up or playing the victim role so that he or she can play the rescuer.

Were you ever wrongly accused of something in your life that you went ahead and took the blame for, thereby creating an unconscious agreement to punish yourself for the rest of your life? Examples of the typical things of which you may have been accused are: being a burden, stealing love that belonged to someone else such as a sibling, abandonment, disloyalty, or being just plain bad.

Run through the list of people who have or have had an influence on you in your life and see if you can think of any unconscious agreements you have with them. To jog your thoughts, here are a list of people or parties with whom you may have some unconscious agreements: mother, father, grandparents, siblings, a teacher or coach, spouse or ex-spouse, children, co-workers, boss or employees, higher authority or God, organizations or government, your family system, friends. Just like you did with feeling the weight of your childhood messages in Key Six, become aware of the cost of these agreements and journal about that. Who might you be without the constraints of these unconscious agreements? Are you willing to break the agreements that hold you back, and keep you from your full potential? If the answer is yes, proceed to the Visualization exercise below.

Visualization – Breaking Your Unconscious Agreements

As with all our visualization exercises, begin by relaxing, taking some deep breaths, and feeling the feelings in your body, which is where they live. Imagine that you are inviting together, all in one place, everyone with whom you have an unconscious agreement. You are calling this meeting with the conscious intention of officially breaking these agreements that are not actually serving you. Pick a place that feels supportive to you. Some people imagine a special table out in nature which everyone can sit down at. Some people visualize everyone standing on an open plain. Some of our clients like to visualize the meeting in a high-powered attorney's office. Take the time to clearly picture the scene in your mind's eye, and choose a location that feels both calm and empowering for you.

Once you have gathered all parties together, inform them that you are officially breaking your agreements with them. If there are only a few agreements, go through them one by one. If there are many, just make a blanket notification.

Feel your feelings as you do this. There may be some sadness, anger, fear, relief, or joy. Also, notice the reaction of these people as you notify them. Do they become angry, protest, cry, or try to stop you? Observe your reaction to their feelings. Feel your own feelings about their reactions. Breathe deeply to help you sit with and experience all these feelings.

Next, choose an action that feels like a powerful way to symbolize freeing yourself from these agreements. Let your imagination get very vivid and detailed. For example, see yourself cutting a cord between you and them, shredding or burning a document, untying yourself, or imagining yourself as a Maypole with rope wound around yourself and having the people move in the direction necessary to completely unwind these ropes.

Use whatever form your imagination wants to use to render these agreements no longer legal or binding.

When you finally feel free, take some time to savor that sensation. Feel the liberation and newfound ownership of your life. Imagine all you can accomplish now that you are free of these unconscious agreements that have been counterproductive to your wellbeing.

Stretch your body and feel it. What you do with it is up to you alone. As you begin to take better care of yourself, you will allow yourself to more easily fill with love and abundance. As you do, you will find that it is natural to serve others from a more truly generous or selfless place, rather than out of a sense of duty or *should*. The giving now is sourced from your own desire to genuinely serve.

If you need help with this exercise, you will find it on Cia's CD *Manifesting Abundance: Consciously Creating the Life You Want*.

Conscious Breathing

We have spoken about adding stature to your sense of self. Conscious breathing can help you do that. For this exercise, please stand in front of a mirror, preferably full-length. Stand erect with your feet shoulder width apart, your arms relaxed at your sides, and your knees unlocked (slightly bent). This is your power position. Let your eyes "soft-focus" so that you are seeing a general image rather than individual parts of yourself the way people tend to look in a mirror. With each deep inhalation, watch how your body physically expands. In your mind's eye, allow that expansion to increase.

Extend your arms out to your sides, loosely at first, gradually allowing them to reach further with each inhale. Feel your right to take up more space in the world—feel your power. At some point, you may wish to close your eyes. Play with the mental image and sensation until you can visualize an energy body that is larger than your physical body and imagine it getting larger and larger until you can picture it filling the room and perhaps even more. Take a sense memory photograph of the sensation, so that you can return to the memory of it anytime you want to feel large and in your power in the world.

9

COMMIT AND FOLLOW THROUGH

Body-Centered Statements

1. I acknowledge that today I committed to _____
_____ and followed through with it.
2. I am building trust in my capacity to honor my commitments that are serving me.
3. I feel strong, and in charge of my *financial* life as I honor my commitments, and each day I renew my commitment to integrity.
4. I feel strong, and in charge of my *entire* life as I honor my commitments, and each day I renew my commitment to integrity.

Journal Joggers

Use the following questions to lead you into your journal entries for this Key.

What agreement with yourself or someone else did you make in the past month that you did not keep? What is the feeling that you get inside as you think of not keeping the agreement? How would you like to feel?

What can you do right now to recreate this agreement in a way that feels good to you?

What agreements have you kept with yourself or others that feel good and give you energy (large or small), such as completing something that is important to you?

What is the feeling that you get inside as you appreciate your keeping your commitment and your word?

How would you feel if you kept your commitments every day—financial or otherwise?

Most people spend more time and energy going around problems than in trying to solve them.

—Henry Ford

9

COMMIT AND FOLLOW THROUGH

LET GO

When I let go of what I am,
I become what I might be.

—Lao Tzu

This Key is about letting go of your past identity related to abundance, money, and the things that stand in the way between you and having them, so you create the space for a new and more positive identity. We have a series of exercises in this Key to help you do this. You may have become comfortable with certain feelings which do not serve you, including possibly the shame or embarrassment about not dealing well with your finances. It might be a role or identity you picked up in your family of origin or a belief system you acquired from your parents or others. You have been exploring this concept of your identity throughout this journey, and specifically in Key Six as you gained a greater appreciation for your money personae and transformed your related self-talk. Now you will be able to consciously determine what you will keep and what you will let go of, so that what remains is what you want—both emotionally and physically.

Your Personal Identity with Money

You have your own personal identity when it comes to money. When in relationship with a family member or spouse, that identity is even harder to shake, because the polarity of the relationship reinforces your identity. Like the game of tug-of-war, the more the other person pulls to stay in his or her position, the more you want to stay put in yours. The disparity magnifies the difference in identities. We often unconsciously choose someone with a pattern opposite to our own with whom to be in relationship, like the old adage "opposites attract." Remember to claim responsibility for your choice in that area too.

Your identity with money may also be tied to how you view your career. Belinda needed to let go of her identity as an accountant, in order to create the space to see herself as an entrepreneur and financial empowerment expert and speaker. It was only through this letting go that she was able to realize her own true purpose. (At this point, you can also acknowledge yourself for getting this far in the process and shifting your beliefs along the way.) This letting go step includes the conscious letting go of the fundamental non-supportive beliefs that do not serve you but have become a part of your energy, including "I am not good with numbers or math." "I do not charge what I am worth." "I'm not good at sales."

Letting Go of Blame

It is all too easy to stay on the surface of blame instead of looking at what is underneath, especially in a relationship. For example, a couple Belinda worked with had never gotten along on the subject of money. Unfortunately, that was the identity they knew and related to. He blamed her for spending frivolously and not being a part of managing the family finances. She blamed him for being controlling, for paying bills late, being generally fiscally irresponsible, and for not keeping her in the loop.

After exploring the blame at a deeper level, we discovered that she had not forgiven him for a few statements he had said in anger several years before. Likewise, she didn't feel taken care of or adequately provided for, given what she was putting into the relationship. That was largely because she saw him as territorial about money, referring to what he earned while she was home caring for their children as "his money." On his part, he felt not heard, trusted, respected, or loved, and was deeply pained by his sense of her lack of trust. This lack of trust was a natural re-creation of what he had experienced early in life. All of these feelings and behaviors formed their combined identity related to money. Once brought to the surface, Belinda had a platform to start their new acceptance and appreciation for the role and identity that each had taken on.

In a relationship, the core of what is needed in order to turn the polarity around is respect, claiming responsibility, and communicating.

To be the most successful in relationships, it is important to be clear on your own identity, what you came into the relationship with, and any conscious or unconscious ways you may have contributed to what appears as conflict. Letting go of the old stories, baggage, and blame will help you start with a clean slate. If you are not willing to do that, you have sentenced your relationship to struggle and suffering.

Allow, So You Can Let Go

This giving up is not a repenting. It's a deep honoring of ourself.

—RUMI

The act of working through all of the previous Keys will churn up past inner material on how you view yourself in relation to your worth and your wealth, as well as in relation to other areas of your life. Old issues and unhealed wounds are likely to come to the surface. When that happens, allow the experience. Welcome it. Allow any accompanying feelings to surface. There may be some sadness. There may be some grieving that needs to be done. There may be some loss. There may be anger. There may be fear.

It's natural for all these things to come up because, remember, you are transforming yourself and transforming your life. Nothing will ever be the same again. So there is some loss. Even if you are letting go of things that are unpleasant, they have become part of your life and part of your identity.

They become part of how you see yourself. So you are really beginning to let go of a part of yourself. If you are not willing to let go, you can't move on.

Getting Caught by Attachment

Sometimes, ironically, what you need to let go of is your attachment to money itself. When you focus on money for money's sake, you lose sight of what it is you TRULY want in life. In India, there is a cautionary tale told about catching monkeys with bananas and coconuts. To trap a monkey, the hunter cuts a hole in the coconut and carefully inserts a banana. The monkey comes along and reaches in and grabs the banana. Of course, the monkey can't pull the banana out, and he won't let go. Thus, he is caught. *Likewise, when your focus and grasp is so tightly on what you have or don't have, you lose sight of the big picture of what is going on around you.* And thus you are caught in your own life. *You may be trying to keep up with the proverbial Joneses, or whatever it is that causes you to lose sight of your own true values.* You may still choose to rehash old losses and injustices. When you think your past connects you with your present, you may feel the need to hold onto it in order to stay alive. Actually, there is no relationship between the past and the present unless you make that relationship happen.

You may find yourself often getting in the habit of living a lifestyle that is close to or beyond your means. The more you make, the more you spend, and in the act of doing so, you lose sight of your own true identity. You lose sight of the fact that you may be getting in your own way in the failure to realize your true goals.

Choose Your Priorities

Overwhelmed? Great! What better time to decide what to let go of in your life. Most people have formed their priorities by default—which is to say, unconsciously. They may come from addictive patterns, such as workaholism, where you don't even realize that you are working to avoid something, but rather have unconsciously convinced yourself that work instead is the priority. These priorities-by-default may have come from observing and taking on the priorities of your parents or friends. They may be something you once *HAD* to do and have since fallen into a well-entrenched habit, instead of asking yourself if this is what you really want.

If you focus on it intently enough, you can probably have whatever you want in life. However, the reality it is important to face is that you can't have it ALL, and you certainly can't have it all at the same time. So, how will you choose to shape your priorities? Will you do it by default—taking the path of least resistance—or by choice—invoking your newfound empowerment, awareness of your right to choose, and renewed sense of who you are?

Fuzzy priorities make for a life of dis-ease, a life without true satisfaction and joy.

> *You can always find time to do what you want to do—if you're willing to give up something else. Life is a series of trade-offs.*
>
> —Barbara Hemphill

Jan Jasper, author of *Take Back Your Time*, says it beautifully: "Despite constant talk about how pressed everyone is for time, I contend that few people really live as if their time mattered. Most people spend more time planning their vacations than thinking about what they want to do with their lives. The way we use time is a combination of habit, the expectations of others, the influence of consumerism, and paralysis caused by too many choices. Few people use their time deliberately. We squander our time doing things because we have always done them, because other people do them or because we're 'supposed to' do them. We spend time buying more and more stuff, and then spend even more time maintaining all the stuff. This is a mistake—we can always get more stuff but *we can never get more time.* Once that really sinks in, it changes everything."

Letting Go of Never-ending To-Do Lists

Daily task lists can grow to become an extensive litany of *shoulds* for many people, until they become an overwhelming, never-ending list of items that could never actually all get done. They can add to a sense of stress and pressure with time and keep us away from living in the spontaneity of NOW. As you learn to loosen the grip of the artificial (and self-generated) pressure from these lists, you can differentiate them from clear intentional action steps that are possible to achieve during any given day. Even choosing only three to five items that you commit to completing each day could be an easy step and a huge win to help you manage your time and focus. Time management is actually focus and priority management.

Cia asked her client, Angela, a busy young mother of two, to stop making to-do lists because she had become a slave to her lists and had lost the spontaneity in life that she was capable of and which brought her joy. She was understandably frightened by the idea, for fear she would forget everything that was important. Despite her fear, she agreed to give it a try. Here are her reports on her homework assignment:

> "So today was day one of no to-do lists. It has gone well. I had some short anxious moments but moved through them with faith. I really "get" what you said to me. I want to be present and I want to trust that I will know what to do. So I have felt lighter and have been breathing more deeply today than I have in weeks. I also was able to spend the day with my husband running errands and we could joke about the lists. I told him that I needed his support in this, and when I feel crazy I may ask for a hug. He seemed supportive."

A week later she wrote:

> "I am accomplishing a lot today, with no lists. I know the goal is not necessarily to accomplish a lot. It is still nice to begin the trusting of myself. I have had a few moments of anxiousness and then I come back to trust. I also felt myself rushing through things and found I got a bit of a rush from it. I didn't change much, just acknowledged it."

Your self-talk may want to come up with a list of every reason in the book of why you can't do what you want. Many of those reasons have

10

LET GO

a strong basis in reality, such as a need to care for your children. But to what extent? For how long? Sometimes well-founded concerns (your stories) get blown out of proportion to satisfy your unacknowledged fears and self-limitation. If you are bound and determined to make excuses, at least take a careful look at those excuses—what is the *benefit* you are getting by not doing what you want? What does it let you avoid? Fear of failure is a common example. Once you have done this, make another list. This list is the list of things you are willing (not comfortable perhaps) to let go of. Once you have made this list, next to each one, write a commitment to yourself. Let that commitment include a specific "by when" and action step so that it is measurable. Each time you check one of those things off your list—celebrate! Write the completed item on a piece of paper and *burn it*, watching it go up in smoke. Doing this with a witness (having a friend or partner to do it with) makes it even more powerful.

Are you willing to lighten your load and let go of terminology such as can't, have-to, would've, could've, should've and should in your life? Just imagine how great you will feel once you have released the weight of that burden.

Living Now

Ask yourself what you truly want in life. If your answer is a specific dollar amount, ask yourself what you want that money for. If your answer is something like "to retire and spend a year on a sailboat," ask yourself what is the feeling you truly want from that. This process helps you source what you are truly searching for. As we interview people in this way, generally their bottom line turns out to be something like peace, free time, or a chance to do a particular activity because it brings them joy. What if you took the short cut?

What is money? A man is a success if he gets up in the morning and gets to bed at night, and in between he does what he wants to do.

—BOB DYLAN

There is a story about an old man taking a walk along the beach. He comes across a young man basking in the sun and strikes up a conversation. "What are you doing just lying here on a weekday?" "This is what I want to be doing today," says the young man. The old man launches into a monologue about how the young man should get up and go to work and save money to raise a family and work hard so that someday he can retire and walk along the beach like the old man. "I am already doing what I want to be doing, basking in the sun," says the young man, finally. "And you want me to work hard for the next 40 years so that I can do this when I am your age?"

We've never heard of a case where someone on their death bed says that they wished they spent one more day at the office, made X more dollars, or bought one more material thing. By most reports, the things people think of are how much love they have given in their lives and the non-material things they have that they are grateful for. At that last moment, that is what we value, and that is, in fact *our* value. What are your values? Are you living by your values? If not, what are you waiting for?

Why not start now by creating space in your life for what you truly want? Practice living in the moment. Meditate. Do less. Give up multitasking. In our society, people pride themselves on their ability to do that. Try NOT doing it for a while and notice an increase in your sense of peace and ability to be truly present to what you are doing.

10

LET GO

Living More With Less

Completions make space for the new—for that which you want to attract into your life. We spoke in the previous Key about reviewing any un-kept agreements with yourself or others. That is a form of completion. So is clearing the clutter from your house or desk, emptying your wardrobe of things you never wear, gracefully bowing out of commitments you made which do not serve your view of the life you want, and literally and symbolically, making room in your life to invite in that which you truly want.

When Belinda returned from backpacking on her own in India in 2006, she had been touched by what she had seen on her travels. One afternoon in Shimla, a small hill town in Northern India built into the side of a mountain, she had tea with her guide Mushy (pronounced "Moi-sha") and his roommate Nazir. They all ate on the floor of their "apartment" which was the size of a 4' x 8' closet. There was no furniture and only a few shelves, including two shelves built into the wall for each of them to sleep on, with one about three feet above the other. No joke.

They cooked for Belinda on a hot plate and served vegetables in gravy with rice and yogurt on top, with a fragrant and delicious homemade tea of cinnamon, cardamom, and saffron. They laughed, told jokes, and read from the adventures detailed in Mushy's postcards from past clients. Amidst the chatting in English, Hindi, and even Hebrew, Belinda realized what pure joy and fun she was having. No one was trying to impress or be anyone other than their authentic selves. Mushy and Nazir were proud of what they had and generous in sharing themselves and their space with Belinda.

On her next stop, Belinda took out nearly half of her backpack and left it all in three large shopping bags with her travel agent in New Delhi. She had decided to live more with less, starting immediately. As expected, it was much easier to travel with the lighter load and she had all the clothes she needed for the remaining three weeks of her trip. She even found some of the room helpful to buy a few items native to India that she would not have had room for if she kept her backpack filled to the rim as when she had begun.

When she returned home, Belinda recognized how well she had lived on half of her backpack, and how it had created the room to expand (especially emotionally and spiritually) that she had been longing for. With that in mind, she came home and looked around her home. It was quite beautiful, yet did have more belongings than she now realized she needed. So much more now appeared to her as clutter. She systematically went through her home and started giving items away—from furniture to clothes to kitchen items. She started to simplify in a whole new way and it felt wonderful.

Organize Your Financial Clutter

Beyond house clutter, you may be holding onto significant financial clutter that is holding you back and dragging your spirit down. Do you know someone who is sitting on a pile of bills and/or unopened statements (bank

10

LET GO

statements, retirement statements, etc.), saying, "I'll start organizing my finances *tomorrow*?" Raise your hand if you know someone like that . . . or is that someone, perhaps, you? If so, you are most definitely **not** alone. We'll help you tackle the clutter, including the pile of paper that bothers you every time you walk by it and seems to get bigger every day!

This does not have to be an overwhelming (or judgmental) process that you dedicate your life to—it's a matter of chunking it down into bite size pieces so that you'll feel accomplished and on the path to being in control of your financial destiny. If yesterday you said you would organize your finances *tomorrow*, then, guess what? Today is yesterday's tomorrow, so let's get going right now.

Start taking control of your financial clutter today with our 5-day step-by-step plan (go to www.OwnYourMoney.com for this plan with related links to resources to support your progress):

DAY ONE: Gather and Sort

- Take a spin through your space (house, apartment, etc.) and gather up every pile of financial "stuff" that has been bugging you and put it in *one* place.
- Open anything that has not yet been opened.
- If you open anything that must urgently be addressed, place such items in an **Active/Time Sensitive** pile and schedule some time on Day 2 to address this pile.
- Go through everything you've gathered and start placing the paperwork into piles. We suggest the following categories:
  - » **Active/Time Sensitive** for important matters such as overdue/current bills, unreconciled or unreviewed recent bank statements, miscellaneous/misunderstood charges for follow-up, etc.
  - » **Monthly statements** including bank statements, retirement statements, pay stubs
  - » **Monthly past (and paid) bills** including credit card bills, utilities, phone, mortgage, etc.
  - » **Permanent documents** including wills, marriage licenses, birth certificates, insurance policies, etc.

DAY TWO: Handle What You Need To

- It's time to handle the **Active/Time Sensitive** pile from Day One so that you can tackle anything that needs your immediate attention. Matters that you may want to address include:
- Review your unpaid bills
  » Review your activity – Are there any unusual or unknown charges on your bills? If yes, call your service provider to understand these charges. Negotiate a credit for any inappropriate charges. (Yes, you can make money organizing your financial clutter!)
  » Pay due/overdue bills – Determine all amounts that are owed and, if overdue, contact the company to let them know you are paying now (and pay it) or work out a payment plan.
  » Review your services – Are there services that you are paying for and you're not sure what the services are or if you use/need certain services? Call your respective service providers and cut back on all extra services not providing you a sufficient return on investment for your money. For example, can you cancel premium cable coverage or right-size your phone plan?
- Bank statements – Reconcile between your checkbook and your bank statements so you understand what checks have not cleared yet, what deposits may be pending, and what your current balance is. Also review your statement for fees. If you are paying any maintenance fees for your accounts, contact your bank and ask for a credit for past fees, and if they can provide you with free accounts. Then be sure to set up alerts for low balances and either block overdrafts or investigate if there is a way to receive complimentary overdraft protection.

DAY THREE: Design a Filing System

- Now that you've handled any urgent or time sensitive matters, you're ready to get back to organizing your records.
- What works best for you in terms of organizing—do you prefer

binders or folders or a combination of both, perhaps? We make the following suggestions for organizing files:

» Check out David Bach's file folder system for a simple and complete set of categories to further divide and organize your financial documents for easy future reference. (Go to www. FinishRich.com for all of David's books and products.)

» For your recurring monthly bills and statements, use a set of 12 monthly folders per year or a 12-slot expandable folder. This monthly file folder system works especially well if you pay your bills at one time each week, plus it makes record retention each year easier too. You are creating a *system* to avoid a big *to file* pile as you immediately file bills away after you've paid them.

DAY FOUR: Organize, Organize, and Organize!

- Compile a list of supplies that you need to get organized. Determine what you already have and what supplies you'll need (hanging folders, regular manila folders, binders, and so on).
- Head to the local office supply store and buy the supplies on your list.
- Use those fancy new organizational supplies and get down to business. Create the system that you designed on Day Three.

DAY FIVE: Peacefully Purge

- At the end of the filing process, you may be left with a pile of records and paperwork that doesn't have a home. Decide what you want to keep and what you can throw away, primarily based on your legal and tax requirements. As a general rule, any invoices, receipts, or statements (bank or credit card) related to items you have deducted on your taxes need to be maintained for the previous seven tax years.
- And finally, it's time to PURGE! Shred the confidential items and throw away the rest of your paperwork you no longer need. You will feel the weight lifting off of your shoulders instantly.

Now that you have reviewed the process, consult your calendar now and set aside some time to complete Exercise A at the end of this Key. Then refer to Exercise A to help inspire you, support you, and to complete this organization process easily. As Naomi, one of Belinda's clients, declared upon completion, "I can't believe it, but I actually finalized all of my filing and organizing. Now I can breathe!" Enjoy the relief of knowing all of your information is caught up, filed, and can easily be referenced.

Letting Go Rituals

It is important to honor your letting go process. Acknowledge yourself for what you have done or manifested in the past that has worked for you as well as what has not. Then create a ritual around letting go of whatever financial identity it is that you are moving away from. It is important to leave the past on good terms. Appreciate the service that you put into becoming who you are at this moment, whatever it took to get here. Make the conscious choice to take the next step. Say to yourself, "That part of my life is past." No blame, no mistake, no recrimination, and nothing wrong. Whatever you are leaving behind was created with good intentions, and now it is over. It is time to move on. Allow yourself to grieve for what you leave behind. Your slate is clean. Now you can celebrate the space you have opened up to receive all the abundance you deserve.

Physical rituals can be helpful in honoring this letting go process. Earlier, we suggested you write a completed item on a piece of paper and *burn it*, watching it go up in smoke. It might be more than just paper you want to burn, such as photographs or objects symbolizing what you are letting go of (safely please). Cia had a startling experience watching her home and her belongings burn to the ground while she sat outside in her nightgown thinking, "What a very interesting letting-go ceremony."

In one of Belinda's workshops, the participants each wrote their *non-supportive* money and success beliefs on a helium balloon. Then, as a group, they went into the center of Copley Square in Boston, Massachusetts, released their balloons, and let go of their related shame, guilt, and negative past with money that had been articulated on the balloon. Rituals work best when they involve a physical component so that your head, your heart, and your body all participate in the letting go experience.

10

LET GO

Even if you think you have fully grieved the loss of something or someone, there may be layers still remaining untapped creating a strong emotional hold on you. You may be in need of a ritual to take you to a deeper level of letting go. In this case, a burial ceremony to allow yourself to presently grieve your loss can be powerful. Gather belongings or objects to bury that remind you of the person or whatever it is that you are releasing. Allow yourself to have a real funeral, complete with grieving. Even something such as grief could be blocking you from real financial freedom.

If letting go feels like a monumental endeavor, don't let that scare you. Letting go is also a moment-to-moment activity. Just as we applied the "baby steps for grown-ups" approach to taking action, letting go may also be an ongoing process. Focus on the journey rather than the destination.

Willingness to Let Go

When you take a moment to reflect, you will likely find that much of your life is lived unconsciously. Correspondingly, most money is spent quite unconsciously. What if you were conscious in all your choices, especially your financial ones, to check that each one reflects who you really are?

The most dramatic test of your willingness to let go, and the importance of living consciously, is captured in the saying of Crazy Horse, the Lakota warrior and holy man: "It is a very good day to die." Saying this gives you a sense of completion and lets you know that you are living, and have lived, your life fully. This saying can help remind and motivate you to live every moment as if it mattered—as if it is simultaneously your first and your last. You are complete. Everything else is just dessert. What would it take for you to feel this way? What is in the way between you and being there?

What needs to be let go of in your financial and personal life? What no longer serves you? Is there a belief system, a career, a habit, or a relationship that you would be better off without? Although until now you may have been unconsciously holding on, this very moment can serve as a new opportunity for you to truly have the life you are meant to have.

10

LET GO

Letting go of what no longer serves you could substantially increase your earning power, ability to save, and/or improve your general financial well-being. Now is the point in the book that it behooves you to look at what you are still holding on to, check in again with your willingness to change, and to feel your feelings. Letting go literally and figuratively creates space for the new. Go for it!

10

LET GO

EXERCISES

Exercise A: Organize Your Financial Clutter

Proceed through each of the days of the 5-step process to organize your financial clutter as outlined in this Key. Under each day below, identify the step you are going to complete and by when you will have it completed. We have provided lines for three actions as a guide. You may have more or less than 3 for each day. The key is that you identify the actual steps relevant for you. Put a check in the box as each step is complete.

DAY ONE: Gather and Sort

Action 1:_____To complete by: _____
Action 2:_____To complete by: _____
Action 3:_____To complete by: _____

DAY TWO: Handle What You Need To

Action 1:_____To complete by: _____
Action 2:_____To complete by: _____
Action 3:_____To complete by: _____

DAY THREE: Design a Filing System

Action 1:_____To complete by: _____
Action 2:_____To complete by: _____
Action 3:_____To complete by: _____

DAY FOUR: Organize, Organize, and Organize!

Action 1:_____To complete by: _____
Action 2:_____To complete by: _____
Action 3:_____To complete by: _____

DAY FIVE: Peacefully Purge

Action 1:_____To complete by: _____

10

LET GO

Action 2:_____ To complete by: _____

Action 3:_____ To complete by: _____

Exercise B: Taking Actions to Let Go

Part I: Make a list

Letting go is not usually easy or comfortable. But it doesn't mean that everything has to end when you let go of something important. Make a list of the things you are afraid to let go of in your life—they can be physical, like a special object, or intangible, like your attachment to a special person. Then go back and look at the list. Look at it honestly and answer these questions for each item: Would I be able to continue living without this thing? How would my life change? What new energy would I be willing to invite into my life to fill the place that this thing was taking up? How might I change my life in order to live with the letting go? Can I ask for some support and, if so, from whom? What might be better about my life if I did let go?

Part II: Let Go of Attachment to the List

Ceremonially destroy your list as a symbol that you are letting go of the things on it. Burning it as a ritual offering is ideal if you have a way to do that safely. Tying the list to a helium balloon and then releasing the balloon outside also works well. Feel your feelings as you do it.

Part III: Let Go of Stuff

Take a tangible step in your life to let go of something that is no longer serving you. It could be something as simple as clearing out one closet. To take this step to the next level, make a date with yourself (and hopefully with a friend for moral support) with the intention of making three big piles: (1) to throw away, (2) to give away, (3) to have a ceremonial letting go process for those pieces that are especially sentimental or hard to release. As you process each piece from that pile, let yourself feel your full range of emotions, and then let them go. Don't ignore the fact that there are feelings involved and that things have symbolic meaning. Really let yourself go through the feelings as you release things from your life. If you choose to include letting go of some abstract pieces of your life during this part of the exercise, write them down on a piece of paper and put them into the appropriate pile.

Exercise C: Live By Your Priorities

Make two lists of your priorities in life. The first list is your priorities by default—in other words the things you spend the majority of your time doing, often rather unconsciously. The second list is what you really WANT to be doing. No excuses. It's just a list. Sit with the two lists and imagine what it would be like to live your life by your conscious choices rather than choices by default. As you become more conscious, you may find yourself making different choices and living more by your authentic priorities.

Your Priorities By Default (How You *Are* Spending Your Time)	*Your Priorities By Choice* (How You *Want* to Be Spending Your Time)

Visualization – Send Your Money Personae on Its Way

In Key Six, we talked about Personae and gave some examples of personae specifically related to money. Do you have more clarity on yours now, as you consider how to let go of its non-supportive aspects on a deeper level? We also talked about how you can befriend your personae instead of fighting with them. This is a gentler way of letting go.

Having identified your primary money personae, draw or describe in detail a characterization of your voice or voices. (Refer to *Key Six, Exercise A – Part II* for your list of personae attributes.) Visualize it as a caricature (like a cartoon figure) or even in a human form. Doing so can be very helpful and very freeing, because this then actually helps to release the grip you may feel they have over you. You don't need to get rid of them; you simply need to meet them with awareness. What are they wearing? How do they stand? What do they say? What do their voices sound like? Can you see the humor in them? Play with your personae. You may even be able to get them into conversation. Pull up a chair for each one and have a talk with it as you visualize it in front of you. You may find it has some interesting things to say!

Next, recognize that you are in charge of these characters, not the other way around. Thank each one for its efforts on your behalf. Let each know that its help is no longer required. Now visualize retiring this voice which no longer serves you. Take the deeper step by imagining you are sending it away on a permanent vacation, storing it away in a closet, or whatever feels thorough, complete, and possible to you.

Conscious Breathing

Have you ever had a deep spontaneous sigh? That sigh was a form of release. You may have been holding in your breath, breathing very shallowly without realizing it. Shallow breathing is related to the famous "fight or flight response" when being still and quiet was a safety mechanism. You may often feel bombarded with stress and your unconscious shallow breathing is likely to have become a habit as a result. Fritz Perls, one of the first great body-centered therapists, said that "Fear is excitement without the breath." In other words, if you are able to breathe deeply through fear, you may notice that it is easy to reframe it as excitement. Dr. Gay Hendricks, in his book *Conscious Breathing,* says "Any trauma you can breathe through loses its grip on you."

Get yourself into a comfortable position, either seated or lying, and loosen any restrictive clothing. Begin to breathe as deeply and slowly as possible. In this exercise, we will be focusing on the exhale. With each exhalation, imagine you are letting go of something from the past or present

10

LET GO

that you have been carrying around and which no longer serves you. Take as many slow deep breaths as you need to feel it fully leaving your body and mind. Spend as much time as you are comfortable going through each of the things you want to release and breathing them out. If you are doing this properly (focused, fully and slowly enough), you will enjoy a deep sense of relaxation and inner peace.

Body-Centered Statements

1. I am letting go of _____ and as I do, I feel an opening to aliveness, prosperity, and abundance.
2. I am willing to grieve and at the same time I am comforted by the idea that for every doorway that closes, another opens.
3. I am creating space for _____ to appear in my life as I let go, fear less, and love (and live) more.

Journal Joggers

Use the following questions to lead you into your journal entries for this Key.

- What is it that you are most afraid of letting go of in your life? Why?
- How might your life be different if you were truly able to let go? Is it worth the risk?
- How did you create your personal identity with money?
- What do you want to keep and what are you willing to finally let go of from that identity?
- Who is the powerful you with money that remains?

The freedom now desired by many is not freedom to do and dare but freedom from care and worry.

—James Truslow Adams

KEY ELEVEN

STAND IN YOUR TRUTH

You never find yourself until you face the truth.
—Pearl Bailey

The closest thing there is to a panacea is truth. Telling the truth is the antidote for just about everything.

In coaching our clients, we like to avoid giving advice, *and* sometimes advice is what is called for. Most of the time, we can sum up the advice into three small words, "Tell the truth." Consistently, when a person takes that advice, miracles happen in the form of a major shift. Observe the fundamental problem of stuck feelings. As you saw in Key Three "Feel Your Feelings," speaking the truth of our feelings allows them to shift. The moment you open your mouth and tell the truth, you leave some baggage behind.

When you find yourself getting irritated, ask yourself what truth needs to be spoken in that situation. When you do not speak the truth of your feelings as they arise, pressure and tension increase. That is the irritation. If the pressure gets substantial enough, it explodes in bursts of anger. The release valve on the pressure cooker of your being is truth telling. Use it often.

Here is an example of when you don't tell the truth about the situation you are in. Imagine this: Your partner keeps buying miscellaneous expensive toys and things for the house, such as a power washer, motorcycle, lawn mower, or toolset. You are concerned about your family finances but you don't say anything about it. One day, he comes home with a new flat-screen TV and you become furious and start screaming at him—not just about the new TV, though. You are also expressing your frustration about what he has purchased over the last two years. He is taken aback and shocked at your response. Clearly, your lack of ability to speak the truth about the little things, combined with your built-up feelings, caused a very angry emotional release. If, early on, you had chosen to stand in your truth and ask for an agreement about joint decisions in purchases over a certain dollar amount, you would not be in this situation. Are you willing to claim responsibility for your part in this, and begin telling the truth in the moment? As an alternative to building up this kind of pressure, would you consider a commitment to ongoing self-responsible communication? (For a refresher, review Key Two.)

Take a Stand

Truth, by its very nature, is grounding. It is supportive. That's why we say "stand" in the truth. Think of planting yourself in it and holding your ground. It is your strength, your pillar. Truth keeps you in touch with reality. If you are not committed to discovering your own truth, the word *reality* has no meaning. Truth is the element which holds all the Keys we have covered together. It acts as the solid foundation for your worth and your being—a foundation you can then build upon.

Standing in your truth is key to getting real about your situation—owning it to its core once and for all—and then having the platform to improve on it. As you gain awareness and a new level of truth about your current circumstances, you then have the power to do something about it. Until that moment, you may be merely glossing over the current situation to only see what you wanted to see about your condition, especially when it comes to financial matters.

Consider this story of Lynda. Lynda attended one of Belinda's workshops and then contacted her afterward to share the actions she was motivated to take. "I did just what you said," she proudly shared, "I went home and talked with my husband, Neil, about our finances. He was shocked and nearly fell out of his chair at first, and then he recounted the brutal stress he has been feeling that has been keeping him up at night. We've been married for 19 years now and 19 years ago I stopped managing my finances and never managed our family finances. I didn't like to do it, and he said he didn't mind doing it, so I handed over the checkbook. That was 19 years ago and I've barely looked at any detail since, although I had a feeling that we were spending beyond our means since we have amassed $30,000 in credit card debt over the last two years. Ignorance was bliss, until your workshop. Now I have guilt about spending and not sharing the stress with my husband. And now I am willing to tell the truth and work together on the management and control of our money." Lynda had been afraid to stand in her truth and have the necessary discussion with her husband. It had been taking a serious toll on their financial, physical, and emotional well-beings. In just the first 8 weeks of Lynda and her husband Neil working both together and with Belinda on their finances, Neil was less stressed knowing that they were in it together—and as a bonus he lost over 18 pounds of actual weight once he felt supported in their efforts.

Although they were not at the extreme of lying to each other about activities with money (see "Financial Infidelity" below), Lynda and Neil were certainly not being truthful about their financial situation. They had each been living in their own dissatisfied financial worlds. It was only through her courage to tell the truth that Lynda initiated a new powerful conversation with Neil, was willing to address her fears, and finally get real about her money and their marriage. Beyond the stress and extra weight that her husband had taken on, Lynda's denial contributed to an inauthenticity that unknowingly permeated their marriage. As you continue to take steps in owning your money and standing in your truth, you will more deeply own and heal the rest of your life.

Living In Integrity

Integrity comes from the word "integral," meaning whole. Truth keeps us in integrity—keeps us whole. When we are not whole, we do not have enough energy for transformation. If we compromise our integrity even in the smallest way, we cut off a piece of ourselves. We create a wound in our psyche. Untreated, that wound tends to fester and grow.

11

STAND IN YOUR TRUTH

Integrity in our life acts like a white tablecloth. It is very easy to see a black spot. Seek out the lies in your life. Hunt them down and take corrective action now. It may hurt to treat that wound, but it will save your financial and personal life. Avoiding saying something, by the way, is the same as lying. The key word is avoiding. Holding something back is what is called a *withhold* and is toxic to yourself and to your relationship. It can also be a form of a lie if it is something that you feel strongly needs to be said. It is not that you need to speak everything that comes to mind. If you are not sure if it is a withhold or not, ask your body. Even a mild sensation of discomfort when you think about it will let you know that it is something you need to share. Your body will provide you clues that you have some truth which needs to be spoken.

Similar to why and how you need to be honoring commitments to both yourself and others, as explained in Key Eight, you are also out of integrity and not standing in your truth when you are not honest with yourself. Others do not need to be involved for you to stand in your truth, as this begins personally—within yourself.

Financial Infidelity

Financial infidelity occurs when one partner isn't honest and open about the financial situation of the family. This is one of the most insidious and destructive marital money conflicts, and it has been on the rise. A 2008 study by Yahoo! Finance and research firm, Decipher, showed that 50% of the respondents had committed some form of financial infidelity, as compared to a 2005 study showing that 30% of respondents had lied about financial information and 25% had withheld information. These deceptive activities include covertly running up credit card debt, lying about the actual cost of a purchase, hiding a purchase from your partner, or maintaining a secret stash of cash.

According to the survey, women are more likely to be dishonest about money than men (or at least admitted to it): 55% of women versus 41% of men say they've committed financial infidelity. Some of the discrepancy might be accounted for by the fact that, unfortunately, there is still an inequality between what men and women earn. If men are earning more, they may feel more entitled, whereas a woman, feeling less entitled, may be more prone to hiding expenditures, for instance. Further, the study found that secrets and lies tend to occur most often among couples in the 35 to 44 age bracket. We have seen financial infidelity in action committed by both the male and female partners. Neither is better or worse—both are inauthentic within the sanctity of marriage and truth.

One cold day in October 2008, Belinda's client, Maxine, was home sick with a bad cold. The doorbell rang and she answered the call. Standing at the door, was a serious-looking woman fully dressed in black. She was an IRS agent delivering a $67,000 lien on their home for unpaid back taxes. This was the first that Maxine had heard about this tax issue. The woman had no sympathy as Maxine started to cry. As she shared this story with Belinda two months later, Maxine again started to cry and said, "That was one of the hardest days of my life."

Her husband Will had not paid the taxes as they had previously agreed together. Nor had he been squandering the apportioned money on philandering, gambling, or drinking. He needed that money to keep up their lifestyle and pay their basic bills. They were living well beyond their means and he hadn't been able to tell her. So instead of being honest about the situation and working on it together, he kept it from her, and it got out of hand.

The good news is that after three months of financial coaching, they had created a united team, hired bookkeeping support, and gotten their back taxes filed. They even had an organizing system with clear roles and responsibilities so that she opened the mail and identified priorities for payment and then he processed and paid the bills.

Belinda worked with another couple who had a similar yet opposite problem. In an effort to not aggravate her husband who was working almost 90 hours per week, she had drawn down their Home Equity Line of Credit (HELOC) by over $45,000. This was done merely to keep up with the bills for their family and three children. Belinda encouraged her to come clean with her spouse so they could solve the problem together.

Many people believe lying about money is actually about the money. *It's not.* It's really about the underlying lack of communication, stress, shame, hiding, and everything else happening in the relationship. A red flag arises with the first cover-up you find yourself beginning to engage in. It's like a thread in a coat that starts unraveling. Sometimes the relationship comes undone: 7% of men and 12% of women have broken up with a partner because of money-related duplicity, the Yahoo! Finance/Decipher survey found.

One of the biggest causes of secret spending is what we call *the covert payback*. There is something your partner did that you think you get to pay yourself back for. For example, your husband was away traveling for the last four days and you had to deal with everything at home, so you feel like you deserve it. Or your wife has been a bit cranky lately, so you can make it up to yourself with a secret purchase you've been wanting. But people often feel guilty afterward. They blame and complain, and then they're ashamed. The lying continues and the financial environment worsens.

Sex, Money, and Power

Many psychologists refer to the sex, money, and power triangle in a relationship. The person who craves sex less in the relationship tends to have more power over the other who wants it more. The person who has more money in the relationship tends to have more power, and feels more justified in getting what they want as priority. Classically, this has put women (typically the partner who can hold out longer or more easily regarding sex) in a position of using that to balance the power in a relationship where, typically, the male has the greater earnings or assets.

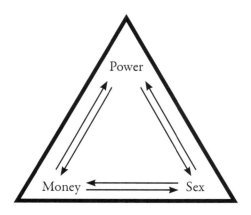

For example, one of Cia's clients, a stay-at-home mom named Alexandra, has a husband who came home after a long day at work, helped with the kids, and then demanded sex. Alexandra felt that if she didn't provide it, she wasn't holding up her end of the relationship. The fact that she complied begrudgingly created increasing friction, distance, and lack of intimacy. Her husband, Ken, was unconsciously using the fact that he is the breadwinner as a form of leverage, giving him the right (in his mind) to demand that Alexandra give back to him in this way. By making what was unconscious into the conscious, supporting better communication and boundary setting on Alexandra's part, and explaining to Ken that her boundary setting would be better for them in the long run, they now have a happier, more intimate sex life and have learned to view each other as equals.

The confrontation between Alexandra and her husband started out as an unhealthy situation. Hopefully, it is something that is changing demographically and with more sexual awareness and respect in society as a whole. However, be aware of any subtle power plays in your relationship based on sex or money and do your utmost not to use them. Higher net-worth individuals or higher earners, please treat your partner as an equal owner. If your partner wants sex more than you do, please do not ever use that as bait or leverage.

Both of you may be doing your best and both of you may be stressed about the financial situation, but how can you come into truthful partnership? (If you are not in a long-term committed relationship, this may also apply to your relationship with a business partner, a parent or child, or even with yourself.) The key is for couples to start with a safe space without criticizing or judging their spouse.

5 Steps for Couples to Build a Healthy and Wealthy Foundation For Your Family, Starting With Conversations With Your Partner About Money

Money is often cited as the number one cause of divorce. Yet instead of using money to divide their relationship, couples can use money as a way to come together and unite to realize their dreams and intentions. A healthy

11

STAND IN YOUR TRUTH

relationship with money feeds feelings of love, empowerment, security, control, happiness, and self-worth—much like a healthy relationship with your partner. Maintaining those relationships together takes work, and it's never too soon (or too late) to start. Here's how:

1. **Understand** who each of you are around money and start to talk about the financial beliefs, concerns, and burdens each of you are bringing (or has brought) to the marriage. It is all about communication. When you have this conversation, mutually agree to create a safe space and listen to each other fully in this very vulnerable time. Couples need to understand that they are not bad people because of poor money decisions they may have made in the past. You may have just never been taught good money management skills. As you gain a better appreciation and understanding of your partner, you will ignite a new sense of hope and help to support you and your actions.

   Couples often bring a lot of *shoulds* into their marriage. For example: He "should" be earning more money and she "should" be spending less, or the reverse cases can also be true. What they are really doing is *shoulding* on their partner. Each has expectations. These expectations are present and yet often not brought to the surface, expressed, and addressed.

   As you stand in the truth and begin a new conversation with your partner about money, your understanding of your Belief Systems already developed through this book will prove essential. Each of you comes to the proverbial table with your own beliefs and stories. If you were each influenced by your parents or grandparents, you could also be bringing the B.S. of four or eight people to the table with you. With this enlightened understanding, you can now open the dialogue. As you do, it is important to keep a safe space where you both ask each other questions without judging your partner's answers. This is a real opportunity to develop deeper compassion and understanding for each other.

   Here are 6 sample questions to help you open the conversation:

1. What does money mean to you?
2. How would you describe your relationship to money?
3. What are your current money habits?
4. What did your parents tell you about money?
5. When you hear the word *wealth*, what comes to mind?
6. What are your worst fears when it comes to money?

Use these questions as a guide. It is not essential you go over them in order. It is more important that you both listen with curiosity and compassion. If this feels especially emotionally charged, start with a more general understanding and appreciation of even having this conversation. Discuss what feelings may be coming up for both of you. Just as we mentioned earlier, money often represents power, control, love, happiness, security, or freedom, especially to the unconscious. Money could be how your spouse feels taken care of, so when you pull the money away, he or she may also feel like their love is being pulled away.

Be sure to complete Step One. If you skip Step One and attempt to go directly to Step Two, the rest of the process suffers.

2. **Evaluate**. Determine your shared strengths and challenges, and where each of you can adjust. Instead of expecting your partner to be someone that they aren't, appreciate what they bring to the table and apportion responsibilities with that in mind. Once you both are owning your money, as described earlier in this book, you will both be able to take 100% responsibility for the success of your family finances. It is a 2-person job. Once you can act more like an offense and a defense on the same team instead of working against each other, you can enjoy money as more of a game. As if it is *you and your partner against the world*—not in an adversarial way, but in a fun way. When couples each understand their own money personalities and their partner's, then they can help each other by compensating for what the other person may not be as good at.

For example, Belinda worked with a couple similar to Maxine

STAND IN YOUR TRUTH

11

and Will, but not quite as extreme. The husband, Steve, was an avoider and his wife, Sarah, would nag him to be timelier in paying their bills. He was good at the spreadsheets but just couldn't get past opening the mail. She wasn't very savvy with computers or banking. He works in a bank. So she offered to be the *mail manager*, and she opens and organizes the mail. He then pays the bills. Everyone is happier. How can you recognize what you have in common instead of just where you seem to differ? Often couples agree on a lot more that they realize.

3. **Align** on values, inspiration, and your combined purpose for money. Talk about your goals for your life together. Since money management is all about choices, your choice to communicate, collaborate, and work together is a key step. This will allow you to be more strategic, thoughtful, and in partnership with your financial management.

4. **Make a Plan and a Money Date.** Your plan will include reviewing your actual activity, making adjustments together based on your priorities and values, and creating a budget (also known as a Savings and Spending Plan, as described in Key Five). Making a plan also includes forward thinking and often consulting a financial advisor to ensure that you are on track for an eventual retirement, as well as affording other longer term goals you may have identified in Key One, such as your children's college education, travel, or a second home.

    Set yourself up for success. Create weekly *money dates* when you manage your money—together. Be sure to add fun before, during, and after each session. Whether you play your favorite song or have a nice home-cooked dinner afterward, making it fun will help bring you back week after week. Each week, consider how you can continue to streamline your processes and reduce the weekly work. If you miss a week, get right back on the bandwagon; consistency and discipline are essential to the success of this process. Automating your savings is also a great step in setting yourself up for saving success.

5. **Be willing to ask for help.** Change fear to fun. Remember, being financially independent does NOT necessarily mean you are doing it alone. (Often, it is quite to the contrary.) There's no shame in acknowledging that you need and want support—from each other or from outside advisors. This can be essential to your acknowledging the truth of the situation to maximize the effectiveness of your process and your finances.

Maintaining Financial Façades

Often in an attempt at portraying a certain image, you may find yourself putting on false financial pretenses. These impressions may be an attempt to cause others to believe you have more or less financial stability and wealth than you actually do. This may hide a basic insecurity, sense of lack, or shame regarding your own self-worth. Not only are you not standing in the truth to others, you are lying to yourself. As you do that, you are actually creating more shame. Further, as you are able to stop this behavior and move to integrity, your shame has a chance to heal. Now is your opportunity to align with your partner, as you get real about your situation and the lifestyle you can actually maintain, and choose how to stand in your truth while in partnership.

How truthful are you to yourself? How truthful are you to others when it comes to the impressions you provide? In actuality, you are the sole person who can be honest with yourself by the choices you make on a daily basis with money.

This quote, from Suze Orman's *The Laws of Money, The Lessons of Life,* summarizes the impact quite well: "I have learned the hard way that financial lies destroy financial lives, and that telling the truth about yourself and your money is the only way to keep what you have and create what you deserve."

Living truthfully with your money is sometimes complicated by interactions with your peers. When a friend of Belinda's wanted to go out with their girlfriends to an expensive restaurant for drinks and dinner for the second time that week, Belinda was uncertain how to respond. At that point in her life, she was choosing not to spend money on eating

11

STAND IN YOUR TRUTH

out twice a week. Should she make an excuse, such as feigning illness, or tell her friend the truth? Belinda told her the truth and offered to host a pot-luck dinner instead. The friend's split-second pause felt like it lasted an eternity—and then came the sigh. Her relief met Belinda's relief as she said, "Thank goodness you said something! I didn't really want to do that but couldn't think of anything else." They made alternate plans, and then they had as long as they wanted to sit at the table, laugh, play great music, eat delicious food, and no tip was necessary!

Commit to Truth

The best mind-altering drug is truth.

—LILY TOMLIN

Truth is transformative. All the work with transforming self-talk and setting boundaries may not mean anything if you are not willing to make a commitment to truth in your life. This may be unfamiliar territory for you. Lying has become such a habit, such a pattern in our society that most of the time we don't even know we are doing it. Someone asks, "How are you?" and you answer, "Fine," when deep down you may feel like you are going to pieces, and you need someone to throw you a lifeline. It's going to take some practice in every aspect of your life. Money is no exception. As we mentioned, it doesn't mean that you have to blurt out everything to everyone. Just make sure that you are not harboring a withhold.

The truth habit may not happen overnight. Again, think of it as strengthening a muscle. You are practicing your commitment to truth each day—each moment for that matter—and reaffirming your commitment to truth in your life. The power of it is tremendous. It will free up vast amounts of energy. It will really put you in touch with who you are. We can't emphasize that enough. If you do nothing else but simply make a commitment to truth, you will transform your life. Truth is the juice that will energize your empowerment and your transformation. Truth is also contagious, so start an epidemic!

People ask us all the time, "You're kidding? Right? You don't really expect me to come out and say _____. I couldn't possibly!" Sometimes, you just have to get those words out of your mouth, no matter how scary it is. Even though it may shake things up, even though it is hard or even terrifying, and even if you are afraid of hurting someone (which, by the way, is usually a euphemism for not wanting to deal with the consequences). We have never yet seen it fail to create a positive, healthy, and enlivening result. The primary reason people don't tell the truth is that they don't want to be inconvenienced by the other person's response, or deal with confrontation. Since telling the truth promotes creativity and aliveness, you may be unknowingly sacrificing an opportunity to have more of those qualities in your life when/if you withhold the truth.

Embracing Feedback—Letting Others Tell Their Truth

A participant at one of Cia's workshops said, "I had an experience the last time I was here. A trusting friend of mine gave me some difficult feedback. He said it was very hard for him to do because he thought it was going to hurt my feelings. He didn't want to be responsible for me and it did hurt my feelings and I cried and I felt the relationship go up in the air, but that was all my shtick. It turned out to be one of the most useful pieces of feedback I ever got because I went directly into feeling 'I'm not deserving. I shouldn't be in the world. I'm defective.' At the same time, I knew he didn't feel that way, and it was really a gift for me to have him be honest—for me to go down into a very uncomfortable place and see where it was, and swim around in it and come back up and out. And had he not shared that truth with me, I might have really avoided and denied those uncomfortable feelings and not gotten down there to know what was fomenting around. I'm very grateful. And I know it was hard for him because he was risking. It was hard for him to speak the truth. It was very painful to begin with but at least it was true. That was great!"

Are you willing to take the risk to open yourself to feedback in this way, and the possible transformation it can bring through the awareness of how you come across to others? It may give you a perspective on yourself that could be tremendously helpful. The key is listening to it in an open way, without needing to defend yourself. Not all feedback will be appropriate. You can decide what to discard and what to keep.

11

STAND IN YOUR TRUTH

Truth as a Relief

> *Telling the truth is like plugging into*
> *an electrical outlet for a dose of aliveness.*
>
> —Douglas DeCarlo

This Truth Key will change your life—while significantly benefitting both your self-worth and your net worth. If you are living a lie, like accumulating significant credit card debt you haven't told your partner about, you may have convinced yourself that it would cause your partner to be furious and you fear it might even destroy the relationship to tell him or her the truth. In most cases, learning (and speaking) the truth—even when it is a bombshell—is a relief. The reality is that, on some level, most people already know, and then doubt their own sanity, which is a replay of the trauma that has occurred to most of us as children—in some cases, with devastating results.

Children are extremely perceptive. They also assume adults will tell the truth. When they are lied to by an adult, they begin to doubt their own ability to perceive reality, perhaps even their own sanity. We urge you: don't do this to a child, or to anyone who ever was a child. The painful stab of being confronted with reality is nothing compared to the long-term consequences of mixed signals and lack of communication.

Ralph and the Poorhouse

Ralph was recalling to Cia what life was like when he was a child growing up in a blue-collar family living in a midwestern city. His parents stayed silent on the topic of money, and like most children, he assumed there were no problems. During the early school age years of his life, however, his bedroom was located next to the kitchen. His parents didn't realize Ralph was awake in the early morning hours before his father went to work. As he started to hear them talk and often argue about money, including how they could possibly make ends meet to "stay out of the poorhouse," he got confused, frightened, and no longer felt safe enough to trust. At an early age, he lost his fundamental security about money.

As an adult, all roads led to the emotional "poorhouse" for Ralph. Once married, with a family, a successful career, and a fine home, Ralph continually felt impoverished and ranted morning and night to his wife, Carrie, about how poor they were. In his mind, he was asking for her to spend less money in the only way he knew how. For her, she got the opposite message. Driven to fear and a nervous breakdown by the continual ranting, Carrie believed her only escape, and way to end his tirades, would be to make a lot of money. Without including Ralph in her desperate plan, she took $150,000 worth of equity out of their home, invested in a high-risk opportunity, and then sadly lost the money. This created a complete circle and, in effect, a self-fulfilling prophesy for Ralph.

You can either choose the route Ralph and Carrie took filled with anguish, loss, and financial ruin based on the regurgitation of the financial insecurity and poverty communication about money, OR you can address your upbringing with money, communicate responsibly, and live in integrity and financial abundance.

How different would this story have been if . . .

1. Ralph's parents had discussed their financial situation and its possible solutions with each other and with Ralph in an open, safe environment?
2. Instead of regurgitating unhealed fears, Ralph had communicated self-responsibly with Carrie and calmly asked her for what he actually wanted, which was for her to spend less money each month and check with him on purchases over $100?
3. Carrie had communicated self-responsibly with Ralph regarding the fear and trauma this was evoking in her?

Cia's Disconnection and Realization

Cia says, "I used to be a chronic liar. I lied so much and was so good at it that I didn't know I was lying; it was just habitual. It was just a way of being in the world. I would most of the time believe what I was saying, because it was not my habit to stop and say, 'What's really true here? What's the bottom line truth?' I didn't know what it was like to live without lying. The result was that my life became so compartmentalized that I experienced total denial of another part of my life at any given moment. When I was with my family, I believed that that was who I was. When I was engaged in business, I was a different person. It was as if those two people were unaware of the existence of each other. I was split off from myself. The left hand knew not what the right hand did. It was like going through life with blinders. I never had a chance to be whole and thus I never had a chance to find out who I really was. Learning to tell the truth was the hardest thing I ever did and the most rewarding. The day I said to myself, 'I'm not going to lie anymore,' my whole life transformed. I can't recommend telling the truth enough—no matter what the circumstances. These days I look at anything I say as being sacred to me. This is healing/whole making, and strengthens my sense of self in a healthy way."

Cia continues, "One of the things which made my learning curve so fast was my promise to myself that if I slipped up and didn't speak the complete truth, I would go back to the person and tell them. As it was so very painful to do that, I quickly learned to think carefully before I spoke." You may experience something like this on a more subtle level. For example, you may find yourself going into a store and charging a purchase when somewhere in your mind you know that you don't have enough money in the account to cover it. At that moment, there is no consciousness of it.

Your Story

We are the hero of our own story.

—MARY MCCARTHY

We each have a story about being out of integrity in our lives. Belinda was so miserable in her old job but she didn't want to admit it. As described in Key Eight, she felt like she checked her personality at the door every morning and reclaimed it when she left. One of the best things that ever happened to Belinda was being laid off. It took nearly a year for it to dawn on her that having been in that job was a lie, and that leaving it was what it took for her to be in integrity with herself.

What is your story? How are you out of integrity in your life, whether you have admitted it to yourself or not? This is a journey that we ask you to start now.

If we asked you to suddenly walk out into the world, and be *totally* in truth, you wouldn't know how. However, we are asking you to begin the process and make the *commitment* to living fully in truth. It's not going to change all at once. It takes practice—it takes watching and listening to every word that comes out of your own mouth.

Be firm with yourself about it. There is a huge temptation to say, "Oh, that's not important," or "I tell the truth, but I just can't do it in this area; it will cause huge problems." It is a slippery slope. Unless you hold firm, you'll lose ground to the force of habit and convention. The gray areas get bigger and bigger until you are awash in them. Cia recognized that her habitual lying was a form of addiction and, therefore, as with any form of addiction, she assiduously avoids anything even bordering on an untruth. Using your new skills in self-responsible communication (Key Two) and in setting boundaries (Key Five), you can be discerning and still be clear and uncompromising in your integrity.

You will find that truth comes in layers. The more you practice, the deeper you will be able to go. Try asking yourself the question about a superficially truthful statement you have made, "What's underneath that? Is there more?" Speaking the truth is a learning experience as you go deeper. You learn truths about yourself as you give them voice.

Keep checking in. Ask yourself, "Where am I out of integrity in my life?" Constantly be on the look-out for how you can step further into integrity—how you can be more whole. If you're not whole, it means you're fragmented. It means you are split off from yourself. You simply cannot afford to be split off from yourself. It robs you of your life. So, come into truth with yourself. It's an amazing experiment. We recommend it highly.

11

STAND IN YOUR TRUTH

EXERCISES

Exercise A: Going Deeper Into Truth

Using all that you have learned from this book so far, answer these questions:

- What is the single biggest lie you tell yourself that keeps you from stepping into a full sense of your own self-worth?
- How does the lie you tell yourself manifest in the level of integrity you are in with others?
- How might it be affecting your net worth too?
- Are you willing to change that story, and shift from being the victim to the heroine or hero?

Now you can consciously choose the truth. If you are willing to change your story, write down an empowering truth to replace the old lie you have been living with. Say it outloud to yourself several times a day until you are able to truly own it and stand in the truth of your full potential as a human being.

Exercise B: Give Yourself Your Own Lie Detector Test

Say something you know is not true. As you say it, carefully note the subtle sensations in your body. What happens to your sense of self-worth? Memorize the feeling. Those sensations will help you know when you are not speaking your truth and to know how it is not truly possible to embrace a sense of self-worth in life without being fully in integrity.

Now, stand in front of a mirror while you say it, and observe your body language. Use this in the same way. What do you look like when you are out of integrity? Do you see the image of a person who knows her or his true value? We doubt it.

Next, try a statement you believe is true. Say it out loud. Feel the feelings. Check it out in the mirror. Do you feel alive and empowered? Do you feel your own self-worth? Is your body language open and coherent?

11

STAND IN YOUR TRUTH

If not, there is a part of you that does not fully believe this truth or is not really *owning* it? Work with the statement as in the previous exercise, until when you say it, all of you is in alignment and accord. (Muscle testing also works well to create a natural lie detector test.)

Now do you see the image of a person who knows her or his own self-worth?

Exercise C: Stepping into Truth

You don't get full practice stepping into truth and your sense of self-worth until you fully claim responsibility for all the times you have lied, and then make a commitment to yourself to be in full integrity from here on out. This is likely to be a painful wake-up call, yet the pain is what makes it life-transforming.

Write out a chronological list of all the lies (big or small) that you can remember having told in your life, or each time you were out of integrity in some way in what you did or said. Next to each lie, make a note of the effect it had on your sense of self-worth and therefore, perhaps your net worth in the long run as well.

Make a commitment to yourself to make amends and to step into your truth regarding each one of those lies. Wherever possible, this means going to the person you lied to and telling them that you lied. Hard to do? Definitely! However once you make a commitment to do this now and from here on out, and experience the challenge of facing people and telling them the truth, it will certainly make you think twice before you say something that isn't true. Since many of your lies may be unconscious and buried, really take time with your list, growing it as you review your life, past and present. The most recent lies will be the most fresh in your mind, and some of them may also be the most difficult to confront as they will involve people you are currently in relationship with.

Remember that as you do this exercise, you are making amends to yourself as well. Forgive yourself for the times you have been out of integrity, while making the decision not to go there again. Good luck. It's worth it!

11

STAND IN YOUR TRUTH

Visualization – World of Truth

Here is an opportunity to enjoy a beautiful daydream. Allow yourself some time for this. Imagine a world where no one lies, ever—a world where people speak plainly about what it is they want and honor the answer, whether it is "yes" or "no;" a world where everyone respects each other's choices and feels empowered to make their own. What would such a world be like? As you imagine this in detail, picture every aspect of life: relationship, work, health, sports, politics, religion, business, etc. In such a world, might people trust and therefore better understand each other? Would there be any need for war? For interpersonal fights? Imagine living in this new World of Truth.

Conscious Breathing

As this Key is called "Stand in Your Truth," we would like you to do this exercise standing, preferably in front of a mirror. Take some full deep belly breaths and imagine that you are getting the feeling of standing in your truth. You are simply and totally who you are, with nothing to hide from the world. Feel the expansiveness and groundedness of that sensation. Now tell a lie. As you do so, observe the difference in your breath and your body. Remember the difference in the feeling. This awareness will help give you a bodily clue when you are not in full integrity. Now fill your lungs again and speak a powerful truth. Fill in the blank of the following sentence as you continue to breathe as deeply as you can: "I am_____." Once again observe what you notice in your breath and body.

Body-Centered Statements

1. I am _____ (state an unarguable truth).
2. When I _____, I get a bodily sensation of _____.

3. I commit to tell the truth about every aspect of my life, large and small, financial or otherwise, in ever deepening layers as my awareness grows.

Journal Joggers

Use the following questions to lead you into your journal entries for this Key.

- What truth have you begun to live as a result of using this book as a transformational tool?
- What truth is not being spoken in your life right now, especially in your financial life?
- What are your afraid would happen if you spoke the truth in this circumstance?
- What positive thing might occur if you spoke the truth?
- Are you willing to take the risk? If not, what is the cost if you continue with your withhold?

Truth is a deep kindness that teaches us to be content in our everyday life and share with the people the same happiness.

—KHALIL GIBRAN

11

STAND IN YOUR TRUTH

DEVELOP A TOLERANCE FOR JOY

Happiness depends upon ourselves.

—ARISTOTLE

Now, why would we use the word "tolerance" for joy? Isn't joy something we all want? Isn't it something that's pleasurable? Well, amazingly, it is usually harder for adults to experience joy than almost any other feeling. It is less familiar and, strangely, you may have resistance to it.

Why? Because you may not be giving yourself permission to feel joy. Most people are simply not "wired" for it. Very literally that means that you have not developed enough receptor sites in the brain for the chemicals of joy. If you think back to the experiment we mentioned in Key Six where it was shown that the messages children received were at least 80% negative, that fact is quite understandable. You have more wiring for pain and unhappiness than you do for pleasure and happiness, so, sadly, the pain often becomes more familiar and thus more comfortable for you.

In addition, you may be resisting joy and abundance because you are suffering from old programming about what joy and abundance actually

12

DEVELOP A TOLERANCE FOR JOY

are, what they mean, and what you believe you do or don't deserve related to them. In truth, joy and abundance already exist within us. You already have them. Yet, you do have to clear the fog of habit, compulsion, and neediness from your vision, so you can see what is already there and grow your gratitude and appreciation, which is part and parcel of your joy.

Like so many, you may have a low set-point or glass ceiling for how much joy and abundance you are able or willing to tolerate. This Key is to help you create a new set-point for joy and abundance, both key components of your self-worth and net worth.

Reasons For Stopping The Flow of Joy and Abundance in Your Life

Joy is generally unfamiliar, and you likely naturally tend to shy away from the unfamiliar. It sets off danger alarms in you, causing you to close down. We all have a certain glass ceiling or upper limit for how much joy we are willing to tolerate. How high or low one's joy/abundance thermostat is set varies from person to person. The good news: You can begin to raise it, no matter what it's set at today! So, let's take a look at your financial thermostat. As it relates to money, your thermostat may be able to tolerate a certain bank balance, a certain salary, and so on.

Similarly, we all have an invisible glass ceiling for how worthy you believe yourself to be and how much income is associated with that. Take a look at your income from the last three years. If it has stayed within a consistent range, might that be the upper end of your thermostat setting regarding what you believe you are worth? Whether it is joy, wealth, success, or any aspect of abundance, you have an unconscious mechanism in place as a shut-off valve to keep you from going over the edge of your comfort zone.

Just as you learned to utilize the I.D.E.A. system to break through your comfort zone in Key Nine to lead you to greater wealth, so too can the I.D.E.A. system help you develop a greater tolerance for joy. As a start, refer to the four steps of the I.D.E.A. system as another tool to support your process of developing joy.

Oftentimes, the reason adults struggle to feel and appreciate joy may stem from old childhood messages. Following are some of the most common reasons why you may have made the decision very early on that it was not okay to celebrate your birthright to the full measure of joy and abundance that you deserve.

Ten Common Childhood Influences Limiting Your Capacity for Joy

As you go through these steps, you may recognize a commonality with some of the childhood messages you noticed through Key Six. Appreciate and acknowledge the similarities and differences.

1. *Being told that joy and exuberance is unsafe or not okay.*

Perhaps, when you were feeling joyful, you exuberantly expressed yourself. You ran all around the house and made noise, or sang loudly, and things broke. Maybe you were yelled at or punished. Whatever it was, somehow you got a message that joy was not safe and that joyous behavior was not okay. You then took on a belief system that it was not okay to get that happy or that excited.

Cia remembers the first (and maybe the last) time she ran around the house celebrating. An antique heirloom lamp belonging to her parents shattered as she knocked into it. Their anger, sadness, and disappointment were so great that Cia never remembers running and playing in the same way again. As another example, when Belinda was a child, she recalls playing on the living room floor with her parents, enjoying the rough-housing and showing off her somersaults. All was happy and fun until Belinda did a tumble and lifted up her head right into the corner of the square glass coffee table. She got an injury on her cheek, which everyone thought would heal so they didn't give her stitches, yet she still bears a small scar today. The emotional scar has been taking longer to heal than the physical one.

12

DEVELOP A TOLERANCE FOR JOY

2. *Outdoing (including fear of betraying or abandoning someone).*

Another common circumstance that may cause you to resist joy begins with receiving conscious or unconscious messages that it is not okay to do better in life than your parents, a sibling, or others around you.

This is particularly noticeable in families where there is a history of suffering. It may have been in the distant past. For example, perhaps your grandparents were Holocaust survivors and carry a strong internal message that it is not okay to celebrate life when so many others suffered and died. Or it might be very recent; for example, you might have a handicapped or less-than-able sibling, or a parent who is severely depressed and feels unworthy. Belinda had a client who was an unemployed young woman in her 20s living at home. She struggled in her job search and in interviewing for positions for which she was well-qualified. Eventually she realized that she was uncomfortable going after a higher level of success than her father. Her desire was there but her abundance thermostat was set too low! Many people either consciously or unconsciously go through a challenging time when they first surpass the amount of income (or its equivalent in current value) than a parent makes or made. There is a parallel here to the feeling you might get when you live to the age that a parent died and perhaps fear that you are not destined to go further.

3. *There is not enough to go around.*

The belief in a finite, or fixed, concept of money and abundance teaches you that if you have more, someone else will have less. This is also known as a "bank concept" of money, as this assumes a fixed amount of money is available for withdrawal and deposit. It is an either-or way of looking at things, common in our culture—if you have, then someone else doesn't.

This may hearken back to the fear of "outdoing" as we discussed above. It may play into a feeling that you don't have the right to have more than someone else, or you may want to give away what you do have out of a sense of guilt. Maybe there were not enough cookies on the plate when you were growing up and someone got left out. Even small and seemingly insignificant moments in your life can have lasting impacts on your beliefs, especially about money and deserving success.

12

DEVELOP A TOLERANCE FOR JOY

4. I don't deserve it.

At an early age, certain reactions from your parents, or others, may have had you feel like who you were and what you did was "not enough" or not good enough. This could come from one of three directions.

1. You may have received overtly negative messages, such as, "Why can't you do as well as your sister?"
2. You may have received very positive messages that, deep down, you never believed you could live up to—and so you have spent your whole life trying. Children sometimes see positive messages as expectations, not encouragement, concluding that their value comes from what they achieve versus who they are. (A tip to parents: praise your children for who they are, for showing up, and for trying—not only for what they do or accomplish. Be sure that the love you express is unconditional.)
3. (This one is often the most subtle.) You felt ignored or brushed aside with phrases such as "That's nice honey," when you were feeling so proud and yearning for praise. Your system may have developed the belief that the only way to get what you were yearning for (recognition and attention) was through mighty struggle and hard work, which may perhaps continue to this day. This is often reinforced by the many negative references associating receiving money *only* through struggle, such as, "Money doesn't grow on trees," "You have to work hard in life," "Nothing comes easy," and "There's no such thing as easy money."

When you believe that you are *not enough*, it often translates to a fundamental limitation you put on yourself about how worthy and deserving you are for joy, love, affection, and abundance. As you continue to believe this, you create a strong identity connection and keep repeating this pattern, thereby reinforcing the alleged evidence that you are correct. Through this process, you may have adopted a powerful identification with a particular way of being that constantly has you feel inadequate. This identity and belief that you are *not enough* has likely created a significant weakening in your self-worth and capacity for joy.

12

DEVELOP A TOLERANCE FOR JOY

Your role in your family of origin may have had a strong effect on that internal sense of worthiness and deservability. For example, there is usually only one position available per family for the "smart one," the "pretty one," the "successful one," the "trouble maker or rebel," the "good-for-nothing" or "burden," etc. As an adult, when you receive evidence contrary to the identity with which you associate, you may tend to ignore or resist it. If you believe you were a burden on your family of origin, you may recreate that role, or a vision of yourself as being that way, with your partner.

5.   I'm too big, too much. I don't fit in. I'm out of place.

Some of us were born larger than life. Your view and your way of being in the world, and possibly in your body as well, were always just a bit bigger than that of those around you. Often you got criticized for this. You may have been bold, spoken out of turn, had a louder voice, taken up "too much space" physically or energetically, been clumsy in our expansiveness, and so on—and have been shut down for it. You may have learned to make yourself small and tone things down to compensate for what seemed to be unacceptable to those around you.

6.   Unpopular, different, or alone.

This one is also sometimes related to the influence of "outdoing" mentioned above. You may have felt unpopular or alone for your successes. Cia, for example, believes she didn't have friends in school growing up because of getting good grades and getting labeled as the teacher's pet. She desperately longed for friends and tried to imitate and please others to attempt to fit in. As an adult, until she realized it wasn't getting her anywhere, Cia continued her peoplepleasing behavior. You may not want to lose your circle of friends by catapulting yourself into a different income bracket and lifestyle, for instance. If you resist success, you can maintain your status quo and the sense of belonging that comes along with it.

7.   I won't get it anyway.

When you have numerous memories—or one strong one—of longing for toys, attention, hope, or an unanswered prayer as a child, your heart may have broken at some point, resulting in a giving up or a sense of hopelessness that stays with you into adulthood. You adopt the attitude that there is no point in wanting because you won't get it anyway, and thus you stop asking or trying. This, then, accumulates additional evidence to confirm your belief that you will be disappointed in your hopes and expectations.

8. Punishing someone.

Somewhere along the way someone hurt you very much. It's possible, even, that the person who hurt you wanted you to succeed for reasons that felt unwelcome to you. You may have been spending a lifetime punishing that person by not succeeding. In fact, that person may not even be alive any longer, and force of habit/belief compels you to continue unconsciously with your punishing strategy—the result being an inability to succeed. You've been drinking the poison and hoping someone else will die. Do you feel sick enough yet? It's time to wake up and realize you are actually only punishing yourself.

9.   It costs too much. We can't afford it.

This is a common message for many of us in childhood. We notice this especially with those whose parents survived the Great Depression. It occurs as well from the many working-class parents, and even some wealthy ones, who struggled for a living and then passed this message either directly, in words, or indirectly by modeling excessively frugal (penny-pinching) behavior. Your unconscious received the message/belief system that you simply "can't afford" the things that might give you more joy or pleasure in your life.

10. It will be taken away (fear of the loss of the source of that joy).

Perhaps you had experiences of deep joy and excitement in your life—real happiness. Then later on, since everything in life changes, it felt as if something went wrong. You lost what you identified as the source of your joy. You may have at that point given yourself the message that your joy is connected to the loss—that joy will create loss became the superstition. Or perhaps the loss made you believe that the joy was not real, so you *shouldn't* feel it. You shut down your *capacity* to feel it. It's time to begin reclaiming that capacity.

Cia's father had a problem with his own tolerance for joy and play. When Cia was a toddler, he would toss her around playfully, getting her all excited until he lost his patience and stopped abruptly. He would quickly let her down literally and figuratively, so that her system became hyper-vigilant, expecting joy to stop abruptly and the negative to ensue.

What you identified as the source of your joy may have been taken away and no longer there for you. This might translate in adult life to developing a fear that if you have something, cash for example, it will then be gone and the related lifestyle lost. A client shared with Cia her discomfort with maintaining any money in her bank account or even in her wallet. She felt a compulsive need to spend immediately as quickly as it came in. She had a belief system that, if she had money, she had to spend it right away before it was gone—ironically creating exactly the situation she was so afraid of! The fear of the loss of joy, pleasure, or abundance can directly relate to a person's inability to maintain cash in her/his bank account.

Any or several of these ten childhood influences could have limited your capacity for joy. Now is your time to recognize the breakdown and choose to breakthrough to embrace the joy that is truly available to you.

Poverty Consciousness and Scarcity Mentality

Everywhere you look you have more reminders of what you don't have—likely leaving you with feelings of limitation, scarcity, and lack. The feelings are often subtle but no less dangerous. The average consumer in the United States today is exposed to, bombarded by, and inundated with, over 5,000 advertising messages *per day*. Many of these messages are encouraging you to buy, become, or do more so that you can have what it looks like your neighbors have. Compound that with a challenging economy and it can be remarkably difficult to stay positive in a generally negative environment. In going after the proverbial American Dream, you may be mortgaging your present—your joy and personal abundance—for an image that was sold to you about what you could have and what your life should look like.

In constantly striving for more, you unconsciously tell yourself that what you have is not enough. This acts as another self-fulfilling prophecy as you reinforce your belief in scarcity as the milieu in which you exist. What would it be like to switch that belief system for one in which you saw abundance and support all around you? When you are so surrounded by lack, embracing abundance and joy can feel strikingly unfamiliar and uncomfortable.

There is a folk story about a man in a small town who lived in a tiny house with his wife and several children. The house was noisy and crowded and the man felt as though he was going out of his mind, but could afford nothing bigger. He went to see the Rabbi of the village and pleaded for advice. "Get a rooster," said the Rabbi, "and bring it into the house with you." Scratching his head, and not wanting to appear ungrateful, the man did as he was told. Within a few days, the man was back complaining that things were noisier than ever. "Get a goat," said the Rabbi, "and bring it into the house as well." The man looked at the Rabbi, as if he was out of his mind now, but did as he instructed. When the man was back in another few days, he was told by the Rabbi to get a pig, and later a calf. When he could stand it no more, he came crying that the situation was totally unbearable. "Now, put all the animals outside," said the Rabbi. The man went home, took the animals out of his house, and relaxed in what felt like peace, quiet, and spaciousness.

Receive with simplicity everything that happens to you.

—RASHI

Developing a tolerance for joy requires stepping out of the poverty consciousness. When you stay in poverty consciousness you are robbing yourself of joy because you will always feel poor.

Transform your poverty consciousness, or consciousness of lack, into a concept of sufficiency: You, and what you have, are *enough*. As you believe that the universe is a place of infinite abundance, your belief will be that "I" can have it all and so can *you*. There is an unlimited amount to go around. You have everything that you need and more. As you model that for others, they may realize that they do as well. It is the consciousness and feeling of

12

DEVELOP A TOLERANCE FOR JOY

having what you need, rather than the amount or monetary value of what you have, that makes the difference.

Being Up Is Better Than Keeping Up

The recession beginning in 2008 was a sharp wake-up call for everyone to realize that even the Joneses could no longer keep up with the Joneses! The sacrifice that people have been making all along to keep up with an image had disastrous results. The silver lining here is a re-evaluation of your actual values and rediscovery of the importance of family, community, and sharing in your life, along with a greater enjoyment of the moment.

Like the proverbial putting the cart before the horse, this is the ironic part. The more you live in poverty consciousness, effort and suffering, the less you feel that you have. The shift to embrace abundance and joy does not begin with gaining more. Many believe that once I have X, Y, and Z, then I can do the things I've been putting off that will bring me the feeling (peace, happiness, joy, fulfillment, and so on) I want.

Similarly, you may have heard yourself once say, "When I get . . . the promotion, find a new job, my rich relative passes away, my "ship" comes in, my lottery ticket wins, my property value rises, find my rich husband, . . . I'll be able to save more money and then finally feel the feeling I crave.

We propose a radical turn-about. Start with the concept of and the belief in your own abundance. As you may recall, you have a choice over your beliefs. Therefore, indirectly, you have a choice over your feelings! You can create your wealth—inside and out—right now. Deepen your transformation as you discover how you can attract and sustain a greater level of joy than ever before:

Eight Tools to Expand Your Tolerance for Joy and Abundance

1. *Recreating your experiences of true joy.*

Imagine, in vivid detail, a moment in your life that you felt extreme joy. If that is hard to find, come as close as possible by asking yourself, "What is my fondest memory?" As you visualize this time and place, use all your senses: the sights, smells, sounds, tastes, and tactile sensations you experienced in that moment of rapture or delight. Allow your body to experience those sensations as closely as possible right now in this moment by immersing yourself in this sense memory. Really take a moment to stay with this sensation. Breathe it in. Fill your body with it.

Notice as you do this that it was a *thought* that created this pleasurable sensation within you. The thought was a memory. A memory is nothing more than a chain of chemicals existing within your brain. What if you could replace so many of the negative memories you carry with a focus on the positive ones? In truth, you can even train yourself to invent positive memories replacing those that were, perhaps, traumatic. This is not cheating, since we've already acknowledged that what you are dealing with are chemicals in your brain. Why not transform those chemicals into ones that serve you?

It is human nature and the way you are wired or trained to focus more on the negative than the positive. Can you remember a time when you received a list of compliments, or good grades on a report card for example, and yet the one negative comment or bad grade stood out so strongly that it replaced the value of all the positive reinforcement?

This is nothing more than conditioning. It is possible right now in this moment to make the choice to begin reconditioning your mind—to begin replacing your memories, images, sensations, with those that serve you better—with those that bring you joy and abundance. Are you willing to choose to do this starting now?

2.   Feel the feeling now and breathe into it.

Once again, conjuring the feeling of joy in your body from the memory you found in the above exercise, use your breath to experience the joy even more completely. How deeply you can breathe is very symbolic of your willingness and your capacity to take in what life has to offer. The more oxygen you are willing to take in is often a parallel to the amount of joy, and other feelings for that matter, you are willing to experience.

12

DEVELOP A TOLERANCE FOR JOY

So use your breath right now to breathe as deeply into your belly as you can and imagine that you're filling yourself up with the sensation of joy. Do this exercise every day if you're working on increasing your tolerance for joy. Simply imagine either something you want or something that you are grateful for, as you practice expanding your ability to take in breath along with expanding your tolerance for joy. As you do it, give yourself the message that it's okay to feel joy. Give yourself permission to have more happiness in your life.

The breathing exercise at the end of the Key, along with the tips on breathing in Appendix I, will help you with the practical aspects of developing this greater capacity and habit of conscious breathing.

3.   Take "can't afford it" out of your vocabulary.

The result of this childhood influence is the belief that you cannot afford the things that bring you joy. You may have convinced yourself that things that bring you joy cost money—more money than you have, in fact. To unwind this belief system, start to notice and appreciate the little things that give you joy. Ask yourself what are truly the most precious things in your life, without which your life would cease to have its meaning? We have never delved into this question deeply with a client and found that the answer was something physical money could actually purchase.

Recognize that you can create your own *magic money moments*, usually with very small dollar amounts expended. Creating joyful experiences often doesn't require spending, as abundance and joy don't have to cost money. Often some of the best times don't. Here are several examples to consider: spending quality time with your cherished family (especially with small, carefree children), stroking your partner's hair or face, going for a hike, daily notations in a gratitude or joy journal, taking a walk on a beach (especially at sunset), writing a love letter, or exchanging a massage with a friend or partner. What are additional examples you can think of where you have allowed yourself to experience pure, unadulterated fun, play, and/or laughter? Sometimes joy may be experienced in poignant ways, as in the "sweet sorrow" to which Shakespeare refers. Consider sharing the most beautiful sunset you ever saw and knowing it will never come again.

12

DEVELOP A TOLERANCE FOR JOY

Does that subtract from or add to the joy of that moment where you are so fully present?

4. Become financially free in your own mind first.

We hear over and over again that people are working so hard to be able to have the money to essentially buy their time back later in life so they can then do what they will want to do, while not allowing themselves to enjoy the present at all. It is ironic that you work to buy back your time. Have you capped out or postponed your joy until later to honor a Belief System you may have that all work has to be hard and painful? Remember the story about the young man on the beach in Key Ten? You can choose to set a new course for financial freedom starting today.

Cia had a client who said that he wasn't willing to stop until he had $5 million saved because that was the amount he believed he needed in order to retire in the lifestyle he wanted. He was working incredibly hard on the floor of the stock exchange, under a lot of stress and hating it. Cia argued against his point from as many angles as she could, encouraging her client to live now as well, to no avail. Sadly, a year later he died of leukemia. Might this be a lesson for all of us on the impermanence of life. You don't have to stop working, especially if you love what you do, but please do start living.

Financial freedom is achieved when your income exceeds your needs. Most often people focus on increasing income to achieve this goal, over-looking the fact that there is another option. If your needs go down, the necessary income to support those needs can also go down. (Recall the *Under-Simplification Syndrome* in Key Eight.) During an economic crisis or recession, although painful, the lesson may be learned perforce and sometimes, in the long run, for the better. Families may stay in starter homes longer or hold off on buying their children unnecessary toys, for example.

Where Cia lives in a small rural village in Costa Rica, the average annual income is the equivalent of a few thousand dollars a year per family. Yet these people are not poor. Cia says that one of the things that made her feel the most comfortable in her town was based on a comment from a close and caring neighbor. The neighbor shared that she didn't envy Cia at all for any of the things she had on her large ranch, because Cia's life appeared much more complicated. Her neighbor valued simplicity and loved her life in the beauty of this caring and supportive community.

The local Costa Rican micro-financing women's organization of which Cia is a member lends a few hundred dollars or so to help women in the community start their own businesses. Almost every woman in the community now has a means of gainful employment thanks to this small endeavor. The contrast between the high stress and fast pace in most of the United States and the rural Costa Rica communities is like night and day.

Who has the higher quality of life? The choice to simplify your life need not come from a place of scarcity. It may instead be created through a new view of abundance and true financial freedom. What would it be like to make a choice that your time and the things you want to do are more valuable than making money for the sake of making money and maintaining a certain lifestyle? Take a breath and consider the impact of such a move.

Two of Belinda's clients posed an interesting dichotomy. One woman earned $50,000 per year and another client was a couple who made $625,000 combined. Ironically, the woman earning $50,000 per year came to Belinda with greater savings than the couple earning over 12 times what she makes, as the couple had a much more complicated and expensive lifestyle. The couple stresses more because they feel so much more pressure to continue to make the money to maintain that lifestyle. Who is happier? Who has more joy?

5. Prepare for the ups, downs, and the gremlins.

Developing a tolerance for joy begs the question of how you deal with upward spirals of positive energy and abundance so that you can avoid an emotional and/or financial crash. As you begin to notice an upward spiral, pause to rest and integrate. Practice staying present with what is occurring for you. As you pause, you gather your resources and build your *container* to support the next upward spiral. Your container is a sense of the largeness of you—that which holds all you have within you. You are bigger than your body. If you take your sense of all of who you are, that is what we are asking you to expand. As your sense of yourself grows, so does your willingness and ability to take in the joy available to you—to truly receive.

Take stock of where you are. Feel how it feels. Each time you do this, the upward spirals get less scary, and you become willing to sustain more positive energy without scaring yourself into a downward spiral. You are in effect expanding your container (and your comfort zone for joy).

When you are feeling good and your net worth is on the rise, start to notice and be alert for the little voice inside you that says, "This is going to be taken away from me," "I don't deserve this," or whatever your programming is. Those thoughts are likely to create a self-fulfilling prophecy. Then when you are losing or spiraling down, you are likely to say, "See? I knew I didn't deserve this or that it couldn't last." What you are less likely to see is that you've created that through your programming and what you were telling yourself.

Becoming aware of the *timing* of your cycles of ups and downs, and thus prosperity and scarcity consciousness, is important so that you can catch them right before a down-swing. (See Exercise B at the end of this Key for a highly useful tool in tracking the timing and impact of your cycles.) Awareness is always important and, especially so, just as you begin your peak. There you will find the clue to your own previous personal non-supportive strategy for bringing yourself down and sabotaging your success.

6. Give yourself permission.

It's time to give yourself permission to have more joy and abundance in your life. Of course you'll have loss and grief, sadness, and all of the feelings that are part of the human experience, and that's fine. That's wonderful just the way it is because the more you have those feelings, the greater your capacity for joy, aliveness, and genuine success. And it's worth it! It's really worth it to be fully alive in a sense of gratitude for all that is and all that you have.

7. Changing your "buts" to "and."

As we mentioned in Key Eight, when you choose BOTH you realize that AND creates a powerful space to experience all you want in life, while BUT limits you from the start. "And" opens up the realm of all possibilities. "But" creates limitation while "AND" is inclusive and creates a sense of expansion. Replace your "Buts" with "AND" and allow your tolerance for joy to expand. You can then say, "I am large enough to be the container

12

DEVELOP A TOLERANCE FOR JOY

for both this feeling *and* that one. I can have this AND this." For example, you could have a 4-day a week job *and* get paid your market salary. You could go on vacation *and* stay within your budget. Your children can enjoy the December holidays *and* you don't have to run up your credit card debt. You can celebrate something in your life with a treat for yourself *and* still have money to save for the month. You can have the job you love *and* the job that pays you well. Your joy may be increasing in this very moment as you begin to appreciate this distinction.

8.   Having your cake and eating it too.

A client of Cia's had a prospective relationship partner ask her if she would be comfortable being with someone who could write out a check for a million dollars. Would you be? Think about it for a moment and don't answer right away. Would you be comfortable if YOU could write a check for a million dollars? Would you be comfortable having a million dollars in a checking, or even a savings, account?

Some people need to spend money as soon as they have it. This is also part of the glass ceiling discussed earlier—a way of not allowing oneself to truly HAVE. Some people will HAVE but have a challenge SPENDING—the other end of the glass ceiling spectrum. Where do you fall on that spectrum? What would it take for you to become comfortable with both ends? Notice if truly contemplating that question brings up some anxiety for you in one way or another. If so, simply "be with" or "presence" the feelings. They may have a message for you.

Gratitude and the Two Types of Abundance

Surely the strange beauty of the world must somewhere rest on pure joy!

—ANNE WILSON SCHAEF

There are two types of abundance: having what you want and wanting what you have. While it may be true that you can have *anything* you want if you focus intently enough and long enough following the Keys in this book, you cannot have *everything* you want at the same time. For example, you may want to have a large family and stay home with the children for as much time as possible and you may also want to be at the top of your profession. You can certainly, with enough focus and energy, achieve either of those goals, but it is unlikely you will achieve them both at the same time.

Therefore, the second kind of abundance is, and always will be, the most permanently rewarding. It is, in effect, the great gift of gratitude. It is what fills us with joy. Focusing on manifesting abundance is exciting and reaps great rewards. However, the peace that is lasting joy comes from a moment-to-moment gratitude for what you have and for all that is—the miracle that is life and the miracle that is your life. When, whatever your challenges may be, you may make the choice to focus on what you have rather than on what you don't—the proverbial glass is half full, instead of half empty and needing to be filled. When your every breath is one of gratitude, you allow "your cup to runneth over" with joy.

What You Want, Give

"What you want, give," is one of Cia's favorite phrases. She reminds herself of it continually. It reaps rewards not only financially but in relationship and other areas of life. Just as giving love to yourself will tend to attract love to you, so too do all forms of giving attract more of what you give. We know of no better way to accentuate the joy in your life and to create the true flow of abundance than by giving back. The happiest people we know are the ones who fill their lives with giving of themselves. Like letting go, giving opens up space for the flow (affluence). Giving money will tend to bring in even more money than you give. Tithing is an age-old practice of giving 10% of everything you earn to charitable causes. We recommend it highly.

There certainly are many worthy not-for-profit organizations to suit your personal preferences. If you are unable to give financially, give of your time. Sometimes hands-on giving is the most rewarding of all. Cia built her own passion for volunteer work with youth in need into a non-profit organization, Visions and Dreams for Creative Learning Youth Programs, Inc., and has turned her volunteer work with communities, animals, and nature in Costa Rica into programs where people can visit and give of both time and money. She has found these activities to be her greatest source of joy, and is currently looking for the right worthy cause to which to give some land. Beyond the direct benefits you receive, this work often yields you even more gifts in the people you meet. When Belinda volunteered in Costa Rica at a human rights Spanish immersion program Cia was leading for underprivileged teens, that gave them an extraordinary opportunity to serve together and build the relationship that served as the foundation of creating this book. Serving can yield you gifts that keep on giving, especially in the lessons you personally learn and the relationships you make, far beyond your time in the field.

You deserve joy, abundance, pleasure, and all the goodness that life has in store for you. This Key is our strong encouragement to seize the moment (*Carpe Diem!*), open your eyes, wipe them clear of limiting belief filters, and take what is rightfully yours. You can do this—right now, here, in this moment. When you know that, you have the choice of how to live. You are worthy of attracting and creating wealth far beyond your previous limitations and barely imagined dreams. This is what owning your money, embracing your worthiness, and expanding your capacity for joy, is all about. The choice is yours.

12

DEVELOP A TOLERANCE FOR JOY

EXERCISES

Exercise A: Your Ideal Life

Use your journal for this exercise. Write a detailed description of your ideal life. Write it in the present tense positive, i.e., *I have* and *I am* vs. *I want to have* or *I will be*. Be as specific as possible. Take into consideration both your internal state (your feelings, including your self-worth and self-esteem) and your external state (imagining your net-worth and what you will be doing with it). You may even decide to describe in detail your ideal day, week, month, or year. If you do this exercise without any preconceived ideas, sometimes what emerges can be remarkably revealing and not always what you expected.

Exercise B: Charting Your Mood Cycles

Use the graph below to chart your emotional cycles up and down for a month. (This is an ongoing exercise.) You may wish to make a copy of the graph so you can re-use it for several months and adapt it to your cyclic tendencies. If you are a person whose mood swings significantly during the course of a day, you might want to create the graph by week, including morning, afternoon, and evening so that you rate your mood at each point of the day. If your cycles tend to be long in scope, it may be worthwhile to make copies of the graph to use for a few months, in order to have a fair chance to fully observe your cycles.

The use of the graph involves rating your mood each day on a scale of one to 10, with 10 being pure joy, and one being a complete lack of any sense of joy. You do this simply by putting a dot or X at the appropriate number for the appropriate day.

Now the most important part to expand your tolerance for joy: Note where the upswing turns around into a downswing. That is a critical point. If you can practice catching yourself just as you begin to spiral down, you can ask yourself, "what was I just thinking or doing that caused this turnabout?" Even if it appears to be circumstantial, remember that it is not the circumstances themselves, but your reaction to those circumstances that determines how you are feeling. Use your journal to keep track of what you notice at each swing.

Use the additional questions at the bottom of the chart to add notes. This may prove helpful to distinguish your swings, particularly what happened when you notice an upward cycle turning down. This chart can also be used to notice what you did, consciously or unconsciously, that helped you get out of a downswing. Once you know what works for you, then you can do more of it. Noting the effect of your mood on your spending can also support a necessary change to your emotional spending. You may also add other lines to consider other factors that may affect your mood, messaging, and spending, such as your menstrual cycle (if applicable), the food you eat, or your travel schedule.

See if you can recognize patterns—across the months, within the month, or even in your mood or what you told yourself. What is it that you do or say to yourself that brings you down when the happiness gets too high for your tolerance zone? Can you start today to change that behavior?

12

DEVELOP A TOLERANCE FOR JOY

EXERCISE B: YOUR MOOD CYCLE CHART

NAME: _____

When copying, please enlarge to 125% for best results.

MONTH/YEAR _____

Day of Month:	1	2	3	4	5	6	7	8	9	10	11	12	13	14	15	16	17	18	19	20	21	22	23	24	25	26	27	28	29	30	31
Rating My Mood 10	10	10	10	10	10	10	10	10	10	10	10	10	10	10	10	10	10	10	10	10	10	10	10	10	10	10	10	10	10	10	10
9	9	9	9	9	9	9	9	9	9	9	9	9	9	9	9	9	9	9	9	9	9	9	9	9	9	9	9	9	9	9	9
8	8	8	8	8	8	8	8	8	8	8	8	8	8	8	8	8	8	8	8	8	8	8	8	8	8	8	8	8	8	8	8
7	7	7	7	7	7	7	7	7	7	7	7	7	7	7	7	7	7	7	7	7	7	7	7	7	7	7	7	7	7	7	7
6	6	6	6	6	6	6	6	6	6	6	6	6	6	6	6	6	6	6	6	6	6	6	6	6	6	6	6	6	6	6	6
5	5	5	5	5	5	5	5	5	5	5	5	5	5	5	5	5	5	5	5	5	5	5	5	5	5	5	5	5	5	5	5
4	4	4	4	4	4	4	4	4	4	4	4	4	4	4	4	4	4	4	4	4	4	4	4	4	4	4	4	4	4	4	4
3	3	3	3	3	3	3	3	3	3	3	3	3	3	3	3	3	3	3	3	3	3	3	3	3	3	3	3	3	3	3	3
2	2	2	2	2	2	2	2	2	2	2	2	2	2	2	2	2	2	2	2	2	2	2	2	2	2	2	2	2	2	2	2
1	1	1	1	1	1	1	1	1	1	1	1	1	1	1	1	1	1	1	1	1	1	1	1	1	1	1	1	1	1	1	1

Day of Month:	1	2	3	4	5	6	7	8	9	10	11	12	13	14	15	16	17	18	19	20	21	22	23	24	25	26	27	28	29	30	31
Mood:																															
What happened today?																															
What was the message you gave yourself today?																															
What was your attitude with shopping?																															
Note your menstrual cycle (if applicable).																															

12

DEVELOP A TOLERANCE FOR JOY

Exercise C: Gratitude

Make a list of things you have to be grateful for in your life.

After making your gratitude list, take a comfortable, seated position and do a whole-body visualization, allowing yourself to feel the feelings of gratitude and appreciation in your body as you imagine the things in your life that evoke those feelings. Memorize this feeling in your body with a sense memory photograph. This is a feeling you can come back to and draw on at any time you desire. We suggest doing it often.

You can expand this practice to be a daily ritual to make a mental and/ or a written notation of what you are grateful for. This can be a rewarding way to start or end your day. Consider starting a gratitude journal and consider including photos and notes of your increasingly joyful life.

Visualization – Your Happiest Time

Sometimes our block to joy comes from the fact that we may not even remember what it feels like. This exercise is a kind of meditation to help you recall a feeling of joy, or as close as you have come to it in your life.

Get into a relaxed position, breathe deeply and relax your body and mind. Allow your mind to wander back in time to a moment or a period of time that was especially joyous for you. Don't over-think this. Simply trust what comes to mind. Often the very first thing that pops into your mind has a special significance for you. Allow yourself to visualize this moment or period vividly and in detail. Involve all of your senses. Recollect as clearly as possible everything that was going on around you, and especially the feelings within you. Allow yourself to fully re-live the experience. As you do so, take another sense memory photograph of the experience. We recommend you spend some time journaling about your experience after the meditation.

Conscious Breathing

Lie on your back with a pillow under your knees so that you feel comfortably supported. Keep your head as flat as is comfortable so as not to block the flow of air. Practice taking deep belly breaths.

With each really deep, full breath in, imagine that you are breathing in everything you want for yourself in your life. Really allow yourself to feel it. The oxygen you are breathing enters every cell in your body. If you infuse that breath with an image—a message—you are infusing the cells of your body with a new vision on which they may re-pattern themselves.

With each full exhalation/release, imagine that you are completely releasing anything, known or unknown, that stands in the way between you and having all that you want and deserve in life.

Continue this cycle of breathing in what you want and releasing any blocks until you feel truly expanded and alive. Now move through space seeing if you can take this feeling with you as you look around you. Can you see the world with different eyes? Do you notice all the potential and possibilities?

Do this exercise daily to continue to grow and expand your container—your tolerance for all the joy and abundance you so richly deserve.

Body-Centered Statements

1. With each in-breath, I increase my capacity to sustain larger amounts of joy, abundance, pleasure, and aliveness in my life.
2. My joy is a gift to myself and others.
3. I choose joy and abundance every day.
4. I attract abundance and welcome in wealth.
5. I believe in my self-worth and am growing my net worth day by day.

Journal Joggers

Use the following questions to lead you into your journal entries for this Key.

- Describe the happiest moment of your life that you recall. Describe the feeling that you felt at that moment, in vivid detail.
- What was it about that moment that made it so happy for you?

12

DEVELOP A TOLERANCE FOR JOY

- What has stopped you from experiencing that feeling more frequently in your life?
- What steps are you willing to take toward eliminating this barrier to joy?
- How would welcoming in abundance feel, look, sound, smell, and taste for you?

Life is not happy or unhappy. I am happy or unhappy,
and life is what I do with these two.

—ANNE WILSON SCHAEF

12

DEVELOP A TOLERANCE FOR JOY

CONCLUSION
TRUE ABUNDANCE

---

*The thing that is really hard, and really amazing, is giving up
on being perfect and beginning the work of becoming yourself.*

—Anna Quindlen

I t is time to draw your sacred journey to a close (for now) and celebrate
its completion. Please now complete Appendix III - Your Net Worth
Belief Assessment - At Completion. This will enable you to truly see and feel
your evolution and transformation and have your feet firmly planted on the
ground with your renewed sense of financial security and independence.

Abundance starts with and, in fact, IS, that feeling you seek—be it peace,
joy, freedom, and so on. Abundance starts *inside* and transcends outside. As you
adopt this distinction, you will truly appreciate that your self-worth leads to your
net worth, and you can have both. You *do*, in fact, have both as they are yours if
you are willing to take them in. Your abundance is something that has always and
will always exist in you, as the infinite abundance of the universe of which you are
a part. Imagine that you have just taken off a pair of really thick dark glasses and
are now able to see a bright new world in front of you—readily available.

As you choose happiness and take greater and greater steps of responsibility for your life, you can also increase your tolerance for bigger doses of happiness and abundance. Start by reminding yourself that currently your nervous system is not used to sustaining large amounts of these life-affirming sensations, and maintain an intention for this capacity to grow.

Your previous concept of lack came from separating yourself from that universal abundance which is your divine birthright. You are now equipped with a new understanding of what was in the way and have moved through those blocks. You are the embodiment of the divine abundance. To whatever extent you stay small, you are blocking the flow of that abundance through you, and doing a disservice, not only to yourself, but to the divine and all that is a part of it. That is the true selfishness—to believe in lack instead of all that is. So instead, let yourself inhabit the infinite space around you, and release the artificially imposed bounds of separation that have created your fear.

Challenges will arise along the way. We encourage you to keep coming back to this book as a renewable resource whenever they do.

Joy, aliveness, reverence for the self, and abundance are sacred. They are part of that creative impulse that is the origin of all that is. To take less than the full dose that is allotted to you, and thus not to live your life to the fullest you are capable of and treat yourself as a deserving, dignified being, is a form of sacrilege. It is not to allow God His/Her full expression and experience in the Spiral of Life through you. Waste not one moment, for they all can be spent in joy, love, and prosperity.

You are as large as the universe. Like the hologram, the whole of it exists within you as you exist within it. There is therefore no separation between you and all that is. Why block the flow, stopping up the current that is in fact unstoppable? Why take less than the universe chooses to channel through you? What would it be like to let yourself be swept away by that current that is the energy of all life, of all the forces of this world, this galaxy, and this infinite space? This is True Abundance. This is your home.

Welcome.

At the center of your being you have the answer;
you know who you are and you know what you want.

—LAO TZU

Getting the Most Out
Of The Exercises In This Book

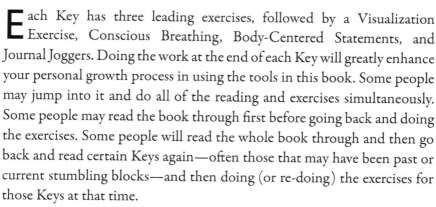

E ach Key has three leading exercises, followed by a Visualization Exercise, Conscious Breathing, Body-Centered Statements, and Journal Joggers. Doing the work at the end of each Key will greatly enhance your personal growth process in using the tools in this book. Some people may jump into it and do all of the reading and exercises simultaneously. Some people may read the book through first before going back and doing the exercises. Some people will read the whole book through and then go back and read certain Keys again—often those that may have been past or current stumbling blocks—and then doing (or re-doing) the exercises for those Keys at that time.

This is not a book to read once and then put down forever. We strongly encourage you to keep it handy to pick up at any time you feel you need extra support with a given area of your life. Likewise, do (or re-do) the exercises again later as you find you need additional support with the principles in a particular Key. It is quite intriguing to note the different layers of understanding you can get from each Key with each reading and the subsequent changes in the way that you do the exercises.

Appendix I

Written Exercises

You will find that the majority of the three leading exercises at the end of each Key will involve some written work. We encourage you to keep this all in one place so that you can revisit it later. As you are working with your intentions, it will be very interesting for you to see how much has come true when you review your original efforts, just as it will be interesting to note changes in doing the exercises a second time.

Although you can write directly in the book, we encourage you to use a separate journal or workbook. You may wish to divide your journal into two parts at the outset, using one part for the journal joggers and open-ended journaling and one part for the written exercises in this book. Be generous to yourself by providing plenty of space to explore and experience the teachings and insights within this book.

Visualization Exercises

We use the term *visualize* in the broadest sense of the word. In reality, the experience is more than simply visual. Our hope is that you will use all of your senses during these exercises. This is getting a *bodily-felt sense* along with whatever *image* you are forming in your mind's eye, as a *full body experience*.

Whatever you imagine and feel, take the time to do it vividly, in full color and with as much detail as possible. Allow yourself to use all your senses, so that it is as close to the actual experience you are imagining as possible. Observe (or create) sounds, smells, tastes, or touch. This may be something as simple as the sensation of the air against your skin. The goal is to create a completely vivid 3D technicolor experience, which you can then lock in with a *sense memory photograph*, and refer back to whenever necessary.

As you observe the externals of the experience, notice, at the same time, any feelings in your body that are generated as a result of the experience. Scientific experiments with magnetic imaging of the brain have shown that the brain cannot tell the difference between something imagined vividly and the actual experience. This is good news because it means that you can actually create new programming, and even change the old, by creating new neuro-pathways in your brain through the practice of detailed visualization.

If you are new to visualization work, we recommend that you begin with what is known as a *safe-space visualization*. You may choose to practice this now before beginning the book, as well as practice throughout the book with the visualization exercises provided at the end of each Key.

Creating a Safe-Space Visualization

Some of the visualizations in the exercises might be emotionally charged for you. If you suspect that will be the case for you, a safe-space visualization makes a great starting and ending point for any of the more intensive visualization exercises. Here is how it works:

Imagine a place where you feel completely safe, secure, comfortable, and at peace. It might be outside in nature, or a special room created just for you. It may be an actual place that you associate with a wonderful experience, or a place you have seen a picture of or simply imagined. Picture it vividly and in detail, using all your senses as if you are truly there. You may even want to imagine/feel a place made to support and hold your body in perfect comfort. Breathe deeply and fill yourself with the awareness that you are completely safe, calm, and at peace.

You may use this visualization at any time in your life when you feel particularly stressed, or if you are having trouble sleeping. As we said, we recommend using it to begin or end any visualization that brings up challenging feelings or memories.

How to get the most out of the visualization exercises in this book:

It may be difficult to read the instructions and immerse yourself in the visualization exercises simultaneously. If you have access to a simple recording device, such as on your computer or mobile phone, read the instructions slowly into your device. Then play it as you do the visualization exercise. Remember to leave plenty of pauses to give yourself the chance to follow the instructions.

Appendix I

Alternatively, many of the exercises are already recorded on one of our CD programs. Look for the related references (within the Keys or in the back of the book) to audio programs to supplement your learning. Using different modalities of learning (for instance, reading and listening) will enhance and fast-track your experience.

Conscious Breathing Exercises

He lives most life who breathes most air.

—Elizabeth Barrett Browning

As you bring consciousness to your breathing, so will you learn to more fully assimilate this understanding into yourself and your life. Our intention is to encourage you to use your breath to help you physically integrate the knowledge/experience you have gained from each Key, rather than remaining on an intellectual level. The *Conscious Breathing* exercises are a combination of breathing awareness and deepening of the breath used in different ways with differing intentions. In the exercises in this book, breath is often combined with visualization to enhance effectiveness. We encourage breathing to enhance bodily awareness and the related awareness of feelings (which live in the body). We suggest you use the practice of conscious breathing often and regularly. A few deep breaths before and after any exercise or body-centered statement will enhance its effectiveness. So, too, will a few deep breaths before and after any challenging task, interaction, or meal. Breathing can serve to greatly improve not only awareness but health and mood as well. It can act as a preventative measure for anyone who has a tendency toward anxiety or fear.

Most of us have our breathing on backwards. We fill our lungs from the top down, expanding our chest before expanding our belly. Imagine breathing like filling a bottle with liquid. The bottle fills from the bottom up. Expand your belly before you expand your chest. Let go of common programming about keeping your belly flat and really see how far you can expand your belly and rib cage as you stretch out your muscles, including the diaphragm, to take in as much air as you possibly can. Get in the habit of stretching and expanding your diaphragm. Shallow breathing (chest breathing) is a metaphor for taking in less than your full measure of aliveness and abundance. Deep breathing opens you to receive all that is so abundantly available around you.

Body-Centered Statements

A body-centered statement is a life-affirming statement that nurtures your inner core and sends a positive message to every cell in your body. It is similar to repeating an affirmation, except we prefer to call it a body-centered statement because when you say the statement, you experience (and observe) a bodily reaction. The point of the exercise is not to repeat the statement over and over again, like a parrot, but to tune in to your bodily sensations, using the statement as a diagnostic device as well as a vehicle for experiential transformation.

Practicing Body-Centered Statements

There are several ways to practice body-centered statements. You may want to use one or more of these methods, depending on your circumstance. The key is to choose one that has meaning for you—one that resonates with who you are.

Before you practice any body-centered statement, take a few deep breaths. Become present in the moment. Notice how you are feeling. We call this getting your *baseline*. Then:

Check in and listen. Read your body-centered statement out loud in an atmosphere that feels safe to you. While you say the statement out loud, tune in to your body's sensations. Keep repeating it, pausing to access your body's reaction each time. If you want to emphasize hearing your statement, cup your hands around your ears as you repeat the statement.

You could also say your body-centered statement silently, especially if you are practicing while you are taking public transportation or sitting at a meeting. Concentrate on your statement and feel it in your body. Let it rejuvenate you.

Recording your voice repeating a body-centered statement can also be a useful way for you to digest your statement in your body. Listen to your voice as you sit in a quiet, safe place. Feel your aliveness grow as the statement is repeated.

Use movement. You can act out your body-centered statement as you are saying it. You'll want to custom tailor your movement to the body-centered statement you are using. If it is about grounding yourself, you may want to walk on the floor barefoot and feel your feet on the ground while you are repeating the statement, stretch your arms and expand your chest. Let the freedom of movement take you into whatever position it will. If your body wants to shake as if you're sobbing, do it. As long as you are tuning into the sensations in your body, each time you say your statement, it will have a transformative affect on your body—and your life.

Try mirror work. Just like the body never lies, the mirror doesn't lie either. If you tune into your body language, the mirror can be your key to assimilating your body-centered statements in your body. Practice saying a statement in front of any mirror (a full length is best) every day, noticing your body language and tuning into how your body feels. Look for progress. You could also use mirror work in a challenging situation to give yourself a pep talk. Maybe you want to confront your partner about something that is bothering you or you have an important presentation to make at work. "I can do it," you might say to yourself in the mirror before you're about to enter into the situation. Or, "I can do this with dignity, honor, and integrity." The mirror reveals the degree to which you have owned the statement. If you are not comfortable with what you are saying, the alignment in your body will be sloppy. Notice your posture. You may slouch or cross your hands over your waist. You may appear lethargic or lifeless rather than dynamic and vibrant. Read your body. Repeat or slightly modify your statement until the feedback you receive in the mirror (or the feelings in your body) lets you know that you are embodying it.

How to Know If a Body-Centered Statement Is Right for You

Make these statements your own. Personalize them. Fill in the blanks where applicable. You may find as you practice these body-centered statements that a particular statement does not feel right for you. Your body might get a clenching or freezing sensation—a resistance. This can happen. Every body-centered statement needs to be tried on for size to see if it feels comfortable for you—but not *too* comfortable (see the paragraph on resistance below). Feel free to modify accordingly.

Maybe you have found a body-centered statement that has potential, but the wording may be a problem. Maybe you have a resistance to certain words and cannot accept what the body-centered statement is saying because of your resistance to that word. If so, consider changing a key word. This may be all you have to do to release your resistance to that statement. For example, you may not like the word "willingness," but once you change that word to "preparedness" or "acceptance" that statement begins to resonate with you. Your body can then believe it.

Resistance to a body-centered statement does not mean that statement is definitely not you. A little resistance can be a good sign—it may indicate you need this statement badly. You have to measure your level of resistance, like a thermometer. If, when you say the body-centered statement, the resistance inside you feels like a door slamming shut with your body saying, "There is absolutely no way I believe this"—then this is probably not the right statement for you. Your body must feel it can potentially believe that statement, even if it's a stretch. A little stretch is good, giving you something to grow into. But if the body doesn't believe that it's possible, try different wording or a smaller aspiration for the statement until you find one that feels possible. As we have said, that doesn't mean make your statement overly easy. You want to stretch yourself, while making it something your nervous system can believe.

Creating Your Own Body-Centered Statement

To create your own body-centered statement, you will want to speak in the present tense positive. *Present tense* means speak as if what you're saying has already happened, "I *am* successful" rather than "I *will* be successful." This gives you the opportunity to try on what you think you want and will prepare your body to accept what you want. *Positive* means what you want rather than what you don't want. A positive body-centered statement says, "I am courageous," rather than, "I am not afraid."

Most body-centered statements begin with the phrase "I" followed by what you want to actualize. A few examples are:

- I love myself unconditionally.
- I radiate self-esteem, inner peace, love, well-being, and happiness.
- I am always in the right place at the right time.
- I trust myself and make smart decisions, especially with money.
- I deserve and welcome abundance in my life.

Use Body-Centered Statements . . . Even if You Don't Want To!

The more resistance you have to doing any exercise, the more your probably need to do it. And when you finally do it, you may find you have a dramatic breakthrough—a life-altering transformation. So, use body-centered statements . . . even if you don't want to.

Journaling

Keeping a journal is one of the best ways for you to recognize your growth and change. It will help you to track how you apply the 12 Keys to your life, and to identify where you may need to put more emphasis on a particular Key. Sometimes, when people are faced with a blank page and the need to write, they freeze, tell themselves they have no talent, and just sit looking at their pen, the paper, or anything else that will get them out of the responsibility of writing.

View your journal as a bankbook of sorts. You will make deposits and withdrawals and you will see the balance rise and fall. In your journal though, you will have set an intention and, if you are consistent, you will see growth and progress towards what you want in life. Just as you don't show your bankbook to everyone, you don't have to show your journal, either. It is a personal record and a tool; treat it as such, and you will be surprised at how much enjoyment you find in it along the way.

Here are some tips to maximize and leverage journaling in your life:

1. Set aside some time each day for your journal writing. The time of day will be important to you for two reasons: If you select an

evening hour, you may find that you put emphasis on what you did or didn't do that day, you may analyze your actions more, and you can set your intentions for the next day. A morning journal session might let you identify stronger, short-term goals which you can reach in the next twelve hours, and then record the next day, after some time for evaluation.

2. In the beginning, you may want to set a specific minimum time to write. Ten or fifteen minutes might seem like an eternity if you have never written before, but even if you only put two words on the page, spend the time you have set thinking about your intentions, the Keys, and so on. In a few days, you will be surprised at how quickly the time passes. You can always have a longer session, or pick up the journal later in the day.

    Write every day, if possible. One journal entry per week may not give you enough thinking time about the Key you are working with. Growth may come slowly and in increments that are difficult to see in one infrequent entry per week. However, as you see changes over a period of time, you will feel a sense of accomplishment. But again, don't treat your entries or lack of them, as something you *failed* to do. This is a learning process, from the inside out, by yourself for yourself. If you miss a day, don't feel like you have to make up for it, simply start where you are.

3. Don't worry about sentence structure—the goal is not to write the Great American Memoir. Even if you only jot down key words, they are key for you and will remind you of your progress later on. No one else will see these notes unless you want them to, so treat your journal as your ideas made real. There will be some days you write a page or more; other days when ten words will seem impossible. There is no such thing as writer's block; the second you have put one word on paper, you have ended the block.

4. If you can't think of anything to write about, don't despair! Everyone wants their first words to be perfect, as in a book, but books go through several drafts before they are put into print and you will do the same thing. You may want to set the same topic to

write about for each Key: "Today, I used Key One, Two, etc. in the following way . . ." or "By following Key One, Two, etc., today I was able to . . ." Or you can write a few words about how a particular quotation helps you.

5.   One of the best ways to start on a journal is to hold an out-loud conversation, with yourself or with an imaginary listener. Sometimes hearing your words flow will make it simpler to put them into writing. After all, we *are* experts at speaking our ideas, and everyone has something to say about what's important in their lives. So experiment with talking out your journal entry first, make a few notes about the subject and then write. It may also be useful to read your entry aloud, which always helps you to focus on what you want to say.

6.   Don't worry if your journal appears as a list of things or ideas, rather than as an essay. Lists are the best way to throw out the excess thoughts and find out what it is you really want to think about, record, or say. This journal is a tool, not a test, and you are learning that growth, whether it is emotional, spiritual, or intellectual, will leave its mark on your writing.

7.   You may want to consider the following statements or questions as guides to your journal entries. But remember, these are examples, not rules, and you are encouraged to write what is important to you. After all, this is your discovery time.

- I believe that Key X will be important to me because if I follow it, it will allow me to . . .
- I can see that by using Key X, I was able to change this about my life today . . .
- Using Key X, I created the following new behavior to grow my self-worth and my net worth . . .
- In addition to Key X, I have been able to bring Keys Y and Z into my daily life as well. I noticed that because . . .
- When I saw the following behavior (you can talk about someone at work or at home), I realized that I am starting to understand the

Keys, and recognize how they can affect my behavior and grow my worth. (Tell what the person did, how it fit into a Key, and why it made you realize your own growth.)

- My relationship with (name someone) has improved today because I used Key X in the following way . . .

- I think that I am having difficulty in applying Key X because . . . (Finish this journal entry with: I will change [name your behavior] beginning today, by [tell what it is you plan to do].)

- Today, I am going to review how the previous Keys have helped me to change my life. (List Keys, and tell why each one has made a change to you.) You may want to do this after every three Keys, just as a reminder of your growth. But remember, that not all Keys will have the same importance or impact on your life, and you do not have to "measure" them at all in order to receive their benefits.

8. Use the Journal Joggers at the end of each Key to provide you with suggestions to spur on your writing about that particular Key as you conclude your reading and completion of the exercises. Each Key has specific questions designed for you to write the responses to them in your book or Journal, so as to support and fast-track your growth and development. They are intended to help get you going. Feel free to make them your own and take off from there.

APPENDIX II

Net Worth Belief Assessment
—At The Beginning

Part I: Rate Your Net Worth Beliefs – At The Beginning

You will first determine what you currently believe, examine those beliefs, and establish new beliefs. You can then be truly open to these new beliefs and manifesting your desires more fully. As this book assists you on the journey from self-worth to net worth, we will focus specifically here on how your beliefs are affecting your net worth. Whether you are seven or seventy, you have some preconceived ideas about wealth and money that have contributed to your current situation.

Note today's date: _____

Rate yourself from 1 through 10 after each of the following statements, with 1=100% Disagreement and 10=100% Agreement with the statement. (See below table excerpted from the Own Your Money LLC Belief Assessment template.)

	Belief	Rating
1	I'm not good at managing money.	
2	I don't deserve to have a lot of money or wealth.	
3	If I try and don't succeed at making money, I will feel like a failure.	
4	If I made a lot of money, I might lose it and then I would feel incompetent and hate myself.	
5	Doing what it takes to make a lot of money will make life difficult and stressful.	
6	Getting rich is a matter of luck or fate.	
7	If I am rich, certain people will resent me, not like me, or I won't fit in.	
8	It takes money to make money.	
9	I don't like dealing with or managing money.	
10	Having a lot of money is a big responsibility.	
11	I should know how to manage my money.	
12	Money can cause a lot of problems in life.	
13	You have to work hard to get money and can't do exactly what you love.	
14	It takes too much time to get wealthy.	
15	Given my background, it would be difficult for me to get rich.	
16	Most people with a lot of money probably did something bad or dishonest to get their money.	
17	Financial security comes from having a steady paycheck and a good job.	
18	It's unlikely I can be rich and happy.	
19	It's better for me to get paid for my time than strictly for my performance.	
20	Having a lot of money will mean I'm less spiritual and pure.	

21	Going after wealth won't allow much time for anything else in life.	
22	Once I have a lot of money, then I'll finally feel secure.	
23	I would never feel secure if I had to be responsible for a lot of money.	
24	I never want people to know I have so much money because people are really mean to rich people.	
25	If I get paid a lot, people will find out that I am a fraud.	
26	I'm a good giver but not a good receiver.	
27	If I ask for help, people will think less of me.	
28	I can make it on my own. I don't need help from others.	
29	Getting rich isn't for people like me.	
30	Realistically, chances are I'll never be rich.	

After you have rated all 30 items, circle the items you rated a 6 through 10. Count how many you have circled of the 30 total items. Even one can serve as the poison to contaminate all of the other positive and supportive beliefs you are carrying.

Part II: Your Net Worth Beliefs In More Detail – At The Beginning

Just as you completed the rating sheet in Part I to serve as a starting point for your transformation, so do we encourage a similar process with this Part II. The questions will be the same between now and at the completion of your *Self-Worth to Net Worth* journey, as your new insights and time elapsed will highlight your shift.

Note today's date: _____

1. What does money mean to you?

2. Do you own your money—or does it own you?

3. How would you describe your relationship to money (for example, making/earning; spending; saving; giving; loaning; borrowing; investing; receiving)?

4. What are your current money management habits and behaviors?

5. What is one habit, behavior, or action that you are willing to perform (but have not yet) to improve your self-worth, your net worth, or both?

6. When it comes to your saving and spending habits, are you a saver, a spender, an avoider, or a money monk (i.e., you just don't care)?

7. When you hear the words *money*, *wealth*, and *rich*, what comes to mind?

8. What did your parents and family tell you about money?

9. How hard do you think it will be to become wealthy and what does that mean to you?

10. Do you feel like you have enough money to start to manage your money? *(Many answer "No" to this question, and ironically any amount of money is enough to manage, and the more that you can gain confidence in managing smaller amounts of money, the more you will attract and welcome in larger amounts.)*

APPENDIX III

Your Net Worth Belief
Assessment – At Completion

Part I: Rate Your Net Worth Beliefs – At Completion

Congratulations on completing all 12 Keys in this powerful program. Now is an important time to reflect on your transformation. When you started this process, you completed Appendix II with your original beliefs. Now you will complete the same form again, below, yet you have changed and evolved with the empowerment in this program.

Note today's date: _____

Again, rate yourself from 1 through 10 after each of the following statements, with 1=100% Disagreement and 10=100% Agreement with the statement.

	Belief	**Rating**
1	I'm not good at managing money.	
2	I don't deserve to have a lot of money or wealth.	
3	If I try and don't succeed at making money, I will feel like a failure.	
4	If I made a lot of money, I might lose it and then I would feel incompetent and hate myself.	
5	Doing what it takes to make a lot of money will make life difficult and stressful.	
6	Getting rich is a matter of luck or fate.	
7	If I am rich, certain people will resent me, not like me, or I won't fit in.	
8	It takes money to make money.	
9	I don't like dealing with or managing money.	
10	Having a lot of money is a big responsibility.	
11	I should know how to manage my money.	
12	Money can cause a lot of problems in life.	
13	You have to work hard to get money and can't do exactly what you love.	
14	It takes too much time to get wealthy.	
15	Given my background, it would be difficult for me to get rich.	
16	Most people with a lot of money probably did something bad or dishonest to get their money.	
17	Financial security comes from having a steady paycheck and a good job.	
18	It's unlikely I can be rich and happy.	
19	It's better for me to get paid for my time than strictly for my performance.	
20	Having a lot of money will mean I'm less spiritual and pure.	

21	Going after wealth won't allow much time for anything else in life.	
22	Once I have a lot of money, then I'll finally feel secure.	
23	I would never feel secure if I had to be responsible for a lot of money.	
24	I never want people to know I have so much money because people are really mean to rich people.	
25	If I get paid a lot, people will find out that I am a fraud.	
26	I'm a good giver but not a good receiver.	
27	If I ask for help, people will think less of me.	
28	I can make it on my own. I don't need help from others.	
29	Getting rich isn't for people like me.	
30	Realistically, chances are I'll never be rich.	

After you have rated all 30 items, circle the items you rated a 6 through 10. Count how many you have circled of the 30 total items. Compare it to how many you circled in Appendix II. Can you see the improvement? (If you would like support to realize even more improvement, you may contact Cia and/or Belinda to take your development to the next level.)

Part II: Your Net Worth Beliefs In More Detail – At Completion

Just as you completed Appendix III – Part I as a reflection on your transformation, this is the time to reflect on your answers now as compared to Appendix II – Part II. Embrace your progress and appreciate how far you have come, as well as areas you may need to go back and delve deeper into.

Note today's date: _____

III

Appendix III

1. What does money mean to you?

2. Do you own your money—or does it own you?

3. How would you describe your relationship to money (for example, making/earning; spending; saving; giving; loaning; borrowing; investing; receiving)?

4. What are your current money management habits and behaviors?

5. What is one habit, behavior, or action that you are willing to perform (but have not yet) to improve your self-worth, your net worth, or both?

6. When it comes to your saving and spending habits, are you a saver, a spender, an avoider, or a money monk (i.e., you just don't care)?

7. When you hear the words *money*, *wealth*, and *rich*, what comes to mind?

8. What did your parents and family tell you about money?

9. How hard do you think it will be to become wealthy and what does that mean to you?

10. Do you feel like you have enough money to start to manage your money?

Now that you have completed Appendix II and III as you began and upon completion of your inside and out wealth creation process, review your shift and appreciate your progress.

Congratulations on your completion
of this sacred *Self-Worth to Net Worth* journey!

About the Authors

Cia Ricco is a well-known, body-centered psychotherapist, teacher, coach, and professional speaker. She is the director of Rancho Ricco in Costa Rica, and a non-profit organization for the benefit of teens and young adults entitled "Vision and Dreams for Creative Learning."

Cia divides her time between her retreat center in Costa Rica, where she is actively involved in community service work and micro financing, and the United States, where she enjoys teaching as well. She is the author of *Living As If Your Life Depended On It: Twelve Gateways for a Life That Works,* and several audio CDs, including *Learning to Love Yourself.* She specializes in individual intensives, helping people create the life they want, teaching clear communication, and is recognized for her powerful work with couples. All of her work takes into consideration the importance of building a sense of self-worth as a foundation.

Cia Ricco is a dynamic public speaker, workshop leader, and writer, as well as a therapist/coach. She is a contributor of advice through radio and national publications. Cia has instituted wellness programs for resorts and businesses, and has provided interactive presentations on stress management, life-care, relationships, and her Twelve Gateways for a wide variety of groups, conferences, and clinics. Her workshops have been offered at Kripalu Center for Yoga and Health, the Omega Institute, Wainwright House, and the New York Open Center among other venues.

Cia supports the whole-health body/mind-centered transformation of individuals, couples, families, and groups, as well as facilitating businesses on communication topics and team building.

For more information on Cia's Costa Rican paradise:

www.RanchoRicco.net

For more information on Cia's coaching, workshops, and retreats:

www.Live-Life.com

For more information on Cia's CD programs such as *Manifesting Abundance: Consciously Creating Your Life The Way You Want It and Learning to Love Yourself:*

www.live-life.com/audio/audio.htm

About the Authors

Belinda Rosenblum, CPA left her thriving corporate finance role to address a major unmet need in our communities—transforming the way people think, feel, and act with money to give them back their rightful power over their money mindset and money management.

She is now helping thousands of people discover how "owning your money" creates certainty, security, and the life of financial independence they deserve. Belinda is the President of Own Your Money LLC, a financial coaching and training company teaching individuals, couples, and business owners how to make personal finance and small business success rewarding, manageable, and profitable.

Her expertise is in high-demand as she hosts her own TV show, radio show, and is a member of the National Speakers Association. She has been called on as the financial expert for Boston's TV networks, Yahoo! Finance, SmartMoney.com, BusinessWeek.com, and *The Saturday Evening Post.*

Belinda's coaching, products, workshops, and speeches address the significant financial stress plaguing most Americans today. Her practical, actionable, and kick-in-the-pants approach to a much avoided topic is refreshing. In her popular home study courses, Belinda personally coaches you with step-by-step systems so you can end any confusion, frustration, or shame around wealth. You can have more than enough money for your lifestyle and life's milestones, while aligning your bank accounts with your level of success.

Belinda inspires, educates, and moves people to action so they can once and for all take control of their own financial future, appreciate their self-worth and realize their financial goals and dreams.

For more information on coaching, keynotes/workshops, press requests, and upcoming events:

www.OwnYourMoney.com

855-8MONEY8 (855-866-6398)

Info@OwnYourMoney.com

To connect with Belinda for ongoing insights, networking, and special offers:

Facebook: Own Your Money

Twitter: ownyourmoney

When you register now at: www.SelfWorthBook.com, you get:

- **Downloadable formatted versions** of the Spending and Saving Plan template, the Net Worth Statement template, and the Mood Cycle Chart.
- Complimentary **Money Breakthrough Session** for personalized next steps to fast-track your financial success.
- A **free subscription** to the Own Your Money content-rich e-newsletter to keep you up to date on new tools and strategies you can use to make money, save money, and stress less about your money.